Religion in Philosop

Editor

INGOLF U. DALFERTH (Zürich)

Advisory Board

HERMANN DEUSER (Frankfurt/M.) · JEAN-LUC MARION (Paris)
DEWI Z. PHILLIPS (Claremont) · ELEONORE STUMP (St. Louis)
HENT DE VRIES (Amsterdam)

11

Eberhard Herrmann

Religion, Reality, and a Good Life

A Philosophical Approach to Religion

Mohr Siebeck

EBERHARD HERRMANN, born 1946; studies of theology and philosophy at Uppsala University; 1977 Dr. theol.; since 1988 Professor of philosophy of religion at Uppsala University.

A grant from the Swedish Research Council has supported the translation of this book.

ISBN 3-16-148375-8
ISSN 1616-346X (Religion in Philosophy and Theology)

Die Deutsche Bibliothek lists this publication in the Deutsche Nationalbibliographie; detailed bibliographic data is available in the Internet at *http://dnb.ddb.de*.

The book was printed by Gulde-Druck in Tübingen on non-aging paper and bound by Buchbinderei Held in Rottenburg.

Printed in Germany.

Preface

This book has emerged in response to what is both a very definite personal, and social need. I am convinced that human life devoid of religious awareness would be considerably poorer than life with it. Not because I believe that every human being must necessarily be religious in order to live a fulfilling and morally good life; but rather, because in my view, the existence of religious awareness in certain people contributes something precious to human life. At the same time, we know that this awareness can take repressive forms. I do not mean that there is a necessary connection, peculiar to religion, between it on the one hand and repression and violence on the other. After all politics, economics, and even philosophy are also things which can lead to oppression and violence. But it makes it all the more desirable to submit religions to critical examination with a view to inhibiting such tendencies. Philosophy can make a contribution to this task by critically examining the philosophical assumptions upon which religion rests. Religious views are among those we never cease from philosophizing about.

Given that this process of critical examination is in principle neverending, this book can be expected at best to provide what, in the context of contemporary society, is a reasonable and well-considered approach to the phenomenon of religion. In this respect, the book can be said to be personal, without thereby dismissing it as the mere product of arbitrary subjective opinion. Philosophizing must surely always be rooted in personal involvement if it is also to be relevant for other human beings. After all, it is human ideas and views which constitute the central concern of philosophy.

Erica Appelros and Mikael Stenmark, my colleagues in the philosophy of religion at the University of Uppsala, have helped to restrain my subjectivity. I am deeply grateful to them for reading the entire manuscript and offering advice which has been both critical and constructive. This has not only made the book more readable; it has also given depth to the analyses which it contains. Considering the vast range of philosophical topics I cover, I am far from confident that I have been able to do full justice to the valuable points they have raised. In the end an author is faced with the choice of either totally refraining from dealing with the many-facetted philosophical questions which arise in connection with the phenomenon of religion – questions which I, like many other people, cannot cease from philosophizing about – or running the risk of failing to give equal thought and analysis to each and every topic under discussion. Faced with this dilemma, I have chosen the latter alternative.

Uppsala, March 2002.

The present work was written originally in Swedish. I am much indebted to Craig McKay for his exertions in the delicate and demanding task of accurately rendering my thoughts in English.

Uppsala, February 2004.

Contents

Introduction

> [I]n any case I think that one's whole view of the
> world is deeply affected if one is a philosopher, by
> one's view of what it is to have a view about the world
> (Putnam 1975, 41)

One of the most exciting philosophical discussions in the analytic tradition
is about the relationship between human consciousness and human language on the one hand and the world on the other. It is a subject that never
loses its philosophical actuality. The complexity of the question increases
considerably if, moreover, it is assumed that we are not merely part of the
world, but are also required consciously to relate to it, and interact with it.
More exactly, the discussion focuses on the question of whether we can
talk unambiguously about objectivity and truth, or alternatively, whether
relativism is unavoidable due to the fact that the human perspective is always tied to a certain context. This discussion arises in part from chal-
lenges from other traditions. For example, feminism emphasizes the importance of gender; pragmatism emphasizes the fundamental role of practice; and postmodernism draws attention to the value of multiplicity. Experience, culture, temperament, our view of life, and our theoretical concepts constitute the prerequisites which we human beings rely upon to understand the world. Does the fact that we can never confront and describe
reality in itself, mean that we can only construct competing accounts and
theories of reality? Is it perhaps more correct to say that what we do is to
create the world, rather than understand it as something independent of our
thought? Although it is up to us how we think about the world, does this
rule out objective knowledge and truth about reality?

   Viewed in a wider perspective, my book is a contribution to this philosophical discussion. At the same time, however, it is also consciously
focussed on the phenomenon of religion. This emphasis is due to the following normative attitude which, because of its general character, obviously also applies to religion. In order to avoid indiscriminately assimilat-
ing every kind of teaching and opinion, it is necessary for us to adopt a
critical stance. Critical thinking can partly be carried out with the help of

techniques and formal methods; but, on occasion, even these themselves require critical examination. Logically valid arguments can be used for both good and evil ends. A critical attitude therefore demands that we also make allowance for normative aspects relevant to the matter in hand. One such kind of normative feature is relevant, for example, when a certain emotional capacity is a prerequisite for being able to identify correctly a certain action as an expression of racism, rather than as a socially acceptable reaction, even if the racists may perhaps make use of arguments which in themselves are logically valid.

Another type of normative feature is to be found in various forms of practical activity. What constitutes a good baker or a good physicist, is something which emerges clearly in the respective practical domain. However, we must not fail to notice that this takes place in the light of a mixture of criteria. Some of these criteria are, so to speak, internal to the practical activity; others are external to it. This is so because our relation to the world around us is extremely complex. If the bread does not taste good, then it does not matter a whit how often the baker refers to his skill, his technically advanced methods, or the superlative raw materials he employs. External criticism, sooner or later, will forcibly bring about a change in the baking of bread; or if this is impossible, perhaps a change in our eating habits so that we eat something else instead of bread. The practice of the physicists also originates in our relation to the world around us. Although physical practice involves extremely abstract theories which are scarcely comprehensible to the untrained mind, most people are aware of the effects which the combustion motor, and still more missiles, have on human life. Our views on such matters can influence physical practice by way of external criticism.

In this respect, the phenomenon of religion is no exception. Criteria which are internal to religious practice are used to determine what kind of religious awareness is good, and who is deemed to be a good exponent of a given religion. However, given that both religions and their secular equivalents make claims regarding the whole lives, not only of certain individuals, but of most human beings, it is necessary to adopt a critical approach to religions and their secular counterparts, in order to avoid either indiscriminately accepting teachings and ideas, or conversely, indiscriminately rejecting everything associated with religion or indeed with any other view of life. Seen from a wider perspective rather than the narrower one linked to a specific religion, there is no reason to accord the phenomenon of religion a privileged status.

In this book, I shall present what in relation to religious practice is an external philosophical critical account; in other words, it is an account from the outside. It is not impossible that this critical account may affect religious practice and thereby what is judged internally, relative to a given religion, to be good religious awareness or similarly may influence who is regarded as a good practitioner of a given religion. I am naturally aware that many believers regard their own religion as a supreme good, and for that reason are unwilling to accept any major change in it. Bearing in mind some of the cruel actions which have been justified in the name of religion, I nonetheless hope that religious practice will not remain unaffected. At the same time, I would emphasize that it is not the aim of this book to devise a suitable strategy for achieving this end. Such issues are beyond the scope of the present investigation. My aim instead is to present a critical, philosophical account and one which is external in relation to religious practice. I do not maintain that this philosophical critique emerges from a vacuum with no reference either to a way of life or ethical system. The philosophical critique we choose is itself partly linked to the kind of person we are and to the way of life that underpins our actions. These presuppositions can in turn be critically studied. However, it is impossible to query everything simultaneously. In the present work, I shall concentrate on putting forward a certain philosophical critique of the phenomenon of religion and its secular counterparts while at the same time setting out and arguing for my own philosophically inspired anthropological assumptions. I shall discuss in some detail what I mean by philosophical critique in the first part of the book which thereby functions as a detailed introduction to the other sections of the book.

Part I

The aim of the book and the nature of the problem

In this book, I set out to philosophize in a certain way about the phenomenon of religion and its secular counterparts. In so doing, it is useful to remind ourselves of the following fact, with which most of us are probably familiar. When human beings begin to philosophize in the ordinary meaning of that word, it is for the most part about metaphysical and existential questions which are not strictly separate from one another, but interconnected. Where do we come from? What is there out there in space? What does it mean to be a human being? The questions concern our understanding of reality, a subject where philosophy, science, art and religion have played, and continue to play a crucial role. As soon as we speak about a view of reality, we are confronted by the problem of what we mean by the word 'reality'? Are philosophy, science, art and religion speaking about the same reality?; or have they quite different functions in relation to our views of reality? Can we speak about a reality in itself which is not merely there independently of us, but exists as something unconceptualized, and is discovered and expressed by us by means of correct descriptions? How far do differing human experiences play a role in our conceptualizations with respect to what we mean by reality? Is there some connection between what is real and what is important or valuable in life? And if so, how are we to determine the connection, without surrendering the logical distinction between description and evaluation?

1 The nature of the enquiry

I look upon the book's central task as one of answering these and similar questions with regard to the function, content and scope of religion. The recurring pattern in the book is first to describe and reconstruct the philosophical assumptions which underpin the various positions discussed, and thereafter to submit them to critical analysis. Many philosophical investigations, in particular within the analytical tradition, are happy to stop once the critical task has been carried out. Sometimes this is quite justified, but it would be a pity if it were to become the rule. Let me briefly explain why I think this is the case, by considering various views about what argument and criticism entail.

An intrinsically important, philosophical question is how the reconstruction and evaluation of arguments is to take place. Should it be conducted exclusively in deductive terms according to which the thesis to be
put forward or tested, must follow logically from the argument? Or should
it be conducted in a non-deductive way where like a judge against a background of presuppositions, support, restraint, various types of rule and so
forth, we reach a judicial decision or verdict i.e. derive a conclusion in this
sense?[1] Another important philosophical question concerns the nature of
philosophical criticism. Certain philosophers in the analytical tradition,
who are afraid of being accused of a lack of objectivity, maintain that only
formal logic should be used since the validity of logic does not depend
upon an ideology or view of life. I am prepared to accept this latter point.
On the other hand, I do not share their fear of normative features. The assumption that only formal logic should be used in philosophical criticism,
is to adopt a certain normative position which, in my view as a philosopher, deserves philosophical scrutiny.

As I shall subsequently show, philosophical criticism should also take
into account the type of problem involved and how it is to be solved. For
this reason, in my critical analysis of so-called metaphysical realism, I
shall not only be preoccupied with criticizing metaphysical realism, but
also with constructively developing alternative conceptual models. These
are intended to allow us to deal more adequately with the concept of reality
than has been the case hitherto in current philosophical discussions about
the status which different kinds of views of reality have, or ought to have.
For example, I shall discuss the issue of how far the contribution made by
our emotions and the acceptance of normative values are necessary for our
ability to develop a view of reality which is compatible with the notion that
we are the biological and social beings that we are. From this perspective, I
want to explain that the question of religion's relation to reality is much
more complex than has been envisaged in the 'trench warfare' about
whether religion should be anchored to a transcendent reality or treated as
a projection of illusion. My hope is that such philosophical analytical
work, even when seen from a social viewpoint, provides a better foundation for a critical approach towards the phenomenon of religion which is
systematic, constructive and sensitive to the subtleties of the issue.

I have already mentioned one respect in which my enquiry will differ
from some other philosophical accounts, namely that I shall supplement
the critical analysis with a constructive step. There is also another respect
in which my enquiry will differ from some others. Although here and
there, I shall present a detailed analysis of subsidiary philosophical problems, or critically analyse the steps in a complex chain of reasoning, it is

---

[1] See e.g. Toulmin, Rieke and Janik 1979.

not the narrow and detailed problems which are the defining feature of my investigation. This is not because I hold that a focus on technical details of a philosophical analysis lacks interest. On the contrary, the results of other philosophers in their often acute and profound analyses provide me with a necessary starting point and foundation for further enquiry.

The way I have chosen to formulate the problem in my investigation requires taking into account several different philosophical domains. This approach is naturally not without risk. We can end up being superficial by removing particular lines of thought from their proper context and, in the worst case, distorting them by moulding them to our own ends. However, the approach also has its advantages. Choosing breadth, as I have done, means not merely the general advantage that it becomes clear how the majority of the central questions of philosophy are intertwined. It also makes for a greater readiness to test several suggestions about the solution of a philosophical problem than is the case when it is only a matter of considering one position and its polar opposite within a limited area. I shall show that the solution to problems which have been developed within a particular philosophical domain can offer new perspectives when they are applied to other philosophical domains with similar kinds of problems. This is the central reason why in my philosophizing about the phenomenon of religion, I have made use of considerably more material from domains outside the philosophy of religion.

My choice of breadth is, moreover, associated with another choice. Throughout the entire book, I shall be working with a number of lines of thought which I am not, however, going to present linearly, one after the other. Depending on the nature of the subsidiary problems which for the time being I am preoccupied with, I shall instead allow the relevant lines of thought to merge in different constellations so that one and the same idea can pop up in different places, sometimes in critical analyses and sometimes in proposals for alternative conceptual frameworks. In the case of the philosophers whose positions in relation to my own I discuss at greater length, this means that I do not first present their thought as a whole, and thereafter critically analyse and possibly apply parts of their reasoning. Such an approach would make it unnecessarily difficult for me to tackle the constructive part of my work. My aim is not the criticism or defence of certain philosophers' arguments, but rather, with the help of these arguments, to get to grips with a definite philosophical issue which I shall shortly identify. Given this general goal, it seems to me that the balance between the reconstructive, critical and constructive stages of my work will be more reasonable if the presentation of the trains of thought of other philosophers does not occur in one section but is partly dependent on the subsidiary problems which I am working with at the time.

Despite the fact that my work is characterized by a certain breadth, from another point of view it is simultaneously very narrow. I wish to create the theoretical preconditions for a balanced critique of religion, by adopting a certain standpoint with respect to the problem of metaphysical realism. On the basis of this standpoint, I shall then develop a defensible concept of view of life which is practically applicable in a pluralistic society. I wish to emphasize that such an outside view – one which is external in relation to the internal self-knowledge of religions and their secular counterparts – is necessary in societies which are increasingly pluralistic.

Clearly the philosophical task I have undertaken can, in part, have far-reaching consequences for how, for example, a theological doctrine of belief is to be formulated and defended, an issue of relevance not only to those who belong to a particular religious group, but to others outside it. However, such consequences are part of the internal discussions of religion which lie outside the scope of the present philosophical work.

2 The philosophical problem formulated

The philosophical issue which is of central importance for the present work, is the following: how can human thoughts which are composed of concepts we ourselves have fashioned, still possess objective validity and deal with something which can be either true or false? What are our possibilities for critical thinking and knowledge when we take into account both aspects of this issue? These questions belong to the eternal questions of philosophy. They occasionally drop out of sight only at other times to pop up and demand our attention. In our own time, they have awakened renewed interest because of increased insight into the normative nature of knowledge. In his critical account of the myth about what is given, a critique which still forms one of the corner stones of the current debate, Wilfred Sellars points out:

> In characterizing an episode or a state as that of *knowing*, we are not giving an empirical description of that episode or state; we are placing it in the logical space of reasons, of justifying and being able to justify what one says (Sellars 1956, 298f.).

We cannot ignore the role that we human beings play as knowledge subjects, when we lay claim to knowledge or, to put it another way, make knowledge claims. Something can certainly be the case without our knowing it; nor is it odd to assume that something can be the case without our even having identified it conceptually. On the other hand, a statement about a given entity which is unconceptualized has no substantial significance for what we reasonably can claim to be real. In such a case we would require access to the unconceptualized reality prior to being able to have access to it via our assertions i.e. conceptualizations.

This immediately raises the following problem, both with respect to religion and its secular counterparts: how can we pass in a defensible manner from holding something to be real to asserting correctly that it is indeed real? Moreover, we need to do this without denying either that our conceptualizations are significant, or that there is a distinction between believing that something is real and the fact that it is real. Something can be real although we do not believe it to be so, and conversely, just because we believe something to be real, does not mean that it *is* real. The question is not merely of academic interest. The way in which we respond to this question in theoretical philosophy, and the answer we provide, has tangible practical consequences for the attitude we adopt at an individual, collective or social level towards various forms of religion. For example, should there be schools or colleges which are based on particular religious teachings? Can any religious group whatsoever be allowed to spread its teachings just because it appropriates the title of religion? In this book, I shall develop a set of conceptual tools which will allow us, so to speak, to strike out in two directions at the same time.

(1) I shall set out to show why it is unreasonable to dismiss religion as something irrational because it has failed to satisfy the demands which have been made in quite different areas e.g. in science.

(2) In addition, I set out to show how religion can be understood as a human phenomenon without thereby eliminatively reducing what is religious to something non-religious.

I wish, therefore, to show that we can philosophically provide a critical account of religion without this account being based upon religious truth claims, ideologically motivated dismissals or by being limited by theology or ideology.

In the present book, philosophy is not, therefore, employed as a tool for theological or ideological aims. This is, nevertheless, quite different from admitting that philosophy is, at least in part, influenced by the framework associated with the philosophizing person's view of life. This connection, as I have said, is not one I deny. In this book, it is a question of treating certain philosophical problems with the help of philosophical tools. Although this certainly cannot be done in a fashion that is absolutely neutral with respect to a basic view of life, nevertheless, it can be presented, I would maintain, in a more neutral fashion than is the case when the philosophizing is explicitly tied to certain theological or ideological aims. Although the same philosophical methods can be used for both purposes i.e. for theological or ideological purposes and for the purpose of solving philosophical problems, the approach and the results are quite different.

The philosophical issues which I shall deal with in this book, fall under the general problem of realism, and are raised specifically by the phenomenon of religion as it occurs *inter alia* in Sweden, a society which like many others, is characterized by a growing multiplicity of both religious and non-religious views of life.

The problem of realism

It is not exactly easy to pin down the nature of the problem since realism has come to mean many things in the course of the history of philosophy and this is still true in current discussions. Let me give a preliminary answer to the question by referring to the role mentioned above which we human beings play as knowledge subjects when we lay claim to knowledge. According to one definition of philosophy which I would tend to accept, philosophical problems arise from human beings' questions about themselves (Stigen 1983, 9). Since human beings are part of a so-called external reality, the concept of nature and not only the concept of human being, is of central importance. A change of meaning in one concept entails a change of meaning in the other. This is evident *inter alia* in the following two respects. It is characteristic of the concept of nature that it does not only play an important role in scientific issues; it also plays a significant role in a human being's metaphysical problems e.g. the place of human beings in the universe. These kinds of metaphysical question are also simultaneously existential. Conversely, it is also characteristic of the concept of human being that it is not only of central importance for human beings' existential questions, but also for their scientific ones. Given that human beings are part of a causal process, questions of how they are influenced by nature and in turn influence nature, are also of scientific importance.

My preliminary answer to the question about the origin of the problem of realism is, therefore, that it is to be found in the tension between how we use the concept of nature and the concept of human being. We are a part of nature simultaneously as we relate ourselves to nature and conversely nature to us, in order to satisfy our needs and to come to grips with the various problems which we encounter in our lives. Our conception of reality is thus concerned with ourselves, our experiences, and our conceptualizations no less than the reality of which we are a part, which we need to relate to, and interact with, in order, not merely to survive, but also to live a fulfilling life.

As I have remarked, philosophy, science, art, and religion have played a crucial role in our understanding of reality and still do. Is this fact sufficient to be able to maintain that philosophy, science, art, and religion are speaking about the same reality? In this case, what is meant by the phrase 'the same reality' and what is the difference between the four domains? Irrespective of how we answer the question, the following fundamental questions arise: can philosophical, scientific, artistic, and religious expressions be understood as referring to a reality which is independent of us, without conceptual and empirical aspects playing some role for how reference is carried out? Do different conceptual frameworks entail different realities? In other words, do they lead to conceptual relativism and ontological relativism? Can we speak of an intrinsically unconceptualized reality, or put slightly differently, of an unconceptualized reality in itself? Furthermore, suppose the answer is negative. What consequences does this have for the relationship between language and reality? How far do different human experiences play a role in our conceptions of reality? And in this case, what sort of view of human beings should form our starting point?

I shall discuss such questions from a semantic, epistemological, ontological, and normative angle with reference, on the one hand, to the relation between what we decide to be real on the basis of the conceptual framework at our disposal, and, on the other hand, with reference to what, so to speak, *is* real. Already at this point, I would like to indicate why I consider it important to maintain this distinction and why I am opposed to an extreme relativist approach which either denies the distinction, or avoids it altogether. As will become apparent, I am not opposed to linking our concept of reality to the fact that human beings are biological and social beings. This is something quite different from relativism in the following unacceptable sense. What is unacceptable is brought out in one of Hilary Putnam's many objections to radical relativism:

> The argument is that the relativist cannot, in the end, make any sense of the distinction between *being right* and *thinking he is right*; and that means that there is, in the end, no difference between *asserting* or *thinking*, on the one hand, and *making noises* (*or producing mental images*) on the other. But this means that (on this conception) I am not *a thinker* at all but a *mere* animal. To hold such a view is to commit a sort of mental suicide (Putnam 1981, 122).

Considering the catastrophic consequences this would have for us human beings such as the right of the stronger to unrestricted domination, I am not prepared to participate in this kind of disengagement of our intellectual abilities. Instead, I intend to take the trouble to develop philosophical tools which will allow us to carry out a critical examination of various notions of reality, knowledge claims and truth claims. These philosophical tools, moreover, are suitable for the constructive aim, where necessary, of suggesting alternative ways of looking upon different types of notions of reality, knowledge claims and truth claims. My work features a kind of relativism, but a desirable one, according to which it would be unwise not to pay attention to the fact that we human beings are the beings we are, possessing both potentialities and limitations.

The problem of the relationship between, on the one hand, what we determine to be real on the basis of the conceptual framework at our disposal, and on the other hand what really is real, crops up in the case of the phenomenon of religion, not least in how the world religions present themselves to their own believers and to their competitors in a society that is becoming ever more pluralistic. In this respect, there is no difference between traditional religions and new religious movements. All consider themselves to be right, which in itself is perhaps not so queer, and the reason that they maintain this, is always derived from their own initial assumptions which is also not particularly odd. Seen internally from within their own religion, it is certainly not a matter of relativism since all other religions are either wrong or can, at least in part, be incorporated within their own particular system of thought. From an external perspective, however, unrestrained relativism is unavoidable since the reasons for the demands for truth, as noted, are always taken from their own initial assumptions.

Given the postmodern challenge to all absolutist claims, including those of religion, we find ourselves in a somewhat paradoxical situation. In a pluralistic society, the anti-relativist claims to absolute religious truth which rest upon the anti-relativist's own initial assumptions, are nonetheless relativist when seen from an external standpoint. Conversely, postmodernism despite its anti-absolutism, is no less absolutist in insisting in general that all expressions, including religious ones, are the product of human cultural and social circumstances, and must be considered in their context. It is to query radically the idea that expressions and concepts have a unique meaning which all human beings can understand or accept regardless of context and interest.

In Part IV, I shall argue that the philosophical choice is not between, on the one hand, metaphysical realism as a guarantee for a non-contextual truth which implies that only one view can be right, and, on the other hand, anti-realist relativism which renounces objectivity and truth. As a third alternative, I wish to propose what I shall often refer to as *pragmatic* or (following Putnam) *internal* realism which allows us to speak of objectivity and truth while at the same time accepting important parts of the postmodern critique of everything going under the name of foundationalism, universalism, essentialism and realism. In the next section, I shall very briefly present the basic aspect of this critique and in the section that follows it, I shall supplement my account with a critique of the realist view of language which is based on the later philosophy of Wittgenstein. The aim of this approach is gradually to pin down the nature of the problem of realism in general and in particular in the case of religion.

The postmodern critique

Although the terms 'postmodernism' and 'postmodern' are both ambiguous and vague, it is nevertheless very clear that postmodern thought is against (a) foundationalism, (b) universalism, (c) essentialism and (d) realism (Magnus 1995, 634). Postmodernists deny that there is one, unambiguous and value-neutral description of existence[2], an assumption which is basic for metaphysical realism and which I shall critically probe in depth in Part II. Instead, postmodernists emphasize that our understanding of reality is determined by the concepts which are available to us by being part of a historically given communicational framework (Henriksen 1999, 23).

(a) The postmodern critique of foundationalism is primarily directed at its vertical structure. Foundationalism maintains that knowledge, no matter of what kind – whether ethical, empirical or religious – is either not derived, and in other words constitutes a foundation, or is derived from such basic knowledge. The only problem is that the principles which are considered to form the basis of ethical knowledge are so general that it is difficult to see how it would be possible to derive anything interesting from them alone. If we want to say something interesting about concrete moral problems, something more than utterly general principles is required.

For example, in the case of the derivation of empirical knowledge from sense-data, the problem arises from the fact that we already from the outset have to have access to conceptualizations of reality in order to derive assertions about reality from sense-data. Depending upon the nature of our investigations, different conceptualizations may be used.

Finally in the case of the world of religions, there is an additional problem. Let us for the sake of argument suppose that it is possible to derive something interesting from some fundamental religious knowledge concerning a transcendent divine reality. In what sense are such claims to knowledge justified? Irrespective of how such fundamental religious knowledge is understood, it is impossible to maintain the superiority of one claim to religious knowledge compared to another claim to religious knowledge, nor can one even critically compare religious claims which are incompatible with one another. For this, external criteria would be required and an appeal to fundamental religious knowledge is not such a criterion. Such an appeal does not work at a general level because the knowledge to which appeal is made is fundamental only for a particular religious group, and not necessarily for other groups. Even the reasons which are adduced

---

[2] See e.g. Farrell 1994.

for arguing that this knowledge is fundamental, are based on the precon-
ceptions of the group. The problem with foundationalism in the world of
religion is that it claims to be the very opposite of relativism, while at the
same time it leads to relativism because the decisive criteria are ultimately
linked to a certain views of life.

(b) The postmodern criticism of universalism concerns the universalist
aim to relate everything to one single entity, be it God, reason or matter.
To make such a claim runs the risk, however, of being meaningless because it is in the nature of the matter that everything can be explained by
this one thing. We do not know any more, or understand any more after
this explanation with respect to our possibilities for interaction with reality, than we did before.

Apart from this difficulty, the universalist perspective entails a further
difficulty, namely that even in the case of limited, clearly defined areas,
there cannot be alternative explanations. From a universalist perspective,
such explanations are ruled out as a matter of definition. There is only one
ultimate explanation and since it is the ultimate explanation, there cannot
be several explanations at the same logical level. Unfortunately, this way
of reasoning has unpleasant practical consequences. When a person or
group on the basis of its strong convictions entertains the idea that it is in
possession of the ultimate explanation and thus the ultimate truth, it follows that people who offer different explanations must be compelled to
give up their delusions and accept the truth. It suffices to mention the Nazi
extermination camps, the Soviet Gulag system, the Inquisition and certain
current applications of the idea of holy war to show what such a view can
lead to.

(c) The postmodern criticism of essentialism is directed against the
metaphysical idea that everything has an essential or intrinsic nature, and
that there is, therefore, a distinction between essential and non-essential
properties of an object. The distinction is based upon a dubious assumption
about the existence of essences. The fact that a chair is a chair only if the
object in question displays certain characteristics, does not entail that there
is some essence which is common to all chairs. It merely shows the limitations we place on the use of the word 'chair'. The distinction is also dubious in another respect which is apparent when we apply categorical assertions about the essential nature of men or women to ourselves as human
beings. Even our views in this respect form part of how we conceptualize
and understand the reality of which we are a part, and at the same time,
which we also need to relate to and interact with. This does not clearly depend on conventions about who, from the viewpoint of physiological reproduction, are men or women. Apart from a few exceptions, we are human beings from a physiological standpoint and of male or female sex in

terms of reproduction. However the physiological difference by itself entails nothing about how we judge normatively what is typically male or female in a social perspective.

(d) The postmodern critique of realism, in particular of metaphysical realism, attacks the idea that we are able to make statements about an object's independent existence and its properties and relations, without being influenced by the linguistic means with which we understand or describe the object, so that ultimately there would only be one true description of reality. In part, it is pointed out that the realist thesis on the independent existence of reality as a guarantee for knowledge in the case of concrete issues, has no practical significance whatsoever. In part, it is emphasized that we are dependent on concepts. When we describe and explain objects, we do so by using concepts and by referring to certain observations which we formulate with the help of these concepts. If realism means that we can assert something about the nature of unconceptualized reality, it forgets that reality for human beings is always something conceptualized and a product of our understanding. A similar reminder also forms the basis of the later Wittgenstein's critique of realism.

Critique of a realist view of language

When Wittgenstein wants to expose what he holds are philosophical pseudo-problems, he does so, as Stefan Eriksson and several other Wittgenstein scholars have underlined, partly by producing clarificatory examples from ordinary language and partly by finding more singular examples (Eriksson 1998, 43).

> Our clear and simple language-games are not preparatory studies for a future regularization of language – as it were first approximations, ignoring friction and air-resistance. The language-games are rather set up as *objects of comparison* which are meant to throw light on the facts of our language by way not only of similarities, but also of dissimilarities. For we can avoid ineptness or emptiness in our assertions only by presenting the model as what it is, as an object of comparison – as, so to speak, a measuring-rod; not as a preconceived idea to which reality must correspond. (The dogmatism into which we fall so easily in doing philosophy.) We want to establish an order in our knowledge of the use of knowledge: an order with a particular end in view; one out of many possible orders; not *the* order. To this end we shall constantly be giving prominence to distinctions which our ordinary forms of language easily make us overlook (Wittgenstein 1953, §130–132).

I shall take one of Wittgenstein's language games as my starting point and present his critique of the assumption about the meaning of words and sentences cited in the above quotation. Wittgenstein asks us to consider the following language-game:

> I send someone shopping. I give him a slip marked "five red apples." He takes the slip to the shopkeeper who opens the drawer marked "apples"; then he looks up the word

"red" in a table and finds a colour sample opposite it; then he says the series of cardinal numbers – I assume that he knows them by heart – up to the word "five" and for each number he takes an apple of the same colour as the sample out of the drawer. – It is in this and similar ways that one operates with words (Wittgenstein 1953, §1).

The purpose of the example is to help us to escape from the grip of certain philosophical assumptions, in this particular case, the assumption that the meaning of words is given by the object they name or stand for. I shall follow Robert Kirk's exposition of how, in the example, the phrase 'five red apples' is used in the constructed language-game (Kirk 1999, 60–63). Kirk himself is critical towards Wittgenstein's view of language, but his reconstruction of Wittgenstein's view of language is well suited to illustrating an important aspect of the problem of realism.

Let us assume that the word 'five' names an object. What might this object be? According to one proposal, it is the number five. In this case, the question arises how this supposed object plays a role in the actual language game. A philosopher inspired by Plato would presumably cite the fact that number is an example of a special class of objects lying outside our world of sense experience. At the same time, the internal relations of such objects among themselves explain, for example, the truths of arithmetic. Thus we can assert that two and two are four because in addition to the numbers two and four there is also a relation of addition and a relation of equality. Although these objects lie outside our sense experience, we can nevertheless know that two and two are four because we can acquire a special kind of intellectual understanding of numbers and the relations between them. Wittgenstein questions whether it is really necessary to introduce numbers as a special class of entities in order to understand how the simple language game in the example works. In his view, in the example it is a question of actions which follow rules serving specific aims in human interaction. No explanation which posits numbers with an existence of their own, is required.

What about colour words then? Are they meaningful because they name a special kind of object? Here the answer is just the same as before. If we observe what happens in a concrete language game instead of becoming ensnared in a general theory, we observe that even here there is no support for the usual view of the meaning of words and sentences. Let us suppose that the expression 'red' means either the red apples or the colour list in the shop in which colour words are linked to colour specimens. The red apples cannot constitute the meaning of the expression 'red'. We assume namely that the word 'red' will retain its meaning even if there are no apples. The meaning of the word 'red' cannot therefore be an individual object like an apple. The same is true of the colour samples. The meaning of the word 'red' is not a colour sample. Once again we presuppose that the word 'red' retains its meaning even if the colour samples were lost. The word's use consists instead in the circumstance that the storekeeper, upon receiving an order for five red apples, selects the apples in agreement with the list of colour words and colour samples. The word 'red' has a particular role in the language game. It is this that constitutes its meaning and not the fact that it is the name of a particular object such as an apple or colour sample.

What of the word 'apple' then? An object word must at least designate an object. Let us see how the matter stands. In the present language game, the storekeeper has a box marked 'apples'. If the word 'apple' is a name for an object which is presumed to exist, then a problem occurs when it turns out that the box is empty because the supply of apples has dried up, due to a natural catastrophe. The word 'apple' therefore ought no longer to have any meaning. That is not, however, the conclusion we draw. The lack of apples does not prevent the word 'apple' from continuing to be used in a meaningful way. Just as in the case of number words and colour words, the meaning of these words is not given by specific objects whether concrete objects like apples or abstract objects such as numbers or the idea of an apple. The meaning of the word consists in the use of the word 'apple' in the language game.

Wittgenstein's discussion of language games is intended to challenge us to question the apparently self-evident assumption that the meaning of words is to be found in their designations. He wants us to see that this general assumption does not help us when we wish to explain what occurs in an actual language game. He does it by illustrating how our use of language is one form of behaviour among others, a rule-governed behaviour which serves many aims and satisfies many needs, with respect to human interaction and the relationship between human beings and the world. In Part IV, making use of this notion of interaction, I shall develop a pragmatic alternative to metaphysical realism and apply it to the domain of religion.

Because of the realist's initial assumptions which I shall criticize in Parts II and III, his fears are still concerned with what happens to the distinction between what we decide is real on the basis of our available concepts, and what really is real. Does the postmodern challenge and Wittgenstein's critique of a realist view of language entail that the second alternative must be dropped i.e. that what is really real is merely what we suppose to be real? Or is it still possible to maintain the distinction between something being supposed to be real, and something being really real? Let me present some examples to show how in the domain of religion, various attempts have been made to maintain the distinction. The first example is an attempt to combine postmodernism with Christian belief; the second is a common philosophical position within Christianity; and the third is an example of New Age spirituality. The aim of these examples is not to give an overview of the internal discussion within religion, but rather to pin down the central problem of realism in the case of religion. Because of my limited knowledge of the history of religion, I shall confine myself to Christianity in the case of the first two examples and to the Swedish situation in the case of the third. I do not believe however that these limitations invalidate the philosophical points which I wish to make with the help of these examples.

Religious illustrations

I shall begin with an attempt in which attention is paid to the postmodern critique of traditional thought while at the same time a realist basic position is retained. I have in mind the attempt by the Anglican theologian, Sue Patterson, to give due weight in the case of Christian theology, both to the postmodern thesis on the indivisible interdependence of language and reality, and to the demand that we treat the truth of God as an absolute truth which holds for all reality. For my purposes, her attempt shows clearly how the problem of realism is raised by specific religious claims about truth and reality.

Although Patterson says that she accepts the postmodern thesis on the indivisible interdependence of language and reality, she nevertheless, wants to retain the idea of Christianity's non-negotiable realist nature (Patterson 1999, 11). She therefore bases her investigation on the following two premises. The first is the minimal theistic requirement that God's reality and truth are absolute and the second is that the human reality which theology deals with is a postmodern reality (Patterson 1999, 161f.). Together the two premises are thought to entail

> that Christian (as well as creaturely) reality be understood as particular and language-ridden while at the same time offering a master-story that draws the rest of human reality inside its linguistic particularity (Patterson 1999, 162).

In spite of the postmodern emphasis that it is always a question of "language-ridden reality", the link with a realist view of reality is nevertheless retained:

> [T]he only *general* theory Christianity should adopt, and then adopt in terms of its own particularity, is its own fundamental claim of the ultimacy and universality of God's reality and truth (Patterson 1999, 31).

As far as I can see, such a position leads to the following dilemma: on the one hand, despite the acceptance of postmodern insights about reality as "language-ridden reality", it is still a question of a universal claim which excludes all other claims since all human reality is absorbed in its own comprehensive account. This would imply that Patterson's position is open to the charge of incoherence. Alternatively, her position is coherent and talk of "the ultimacy and universality of God's reality and truth" is really a part of linguistic particularity and nothing else. In this latter case, words such as 'ultimacy', 'universality', 'reality' and truth lose their established meaning which extends beyond particular contexts.

Patterson gives the following argument for the necessity of theological realism. "If all human attempts at establishing truth are 'contaminated', as Putnam puts it, realism must be theistic to be coherent" (Patterson 1999, 163). Our always limited and slanted views of reality and our far from reliable attempts at arriving at the truth require something non-human as a counterbalance. Given that Patterson requires a theistic realism, and in this connection speaks of universal truth, as far as secular reality's radical dependence on God is concerned, I hold that she is advocating a type of metaphysical realism which I have set out to criticize in the present work. The relationship between secular reality and God is considered to be ontological, and is supposed to exist, irrespective of how we conceptualize it. The problem, however, is simply that we cannot say a word, not even about God, without conceptualization. Divine reality is also a reality which is comprehended and conceptualized by human beings. It is either inconsistent merely to treat secular, but not divine, reality as a linguistic one, or else a further argument is required to maintain that divine reality is intrinsically unconceptualized. I have been unable to find such an argument in Patterson.

Seen from our human perspective, all our views of reality require conceptualizations. It is somewhat ironical that Patterson refers to Hilary Putnam. It is certainly the case that Putnam has changed his opinion on a number of philosophical issues in the course of time; but on one point he has not altered it. Metaphysical realism, that is the view that there is only one true description of reality, or to employ Patterson's own terminology only one true "master-story", is the one type of realism which Putnam in numerous writings has never ceased to question. If Patterson wishes to hold on to a position of metaphysical realism, as I believe the above quotations show that she does, while at the same time making use of the basic postmodern assumptions, she is faced with the foregoing dilemma. Given the crucial role that this dilemma has as a starting point for my critique of metaphysical realism, I shall repeat it in a somewhat modified form. If Patterson means what she says when she speaks about "language-ridden" reality, then she must abstain from the truth claim that there is a divine reality which is independent of us, that is, independent of all our conceptualizations. To refer, as Patterson does, to God's incarnation in Christ as a means of conceptualizing divine reality, and thereby allowing us access to it, does not suffice to save the situation. Even in this very reference, there is namely a claim to know how it really is, quite independently of the Christian conceptualizations of God's incarnation in Christ. On the other hand, if Patterson treats metaphysical realism as a non-negotiable part of Christianity, this rules out incorporating the basic postmodern insights within her position. I cannot see how Patterson can avoid inconsistency, given her choice of premises.

It seems to me that Patterson, despite her postmodern influences, still holds on to the assumptions of metaphysical realism. As a result, the difference between her position and a more traditional Christian one is only a matter of degree, with regard to the issue of the relationship between language and reality. A good illustration of the traditional position can be found in Peter Vardy's *The Puzzle of God*. Here, there is no attempt to reconcile realist components with postmodern – or in Vardy's terminology – anti-realist ones. Realism and anti-realism are presented as two mutually exclusive points of view. I shall confine myself to quoting Vardy's definition of realism and its application in Christian belief:

> The realist claims that a statement is true because it corresponds to a state of affairs that is independent of language and the society in which we live. To say that a statement is true is to claim that it correctly refers beyond itself. ... When we come to apply this to God, we shall see that the realist maintains that the statement, "God exists" is true because it corresponds or refers to the God who created and sustains the universe (Vardy 1990, 23).

The majority would certainly agree with this, with most atheists subscribing to the first part of the quotation and most Christians accepting the rest.

The belief in the absolute reality and truth of God or the divine being seems so widespread that it is not only in traditional religious contexts that it is used as a foundation for the view of language expressed in the quotation above and for the metaphysical realism associated with it. The same thing is true of a modern spiritual movement like New Age. As Olof Franck has shown, this movement also interprets the relation between language and a transcendent reality from a realist perspective. The relation between religious language and transcendent reality is said to be given, and can therefore be discovered. Human beings are said certainly to partake in the omnipresent divine power, to constitute the meeting-place where the divine can be encountered, and to be fellow creative agents who form part of the cosmic whole. However, *what* is true as far as spiritual questions are concerned, is assumed to be unhesitatingly given. The truth claims concern among other things the existence of a divine power which operates both in and outside human beings, the existence of extra-terrestrial beings and worlds, the existence of moral values and the expectation of a life after death (Franck 1998, 59f.). Not a word is said to suggest that human beings contribute something as far as the relation between religious language and transcendent reality is concerned. This relation is something given and is there waiting to be discovered.

As can be seen, there is in this respect little difference between more traditional religion and a modern spiritual movement like New Age. Some people will undoubtedly wonder what there is strange in this. Is it not characteristic of religious belief to hold that there is a divine reality which exists independently of us, and upon which the secular reality depends, and to argue that there exists an objective, referential relation between religious language and divine reality? It may be that many hold such a view, and have also spoken up in defence of metaphysical realism as a basis for this view i.e. it may well be that this happens to be the most common view of the relation between philosophy and religion. I would, however, criticize the rationale behind this view by focussing on the general problem of realism in Part II and on the particular problems associated with religious realism in Part III. Before I do this, however, I need to present my view of religion and the philosophy of religion.

3 Religion and philosophy

When in this book I discuss the problems of realism in general and of religious realism in particular, I do not adopt a perspective which is internal to religious belief. As I have said, I am interested in the problem of realism as it is also manifested by the phenomenon of religion, with a view to developing conceptual instruments which will help us arrive at a better understanding of this phenomenon's function in the lives of human beings, while at the same time retaining a critical distance to it. We know from certain frightening examples that not all variants of religious belief are good for us. These words already reveal naturally certain views about religion. The question is whether these views precede or succeed philosophical reflection about the phenomenon of religion. If we, for religious reasons, wish to criticize certain variants of religious belief by making use *inter alia* of philosophy, a definite view of religion precedes philosophizing. In this case, philosophy is, however, subordinate to religion. On the other hand, if we wish to assign philosophy an autonomous position in relation to religion, philosophical reflection about the phenomenon of religion precedes a definite view about religion in the sense that our view of religion can be altered as a result of philosophical reflection about the phenomenon of religion. I shall work within the latter framework, but at the same time, I wish to draw attention to the fact that there is a kind of circle involved in philosophical reflection about the phenomenon of religion.

An unavoidable circle

The circle can be entered at two points. (1) One entry point arises from adopting explicitly or implicitly a definite view of religion. The task consists in clarifying the underlying philosophical assumption which such a view obliges us to adopt. If we accept, for example, the Roman Catholic view of belief, we are obliged to subscribe to the basic assumptions of Thomist philosophy. If we accept Rudolf Bultmann's programme of demythologization and the associated view of religious belief, we are obliged to accept certain philosophical assumptions which derive from Martin Heidegger's existential philosophy. Further examples could be given.

Once we have clarified the philosophical assumptions that a particular view of religion imposes on us, it becomes time to submit them to critical analysis. This analysis has then consequences for the plausibility of the view of religion with which we began. A pre-requirement is naturally that our view of religion is not considered to be non-negotiable because of revelation or for some other reason. If a non-negotiable and dogmatic position is adopted then philosophy is entirely used to defend our own religious standpoint. However, given that there does not seem to be any accepted definition of religion, varying views and explanations of religion as a phenomenon in human life, are possible. These various views and explanations can be critically compared with one another indirectly, by examining the philosophical assumptions which the views and explanations compel us to accept.

(2) The second point of entry to the aforementioned circle is to begin, as I do, with certain philosophical problems e.g. the problem of realism, because they repeatedly crop up in the philosophical literature. There is the debate about scientific realism which discusses whether scientific theories describe reality, and are thereby true or false, or are instead more or less adequate instruments for saying something about what can be observed. We have the debate about semantic realism which raises the question of whether linguistic meaning is to be exclusively defined in terms of truth conditions which hold no matter whether we have knowledge of them or not, or instead is to be defined on the basis of our capacity to create procedures which allow us to determine the statement's truth value. There is the discussion about epistemological reasoning: are there truths which go beyond the evidence i.e. "truths whose obtaining lies beyond our powers of recognition" (Dancy 1985, 19), or is the knowable world the only world which can be linked to the concept of truth. We have the debate about moral realism which takes up the issue of whether values have an intrinsically real existence, or are instead created when, for example, emotions are conceptualized. Finally we have the debate about religious realism which depends in turn upon the positions adopted in all the other discussions

about realism. I have already mentioned the broad nature of my philosophical enquiry and this will be manifest when I discuss how the debate
about the problems of religious realism are interwoven with the other discussions of realism and anti-realism.

In the second entry point to the circle, the relative ranking of philosophy
and religion are reversed. We start instead with the philosophical positions
which are adopted with respect to the philosophical problems raised by religion and its secular counterparts, and thereafter investigate the question
of what views of religion follow from these philosophical positions. The
critical investigation of the implied view of religion is then about, among
things, the question of how this view stands in relation to the personal
view of the believer and religious critic. This certainly lies outside the
framework of philosophical enquiry, but a solid basis for our attitude to
religion as a phenomenon in human life requires us to give some thought
to this issue. I do not mean that the criterion for deciding which view is
acceptable should be that all believers and critics of religion ought to be
able to accept the view. I simply mean that a view about religion as a human phenomenon has no worthwhile explanatory value, if it is not the case
that a large number of believers for whom religion is as vital as the air they
breathe, can in some way identify themselves with the view.

In what follows, it will become clear that although I certainly take note
of both of the aforementioned entry points, it is the second one which is
primary for my own work. It is thus not the case that I set out with a definite view of religion which I shall defend or recommend, that I then formulate the philosophical assumptions which this view requires, and that I
finally criticize other philosophical assumptions which are inconsistent
with them. Instead, it is my philosophical reflections about the problem of
realism and its ontological, semantic, epistemological and normative aspects which have led me to view religion as a phenomenon in human life
in the way that I do. I shall briefly present my view of religion and then in
the course of the work, I shall show in more detail how I have arrived at it.

Religion as a human phenomenon

First of all, I have come to look upon religions as views of life. For this
reason, I do not distinguish between religion and view of life, but only
between religious and non-religious views of life. Conspicuous social
changes serve to motivate the identification of religion and view of life.
Sweden is very far from being the only society which is assuming a stead-
ily more pluralistic character. Given the role as a view of life which religion plays in the lives of men and women, it is precisely life and what it
means to be a human being which religions and their secular counterparts
are concerned with. The term 'view of life' is not entirely felicitous since it

risks being associated with a mere observer's position and not with the life of personal involvement which it is really about. A view of life can be formulated verbally, and this is quite usual; but it is in the way we live that a view of life becomes evident. In Part IV I shall show that this functional interpretation of religion does not entail an eliminative reduction of the religious to the non-religious.

Secondly, given this background, I have come to interpret views of life, and therefore also the task and function of religion, as being one of expressing and communicating what it means to be a human being, that is to say, to live with such inevitabilities of life as happiness, love, joy, suffering, guilt, and death. These components in our lives are unavoidable and inevitable. We cannot understand them completely. There is always something overpowering about them which affects us deeply. Nor can we eliminate them by reducing them to something else. When we consider love, for example, and why we are drawn to certain types of people, although it is wise sometimes to note that it is in part a matter of chemistry, it would be absurd to maintain that love is no more than chemistry. Life also involves qualitative experiences which have a value irrespective of their causes.

Insights into life's inevitabilities also need to be expressed for otherwise they cannot be presented as insights. At this point, views of life enter the picture, since they offer conceptualizations and other expressive means which we can existentially experience as adequate expressions for what it means to be a human being, in particular with reference to life's inevitabilities. In what follows, when I use the phrase 'what it means to be a human being', sometimes with the added phrase 'i.e. to live with life's inevitabilities' and sometimes without, I mean simply that. Of course there is much more involved in being a human being, which I shall nevertheless disregard, as far as view of life conceptualizations about what it means to live with life's inevitabilities are concerned. I shall not consider, for example, the concrete consequences which views of life can have for the preparation of food and diet, our personal economy, and relations between the sexes.

If, as I shall advocate later on, we look at views of life from the perspective of the participating or acting agent, four distinct, but interrelated uses of the expression 'view of life' can be identified:
(1) The first use refers to the images, narratives, and ideas which allow us to express what it means to be a human being i.e. to live with life's inevitabilities.
(2) The second use refers to those images, narratives and ideas which have been institutionalized through social intercourse and which are taken as paradigms of how life can or ought to be lived.

(3) The third use refers to those images, narratives and ideas which are summarized and structured in teachings, systems of dogma and similar.
(4) Finally the fourth use refers to institutions in the literal sense such as churches, political parties and similar entities.

The present state of the philosophy of religion

Some people consider that the task which I have set myself, does not belong to the philosophy of religion. They hold that the philosophy of religion is an activity which belongs alongside such theological disciplines as fundamental theology, dogmatics, theological or practical ethics. This viewpoint is opposed by those who hold that the philosophy of religion is a philosophical and not a theological discipline. At the same time, within the ranks of those adopting this latter approach, there are diverse opinions about what the philosophy of religion is, depending on whether philosophy is linked to hermeneutics, existentialism, phenomenology or analytical philosophy. An influential demarcation line can be illustrated by considering the situation of the philosophy of religion in North America which, together with its British counterpart, has had the greatest impact in Sweden in recent years. A clear division in approach can be discerned in the proceedings of a colloquium held some years ago, between philosophers of religion belonging to the American Philosophical Association and those belonging to the American Academy of Religion (Wainwright 1996).[3]

Put rather simply, we might say that the philosophers of religion in the American Philosophic Association are concerned almost exclusively with philosophical problems which are associated with traditional Christian theism, and the majority of them are in fact theists. The theistic philosophers of religion focus on God, the object of religious belief, and on the truth claims which arise wit h respect to a divine being. This type of philosophy of religion is primarily concerned with epistemological issues. The philosophers of religion who belong to the American Philosophical Association are in general to be found in university departments of philosophy. They are often prominent in other philosophical areas, and are thus able to immerse themselves in theistic issues without their philosophical professionalism being called into question. Moreover the theistic philosophers of religion hold that it is perfectly natural to devote oneself to Christian theism, rather than to some other form of theism, because Christian theism constitutes an important part of the Western philosophical tradition. In addition, a very definite view of analytical philosophy appears to be dominant in the philosophical departments where they teach. Analytical philosophy is often related to science and to the objects and entities which

---

[3] See also Koistinen 2000.

science finds interesting. The object studied in the theistic philosophy of religion is God. Because reason's capacity to discover truths is held to be reliable, it is important to determine the truth or falsity of theistic claims with the help of reason and logic. A theist will tend to be more interested in determining the truth of theistic claims and in critically analyzing atheistic objections. Atheists on the other hand tend conversely to be more interested in providing a critique of the truth claims of theists.

Appealing to an analogous generalization about the philosophers of religion belonging to the American Academy of Religion, we might, once again putting things somewhat simply, say that most of them are active in departments of religious studies. They do not enquire into God, nor do they attempt to establish the truth of statements about God. They are more concerned with people who practise a religion. They look upon religions as a complex phenomenon composed of rites, texts, myths, social relations etc. The philosophers of religion at departments of religious studies have in principle nothing against the notion of philosophically analyzing religious views. On the other hand, they are sceptical about the way in which their colleagues in the first group are specifically concerned with theism and Christian theism at that. They hold that the theistic philosophers of religion do not simply view theism descriptively as a part of the history of Western philosophy but also use it as a metaphysical theological norm.

Whereas analytical philosophy forms the philosophical background for the theistic philosophy of religion, the departments of religious studies are based, above all, upon the type of European philosophy which is essentially anti-metaphysical i.e. the philosophy of Immanuel Kant or Martin Heidegger. This leads to a rejection of theism as metaphysical and thereby also to a rejection of a one-sided focus on the question of truth. Instead there is more interest in the human subject and in the institutions and various types of practice which human beings have developed in various situations.

Let me try to say where my own work fits into this broad picture of the philosophy of religion. In contrast to theistic analytical philosophy, and for reasons which I shall set forth in Parts II–IV, I share the anti-metaphysical attitude which is to be found not only in certain Continental thinkers but also in the philosophy of the later Wittgenstein, in pragmatism and in parts of analytical philosophy. I look upon myself as an analytical philosopher of religion in the sense that I hold, despite postmodern objections, that questions about truth and rationality are still important. There is a difference between, on the one hand, our maintaining that something is true or reasonable, and, on the other hand, its actually being true or reasonable. Although I shall defend a certain form of relativism, I shall also show that that our actions and our attitudes to our fellow human beings will differ greatly, depending upon whether we accept this distinction or not. I shall keep to this distinction, but at the same time, I shall devise an alternative to a metaphysical realist philosophy of religion. I shall do this by fixing my attention on the human subject in the sense that reality for us is always a reality which is interpreted and conceptualized by us. By 'us' I mean the biological and social beings that we are.

By the philosophy of religion, I mean the philosophical discipline which treats philosophical problems raised by the phenomenon of religion and its secular counterparts. This sounds simple, but it is in fact far from simple since there is no generally accepted definition of philosophy. Let me explain my position with regard to the fact that some people think of philosophy as a doctrine, some consider it a theory, some regard it as a way of life, while still others view it as a type of reflective activity.

4 Philosophy

It is not unusual that by philosophy is meant the striving for wisdom in the sense of a search for a insightful and harmonious way of life. Philosophy thereby merges with a definite ethical or religious attitude to life and we find expositions of Marxist, Christian, Buddhist, Moslem, and Jewish philosophy etc. Sometimes, when philosophy merges with a religious attitude to life, it is seen as constituting a philosophy of religion. My own opinion is that it would be unfortunate to identify philosophy or the philosophy of religion with a religious or secular attitude to life. The question of deciding what attitude to life we should adopt, involves much more than philosophy can deliver. It can help us on our way, but precisely because of its strong emphasis on reason, it cannot in itself constitute an attitude to life. The development of a viable attitude to life requires many more capacities than merely an intellectual one. I shall return to the question *inter alia* of the importance of the emotions for this matter in Part V. Very roughly we can say that some philosophers hold that philosophy is incapable of producing knowledge. Other philosophers, by contrast, use the term 'philosophy' for reason's ability to arrive at knowledge purely with the help of conceptual analysis and logic.

Philosophy and knowledge

Those who maintain that philosophy can deliver knowledge, can themselves be divided into two groups. One group maintains, in the spirit of classical metaphysics, that the knowledge about intrinsic existence or about the fundamental principles of reality which philosophy provides, is basic for all knowledge. The criticism which I shall make against metaphysical realism, is a blow to this view. In the other group which aims at developing a scientific philosophy, logic and conceptual analysis are placed in close relation to the knowledge accumulated by the sciences (or more specifically the natural sciences) and founded upon mathematics and empirical observation. Some would even go so far in the name of science and scientific philosophy to maintain that scientific reason holds dominion even in the sphere of issues pertaining to attitudes to life. In its most extreme form, it is evident in what has come to be called 'scientism' which holds that the sole rational attitude to life is one where we accept only that which can be accepted on scientific grounds.[4]

There are, above all, two objections which I have to scientism, and thereby to the one-sided emphasis on scientific reason in general. First of all, many of our most customary and indispensable activities do not rest merely on a scientific basis. For example, a great deal within medicine is based not on strictly scientific grounds but upon tested experience. There is nothing wrong with this because from the viewpoint of results we can very often rely on tested experience even when it lacks strict scientific support. Secondly a purely scientific basis is insufficient for another reason. In our views of ourselves and other beings in our world, experiences of meaning and value play an indispensable role. It is certainly possible, and for certain explanatory purposes it is obligatory, to objectify this function also, and explain it e.g. in evolutionary terms. In our daily life, where we are faced with problems of different kinds, and have to make a decision, we cannot get away from the fact that we have these experiences, and that they play a part in determining our lives and actions. In order to give this fact its due, we therefore require also to conceptualize these experiences of meaning and value, and at the same time submit them to critical appraisal. In this respect, we derive no particular benefit from resting our case on scientific grounds. We need also to take into account the traditions in which we have learned to express and recognize experiences of meaning and value. Science can help us to understand how we have learned this and this understanding can and should be used in philosophy and the philosophy of religion, when we set out to give a critical account of how expressions for meaning and value, for example, can be appropriately conceptualized.

I have said that it would be unfortunate if we identified philosophy or the philosophy of religion with an attitude to life. At the same time, I would not deny that there is something in the assimilation of philosophy to an ethical, religious or secular attitude to life. Greater room is then accorded to the inevitable question of what it means to be a being with the capacity for self-knowledge. The questions of how we can be better human

---

[4] See e.g. Stenmark 2001.

beings, and how we can achieve a fulfilling life in relation to the world around us, should not, in my view, be divorced from philosophizing. Nor, for this reason, can I accept a purely technical view of philosophy, according to which the philosopher is some kind of paid employee, charged with carrying out prescribed theoretical work. From this perspective, the issue of how philosophical work is related to our lives and those of other people seems obviously irrelevant. The main point is exclusively supposed to be the solution of a technical philosophical problem with the help of certain accepted means, irrespective of whether it is relevant for further philosophical issues or for non-philosophical ones.

As a justification of my rejection of such a narrow view of philosophy, I would like to refer to how Putnam, according to James Conant, on the basis of the Kantian distinction between "the scholastic concept of philosophy (*der Schulbegriff der Philosophie*) and the universal or cosmic concept (*der Weltbegriff*) (Conant 1990, xxiv)" strives for a synthesis of the two concepts:

> The *Schulbegriff* (the scholastic concept) embodies philosophy's aspiration to the systematicity and the rigor of a science. ... It is sought and valued as a science ... for two reasons: first and foremost, because it strives to clarify the foundation of the other sciences (properly so-called) and to lay a groundwork for them; and second, because it provides a fertile breeding ground for scientific ideas. ... The crucial feature of the *Schulbegriff* of philosophy that Kant pauses over here, however, is its esotericism – the fact that it is in the province of a few professionals (Conant 1990, xxv).

In contrast to this, the other concept of philosophy embraces rational thought about all kinds of questions which are of interest for nearly all of us.

> Philosophy, viewed under the aspect of this concept, is radically *exoteric*: both its sources and its aims are rooted in the very nature of what it is to be human. ... The *Weltbegriff* of philosophy is grounded in the fact that every human mind, by virtue of its sheer capacity to reason, harbors a philosopher (Conant 1990, xxviii).

My reason for rejecting the purely esoteric concept of philosophy is that many philosophical problems have originally arisen in non-philosophical contexts. Consider for example Kant's classical questions: how is knowledge possible? How is morality possible? Such problems could probably never have been formulated if we did not for the most part actually behave correctly and knew a great deal, while at the same time there are occasional collisions between various views about what is right and what is to be accepted as knowledge. These collisions are serious because we act on the basis of what we consider to be right and what we believe we know, and sometimes, for practical reasons, there is no room for more than one alternative among the possible courses of action. In the case of capital punishment, for example, a country either has it or does not have it, irrespective of how divided opinion may be on the issue, and acts in accordance with this. The question of what is really right, can arise. Physicians are sometimes confronted with situations in which they do not know what diagnosis to make i.e. to determine the cause of an illness. Nevertheless they must decide what they are to do. The question of what knowledge is, can then arise. The sceptic likes to seize on such situations to generalize about the difficulties, and to question our very capacity to know anything.

The opposite to scepticism is sometimes expressed in another view of philosophy. In this view, philosophy is treated as being identical with one or other view of the world. Philosophy in this sense treats reality as a whole, and gives answers to questions about the foundation of reality, about values, about the place of human beings in reality and their capacities for knowledge and action. Philosophy for which this is claimed, is often presented as the primary science, or as the precondition for scientific knowledge in general. Such a claim is synonymous with the claim to know how things really and ultimately are, and thereby presupposes what Putnam and many in agreement with him call "a God's Eye point of view."[5] The problem with such a perspective is that it is not one which we, as human beings, can adopt. As soon as we try to conceive how really or ultimately things are, we do so by necessity within the framework of our language and our cognitive capacities. I shall return to consider the question of what conclusions can or cannot be reasonably drawn from this criticism.

Philosophical reflection

I have no more desire to treat philosophy as one science among others than I have to treat it as the primary science or the unshakeable foundation of all scientific knowledge. It is obvious that philosophy cannot attain knowledge as the sciences, for example, do. Some have, therefore, drawn the conclusion that philosophy in the traditional sense ought to be given up and replaced by science. This, however, is to cast out the baby with the bathwater. It does not follow from the fact that philosophy does not produce scientific knowledge, that it is useless or unnecessary. It is needed in the form of reflection about existence which also naturally includes the sciences. In all scientific disciplines, we are preoccupied, for example, with theories. But the sciences themselves are not in a position to answer the following questions. What is a theory? How are we to interpret a theory: as an instrument or as a description of reality? There is no one answer to such philosophic questions, but the answers we give, determine the way in which scientific work is actually carried out, and the claims, not only with respect to knowledge but also with respect to values, we can make on

---

[5] E.g. Putnam 1981, 49.

this basis. For this reason, we require continual, ongoing reflection about such philosophical questions.

If we look upon philosophy as a reflective activity, it is then quite natural to speak of the philosophy of science, the philosophy of art, the philosophy of law, moral philosophy, the philosophy of language, the philosophy of mathematics and so too of the philosophy of religion. In the case of the philosophy of religion, we reflect about the phenomenon of religion and about the philosophical problems this phenomenon raises.

Now it might be thought that such reflection would require a well defined concept of religion. As we have said, however, there does not seem to be any generally accepted understanding of religion. It would seem to be a characteristic of words such as 'religion' or 'democracy' to borrow an example from the social sciences, that we continually require to discuss how such words are in fact used, and how they ought to be used in relation to the problems we have to confront in our lives. Our need for a definition of the word 'religion' depends on the situation. It depends on whether we have philosophical, psychological, theological, political or other aims. All of this contributes to what we mean by religion and determines the problems which arise and about which we wish to reflect. The object of reflection in the philosophy of religion can thus vary. It can be a certain religious way of life, an abstract view about the essence of religion, or a definite theological standpoint. A precondition for this flexibility is, however, that the philosophical reflection adopts an independent position with regard to religious belief.

What then is the difference between philosophical and theological reflection for example? Both make use of explicit argumentation. If we ignore philosophy in the sense of teachings or as a standpoint which can be summarized in a number of theses, the difference between philosophical and theological reflection is to be found above all in the following. Theological reflection which explicitly or implicitly starts out from a given denominational or religious framework, aims at defending a definite point of view, rendering it more secure or at least undermining objections to it. This does not mean that I am claiming that philosophical reflection has no presuppositions. It too begins with personal interests, with what one considers valuable and wishes to preserve, and with what one is afraid of and therefore wishes to dispel. The aim, however, is more a matter of being able to raise certain questions which help us to understand how things are related, and to solve problems, rather than a matter of defending a particular viewpoint. In simple terms, we can express the difference like this: whereas in philosophy we concentrate on questions without knowing the answers in advance, in theology we adopt a position towards answers that have already been given. Something similar applies to various types of ideology where philosophical methods are subordinated to the aim of confirming one particular position and refuting competing alternatives.

Very often philosophical questions revolve around things which are taken to be self-evident e.g. to treat the assertion 'God exists' as a statement of fact, a necessary precondition for being considered a believer according to many believers and also critics of religion. Metaphysical realism functions for a number of theologians and theistic and atheistic philosophers of religion as a precondition which is not open to debate.

Let me illustrate how I shall reflect philosophically about metaphysical realism and other philosophical standpoints relating to this issue. It is indubitably true that we have realist intuitions which would be meaningless to question. Such intuitions are to the effect "that human experience is only a part of reality, reality is not part or whole of human experience" (Putnam 1975, 273). What we hold to be true, as well as those experiences which help us to formulate our beliefs, are however internal in relation to our language. This does not mean that with the help, for example, of some kind of agreement, we could ourselves decide what is true. Neither does it mean that we are aware of everything which is true, or conversely that only what is true is known to us. It means instead the following. In order to claim that something is true, we have to understand what we mean by 'true'. Understanding what 'true' means, involves a relation to what, in Putnam's terminology, is for us human beings ideal or (in later writings) sufficiently good epistemological grounds for a justification of a given belief.[6] Existence embraces more than what we are and what we can understand.

In spite of the fact that reality, so to speak, offers resistance and is both the practical and logical basis for all that we say, think and do, it is still problematic if we, for this reason, were to make pronouncements about reality, at the same time claiming that we are making statements about reality as if it were something unconceptualized in itself and not already understood by us. My philosophical reflections pay no regard to whether it is metaphysical realism or metaphysical anti-realism which is true or false. The aim of the critical part of my work is instead directed at that which makes both metaphysical realism and metaphysical anti-realism philosophically dubious positions, both in general terms and particularly in the sphere of religion. If realism is taken to mean that we can say something about reality as though it were intrinsically unconceptualized, we are forgetting that reality is always something which is conceptualized and understood by us. Conversely, if anti-realism means that there is no reality which is independent of us, we are forgetting that reality offers resistance, in the sense that there are limits to our possible actions. Moreover since we act on the basis of our conceptualizations about reality, this means that

---

[6] See e.g. Putnam 1987, 19f.

conceptualizations which are suitable with respect to the reality in which we move and have our being and which we need to interact with, cannot be entirely arbitrary. The philosophical work involved in critically examining the different types of conceptualization and their preconditions needs to be adjusted to the underlying tension between on the one hand the fact that reality, so to speak, offers resistance to the arbitrary dictates of our will, and on the other hand, the fact that reality for human beings is always something conceptualized. The adaptation of the philosophical work to this tension implies that any claim to reveal timeless universal philosophical theses about reality as such, is pointless. When such theses are set forth, they merely reproduce the problem of realism by onesidedly emphasizing only one of the components contributing to the state of tension.

A philosopher who is subjected to this kind of criticism, may perhaps raise the following objection: if philosophy and the philosophy of religion cannot produce timeless universal philosophical theses about reality, what is its value? I would reply by saying that philosophical work is something which we have to apply to ourselves, to our own view of how we look upon things, and to our expectations of them. In this sense, philosophy has a personal dimension which is emphasized by Wittgenstein among others. Philosophy is not something which can be left to someone else. It is a question of our becoming aware of the concepts which have caused our philosophical perplexity and of how these concepts are linked to the way we live (Wittgenstein 1989, 132).

In my view, this is best accomplished by starting with the way in which we, as philosophers, use certain expressions, and how these expressions occur in the arguments and motivations which are adduced for various types of belief. It should be noted that the word 'belief' is already in itself a word which is assigned different meanings and which can cause philosophical perplexity. We are concerned both with beliefs which function as claims to knowledge and with beliefs where this is not the case. The latter kind of belief represents what we more or less take for granted, and together with explicit claims to knowledge forms part of the basis for our actions. They are of such a character that their import is revealed in the reactions we display. When these beliefs are verbalized, it does not necessarily have to be in the form of a factual statement. Thus the belief that there is an external world is an example of the latter type of belief. Given the type of beings we are, it specifies the practical and logical presupposition for all that we do, say, and think. However, the belief itself is not a statement of fact.

One of the possible tasks of the philosophy of religion with reference to so-called religious language, would therefore be to investigate what sort of belief is involved. If it is a question of a knowledge claim, any criticism has then to discuss what we mean by knowledge, and how we test knowledge claims. If it is a question of reactions, in which the very use of certain formulations constitutes reactions to life's inevitabilities, for example, any criticism has then to address itself to questions about the significance of the reactions for our understanding of reality.

The philosophical methods for clarifying such conceptual matters consists not only in logically reconstructing arguments, but also in bringing into the clear light of day what is apparently an argument but in fact is more the presentation of an idea. There is nothing wrong in our having ideas. We indicate by their means both our actual lives as well as the lives that we consider are worth living. Certain ideas in philosophy can, however, be misleading, and give rise to so-called philosophical problems such as the existence of the external world. Certain kinds of philosophical problem which can be treated without implications for how we live as the beings we are, are avoided by developing for critical purposes, distinctions which allow us to see that there is a difference between what we hold to be true for particular objects and what we hold to be true for, so to speak, the whole of reality, and that these different beliefs do not therefore belong to the same category.

Another important distinction which philosophical reflection can make us aware of, is the difference between, on the one hand, conceptual distinctions, say between dark and light, where we cannot conceive how we could ever doubt that black is darker than white and white lighter than dark, and on the other hand dualisms which have definite ontological or ideological associations, and which are open to question. The latter is true in particular of such divisions as those between culture and nature, objective and subjective, rational and irrational, male and female.

Philosophy's contribution to achieving knowledge consists in criticizing conceptual confusion and logical errors and in devising alternative conceptual tools. With respect to the latter, philosophical work is concerned, not with how things are, but with how things could be understood. In order not to become lost in fruitless speculations, the starting points of our investigations should be specified: the philosophy of science is concerned with science, the philosophy of law with law, the philosophy of language with language, the philosophy of religion with religion and so on. The fact that it can be difficult to specify exactly what it is in these many-faceted phenomena that one is trying to capture, is of course another question. Because the phenomena are many-faceted, it is more appropriate to present a philosophical critique of e.g. ideas about the essence of language, religion, mathematics etc and to concentrate on the problems which are raised by these phenomena in various situations.

Philosophical problems

For the sake of clarity, I want to underline that a problem is always a problem for a particular person, at a particular time, and in a particular theoretical or practical context. In order for something to constitute a problem, it must be experienced as a problem. That is the subjective aspect. There is a problem in this respect when we feel troubled or challenged, and want to get to grips with what is worrying or challenging us. On a subjective plane, the problem is solved or disappears when, so to speak, our peace of mind has returned.

The reason why our peace of mind is disturbed and we experience something as a problem is the existence of a logical or some other tension between two different poles; or, to put it another way, we are aware that something fails to add up. Very often such problems can be formulated with help of the somewhat trite phrase 'on the one hand – on the other hand'. For example, on the one hand, God is said to be totally different in nature, with the implication that we cannot really say anything about God. On the other hand, believers claim to know a great deal about God and based on this perspective, a great deal about the world, history, and human kind. There is something which does not add up here. This is not, however, a problem in itself: it becomes one for people, for example, who feel themselves constrained by political decisions or social norms which are based on God and God's will, but who suspect that it is not simply a question of God but also of other factors such as economic ones. Consider another example. On the one hand we speak of religious knowledge of God, as if this knowledge is true and objective in the same sense that applies in the case of knowledge in other contexts. On the other hand, knowledge of God is described as something exceptional which does not allow the usual procedures for checking a knowledge claim. For certain believers, this is not a problem at all. However, it is a problem for any person who does not want to have the dissemination of religious knowledge of a fundamentalist type on the school curriculum, but wishes instead to be able to submit knowledge claims to critical scrutiny, irrespective of their provenance.

What is it that more exactly defines a philosophical problem? Despite the fact that there is no generally accepted definition of the word, 'philosophy', this does not mean that any answer whatsoever to the question will be a reasonable one. The way that we react similarly, indicates that there are questions which are part and parcel of human existence. It is linked to the fact that we are part of it and at same time we must consciously relate to it and interact with it. We are biological beings, and are therefore forced to acquire food. We are social beings, and are therefore compelled to develop relations with other human beings. In one respect, it is therefore not we who create the world, and bring about what is true. In another sense, however, the world and the world around us is our creation: it is constituted by us in the sense that reality is always reality as understood and conceptualized by us. How do these two aspects fit together?

It is characteristic of such philosophical problems, first of all, that they have to do with human existence, namely that we have consciously to relate to it, while at the same forming part of it. Secondly, given that these philosophical problems belong to human existence, they constantly recur. In this sense, they are eternal questions. Philosophical questions raised by the phenomenon of religion are thus questions which are brought about by the circumstance that the possibility of religious reactions, that is to say, the ability to see the world in religious terms, seems to be given as an integral part of human existence.

Since the problems I hold to be philosophical are intrinsically part of our human existence, we do not start out with certain fundamental principles about the nature of religion, ethics or mathematics from which we then deduce statements about the existence of God, the absoluteness of values, or the existence of numbers, and subsequently pass to a philosophical discussion of their deeper meaning. Nor is it a question of a causal relation whereby starting from various concrete religions and different secular views of life, different natural languages, different group languages, different means of expression which we call languages, different ethical systems, and different legal systems etc we then try to discover genetic explanations of how, not only these differences, but also how religion, morality and knowledge etc. themselves have come into existence. Nor is it a question of taking Kant's transcendent explanation that knowledge is impossible unless our sensations are ordered in certain forms of sensory experience and categories of understanding, and transforming it into some kind of quasi-causal explanation. Such an explanation consists in referring to the theoretical entities, forms of sensory experience and categories of understanding, as though they were actually existing entities which although certainly incapable of being discovered, nevertheless can be conceived as existing, in the sense that we have access to them by means of reason. By reasoning in this way, philosophy creates its own problems. We become bogged down in discussions of theoretical principles e.g. how far sensory experience or reason is of primary importance in determining questions of meaning and truth, while at the same time, we ignore the consequences which the outcome of these discussions could have for human life. In order to ensure that philosophical problems do not run the risk of becoming empty debate or a fruitless species of internal bickering, they must be viewed as problems which are intimately bound up with human existence.

Religion is also something intimately connected with human existence in the sense that the possibility of religious reactions, that is to say the possibility of seeing the world in religious terms, seems to given as an intrinsic part of human existence. Perhaps this can explain why there is such agreement about identifying particular ways of living as religious, irrespective of whether we ourselves are religious or not. For a person who, for example, takes life as a gift, it is not a question of first living, and then interpreting existence in religious terms as a gift. Rather reacting to life as a gift and expressing this fact verbally and non-verbally in our lives, are two sides of the same coin. Not all people react in this way, and for this reason, religious experience is more problematic than our experience of our physical environment. For those who react religiously, there is such commonality in reaction, that they are able to recognize a religious reaction, and to critically discuss its genuineness or its ability to integrate different aspects of life. Despite conspicuous differences, we can compare this with the reaction of showing pain.

There are a few people who do not feel pain, but the majority do. In this respect, showing pain is a primitive and spontaneous reaction. As children we shriek when something hurts. Gradually we learn to express our reaction to pain in a different way. Nevertheless, it is behaviour which originates in our primitive reaction to pain which we experience, as the creatures we are. Because there is a commonality of reaction, we are able to recognize behaviour associated by pain, and can critically discuss people's sincerity in speaking of their pain in situations where we have our doubts. A religious reaction is something that is learned, and can therefore not be numbered among the primitive reactions. Nevertheless, it is not something accidental in the sense that the very possibility of religious reactions i.e. of seeing the world in religious terms, would seem to be part and parcel of our human existence. The close relationship between reactions to pain and religious reactions consists in the fact that both are spontaneous reactions. Given the function which religions have in our lives, a function which applies to us as the beings we are, with a need to live a morally good and fulfilling life, there is also a commonality of reaction on this point. This explains why we can recognize religious reactions, and can also discuss critically the degree to which religions are able to satisfy this function, irrespective of whether we are religious or not.

But what has all this to do with philosophy? Naturally nothing at all, if we believe that philosophy, in the manner of the scientific disciplines, or in some metaphysical sense, supplies us with knowledge. However matters are quite different if we look at them in the following way. If we wish to speak about our different reactions, and how we express them in different situations, we need concepts and distinctions which help us to distinguish what we are speaking about. Thereby we define or constitute what we are speaking about. We do not cause pain or religion or our other reactions through our expressions for them; but what we have to say about all this, is a result of our conceptualizations of what our reactions are reactions *to*. These conceptualizations have a tendency, so to speak, to begin to live a life of their own, and give rise to problems which could be resolved if we perceived the danger of disengaging these questions from our lives. Here we encounter one of philosophy's critical tasks. Nevertheless, it does not presuppose that we can exactly define what is meant by religion, mathematics, language etc in order to identify the philosophical problems which are raised by religion, mathematics, language etc. In order to be able to speak about philosophical problems which are raised by, for example, the phenomenon of religion and its secular counterparts, it is not presupposed that we can give necessary and sufficient conditions for calling something a religion. Nevertheless we shall be able to make fair progress in solving philosophical problems when we know how various words are used, and know the function of various phenomena in human lives and the problems raised by these phenomena.

Religious and non-religious views of life

In spite of the lack of necessary and sufficient conditions for calling something a religion, there is nevertheless amazing unity about when to say that someone is religious, and even when to describe someone as being sincere or merely hypocritical. As long as we reserve the adjective 'religious' for human beings, there does not seem to be any great problem. Problems arise, however, when from a Western perspective which holds that religion's core is made up of teachings about God, we discuss whether certain forms of Buddhism are religions or not. The desire to avoid such problems is naturally insufficient reason for reserving the adjective 'religious' primarily for human beings. My suggestion that we do so, is based on the following considerations.

A religion or some secular counterpart is interesting only if it is a part of a person's life, or more exactly, if it has to do with what I shall call life's inevitabilities represented by suffering, guilt, death, love, joy and happiness. They are the undeniably central realities in our lives, but we cannot explain them, far less explain them away. In order not simply to have experiences of pleasure or discomfort and to be able to express that even in this existential sense, we respond to something of which we are simultaneously a part, namely life, we also require linguistic tools. It is not only we human beings, but also the conceptualizations, which are relevant for this purpose. These have evolved in such a way that our language supplies the means for, so to speak, creating and living with expressions which adequately express what it is to be a human being. An emphasis on this perspective means that in a definite sense there is no difference between religious and non-religious views of life. When we say something about reality, even in an existential sense with life's inevitabilities in mind, we do so with the help of the conceptualizations which are available to us. They can be altered when we discover that they are misleading or no longer fulfil their function in some other way. However, we are never without conceptualizations. In this sense, reality is constituted by us. I shall return to the question of what this means more exactly. Nor is religion any exception in this respect. Views of life, including religious views of life, are human beings' way of expressing what it means to be a human being, in other words, to live with life's inevitabilities.

In another respect, on the other hand, there is a difference between religious and non-religious views of life. When human beings display a religious response to life's inevitabilities by seeing them in religious terms, they seem ready to allow for the possibility of something which is 'not of this world' to use a religious formulation. The readiness to accept such a possibility implies that human beings are transformed or are 'converted' to employ another religious term. Worldly things are still important, but are not an end in themselves. Nor are the things the possibility of which they are now ready to accept, ends in themselves, but form a part of the religious person's life. The expressions used to describe this are supplied by the religious traditions in which they live. I would underline that my philosophical position of looking at religion, so to speak from the outside, does not imply a denial of the religious. My perspective only implies that I shall confine myself entirely to the philosophical problems which are raised by the phenomenon of religion.

Irrespective of whether we adopt a religious attitude in the above sense or not, both religious and non-religious views of life share the fact that in expressing how life could be when it is at its best, they offer real life alternatives. Even if there can never be a life without suffering and death, injustices and oppression, it nevertheless makes a significant difference if there are people who work for a life dedicated to peace and brotherly love or to a life devoted to the production of goodness according to capacity and the distribution of goodness according to needs.

If we want to say something about life when it is at its best, we need to have recourse to ideas, images and narratives which manifest themselves as natural responses to life. If our ideas, images and narratives do not function in this way, they must be modified or replaced. It is not the task of the philosopher or the philosopher of religion to construct existentially adequate ideas, images and narratives. Such arise in the shared life of human beings. On the other hand, the philosopher is able to clarify what it is in the ideas, images and narratives that has led them to cease to function in our lives, and are no longer experienced as adequate expressions for what it means to be a human being or to live with life's inevitabilities.

Religion is a human phenomenon in the sense that the possibility of religious responses would appear to be part and parcel of our human existence, even although not all human beings share these responses. It becomes, therefore, important to examine the philosophical problems which arise in particular from these responses, and how we relate to them. At the same time, they ought to be seen as a subset of the philosophical problems which are bound up with the fact that we are beings who must relate and interact with something we are simultaneously part of. Among other things, there is a state of tension between

(1) the fact that, on the one hand, we are part of a causal chain of organic life while, on the other hand. by the choosing to direct our lives along certain lines, we can influence this chain,

(2) the fact that, on the one hand, we are steered by instincts, reflexes and emotions while, on the other hand, we can train our emotional and intellectual capacities to be able to deal with these,

(3) the fact that, on the one hand, we cannot assert whatever we like about reality and behave accordingly since reality, so to speak, offers resistance while, on the other hand, we can create theories with the help of which we can say something true about what is observable, and thus are able to participate in determining or constituting reality,

(4) the fact that, on the one hand, we cannot deny life's inevitabilities while, on the other hand, we are not compelled to accept unconditionally the view of life we are born into and its expressions, but can critically test to what extent the ideas, images and narratives of existing views of life offer an existentially adequate expression for what it means to live with life's inevitabilities.

In all these respects, the phenomenon of religion and its secular counterparts give rise to philosophical problems.

Given the reflections and arguments about the nature of philosophy which I have set forth, I look upon philosophy, and thereby the philosophy of religion, as having three tasks – an analytical, a critical and a constructive one. In the case of the philosophy of religion, the analytical task consists in clarifying the structure embodied in religious ideas of various kinds, including very theoretical theological ideas such as theistic ones, and at the same time in clarifying what is an expression for responses, propositional assumptions, arguments for possible positions or motivations why certain things are more important than others. The philosophy of religion's main critical task is to point out logical fallacies, conceptual confusions, category mistakes and philosophical empty rhetoric which takes place when the philosophical questions are disengaged from the fact that we are the biological and social beings that we are. This ought to be seen against the background of philosophy's more general critical task of investigating the conceptual presuppositions underlying various human activities and social phenomena. We can then be more observant about what kinds of argument are relevant for a revision of the various activities. Finally the constructive task in the case of the philosophy of religion consists primarily in proposing distinctions which are relevant in developing existentially adequate expressions and in suggesting possible conceptual alternatives which allow us more easily to adopt a position with respect to – in our case – the phenomenon of religion. For this, it is necessary that philosophical reflection is not made subservient to religious or ideological ends, but remains quite independent of them.

In this book, I shall apply myself to all three tasks with respect to a central complex of philosophical problems which arises from the phenomenon of religion, namely the problem of realism. The four remaining parts of my book are organized as follows: II will deal with 'Realism's problems in general'; III will treat the 'The problems of religious realism' where I shall chiefly devote myself to the analytical and critical tasks; IV will deal with 'Pragmatic realism with respect to religion'; and finally V is devoted to 'Views of life and a fulfilling life' where I shall be primarily concerned with the constructive task.

Part II

The problem of realism in general

Anyone acquainted with developments in English-speaking philosophy, cannot fail to have noticed the steady increase in publications relating to the problem of realism. We have the discussion about scientific realism, that is to say, the question of how far scientific theories describe reality and thereby are either true or false, or whether instead, they are suitable instruments for formulating hypotheses about what is observable.[7] There is the discussion about semantic realism, that is say, whether linguistic meaning should be defined in terms of a statement's truth conditions, or rather in terms of use.[8] We have the discussion about epistemological reasoning: are there truths which transcend evidence?; or is truth instead to be explained in evidential terms?[9] There is the discussion about moral realism: namely, how far do values exist independently of human beings?; or can they be better explained as the result of a process of conceptualization?[10] Finally, we have the discussion about religious realism: can a divine being be said to exist in itself?; or is it more appropriate to interpret talk about such a divine being as the result of a conceptualization process.[11] All these discussions are in various ways closely related to the discussion about metaphysical realism, namely whether there exists a unconceptualized reality in itself which is independent of us, or whether instead reality is more adequately interpreted as something which is conceptualized and constituted by us.

In my view, it would not be particularly prudent to deny our realist intuitions. We possess a body which is continually bumping into other bodies. Reality also offers resistance in the sense that it imposes a constraint on the our possible actions. In the majority of cases, we can get along pretty well on the basis of our realist intuitions and the experiences which they give rise to. In spite of the difficulties which, in my view, are inherent in metaphysical realism, I shall not turn my back on realism as such. I am simply dissatisfied with many of the philosophical arguments for realism

---

[7] See e.g. Agazzi and Pauri (eds.) 2000, Churchland and Hooker (eds) 1985, Cohen, Hilpinen and Renzong (eds) 1996 and Leplin (ed.) 1984.

[8] See e.g. Dummett 1978, 1991, 1993, 1995 and Wright 1987.

[9] See e.g. Dancy 1985 and Kirk 1999.

[10] See e.g. Blackburn 1993 and McNaughton 1988.

[11] See e.g. Herrmann 1995 and Runzo (ed.) 1993.

which I have encountered. As I shall demonstrate, some of those arguments which in the name of realism are taken to be unproblematic, are not at all evident. This becomes clear if we, from time to time, take a detour via the so-called anti-realist or non-realist alternative. In the case of realism, anti-realism or non-realism, I have no intention of taking up a position for or against some ready-to-use philosophical package. Instead I would like to make the most of our realist intuitions in general, and in relation to the religious domain in particular, in a way that is philosophically defensible.

It is customary to define metaphysical realism in the broad sense as the view according to which

(1) Real objects exist (although it is a matter of debate what sort of objects they are).

(2) These objects exist independently of our experience of them, or our knowledge about them.

(3) These objects have quite determinate properties, and have quite determinate relations to one another, independently of the concepts which allow us to understand them, and independently of the language we use to describe them.

By anti-realism, we mean in general a view which denies at least one of the three foregoing theses.[12]

1 Reasons for and against metaphysical realism

The foregoing definitions of metaphysical realism seem fairly unproblematic since they reflect our inescapable realist intuitions. It is obvious that the table at which I am sitting and writing exists, and remains where it is when I leave the room, and furthermore that it looks the way it is, irrespective of whether someone describes it, and irrespective of the way in which they describe it. Such definitions of metaphysical realism no longer appear quite so self-evident when they are considered in the light of another view which also seems reasonable, namely, that what is reality for us is a reality which is conceptualized and understood by us.

Human limitations

Because we are the beings we are, we are subject to various limitations of a communicational, conceptual and epistemic kind.

(1) The communicational limitation consists in the fact that we have to use the linguistic means which are available both to ourselves and to those

---

[12] See, e.g. Butchvarov 1995, 488f.

with whom we are communicating, in order to be able to communicate at all.

(2) The conceptual limitation comes about as follows. As far as processes of understanding are concerned, our actual understanding of our various experiences is attained by means of concepts we have learned. This does not mean that our concepts are unshakeable. Disturbances and impediments affecting our understanding can lead us to alter our concepts, or replace them with new ones. On the other hand, we would neither be in a position to understand nor to make claims to knowledge about objects and their properties, if we lacked concepts altogether.

(3) Finally there is the epistemic limitation. As far as claims to knowledge are concerned, both when we make them and justify them, we do so in relation to what appears to us to be evidence. Evidence is partly a result of socialization and partly the outcome of the experiences which are available to us, as the beings we are.

By way of illustrating the manner in which these three limitations are significant, let us consider how Catherine Z. Elgin links Wittgenstein's argument about how we learn to use the word 'pain' with his view of knowledge. It is the interaction between socialization and the fact that we are the beings we are, which is important. According to Elgin, Wittgenstein means that that we would be incapable of grasping pain, or in other words be conceptually incapable of stopping the flow of experiences, if we lacked language's conceptual schematization. Without this, there would be no way of differentiating between different mental states. What allows us to speak of mental states, is namely that we conceptually grasp certain regularities in publicly observable behaviour. These regularities give rise to criteria for the correct use of mental terms. When we say that someone is in pain on the basis of their behaviour, this is not simply an expression of some reductionist formula of the form 'x is in pain' if and only if x exhibits behaviour y. Nonetheless it is precisely because of human behaviour that we recognize when people are in pain. If we were unable to perceive any regularity in human beings' behaviour when they were in pain, we would be unable to learn the word 'pain'. There would be no such word and we would not have developed the concept of pain. Naturally we would still have pain when it did indeed hurt us, but we would not be able to talk about it. That becomes possible when we learn through socialization, partly how to express pain by saying that we are in pain instead of simply shrieking, and partly how to ascertain if someone else is in pain. When we have to decide whether someone is in pain, it is a question of competence with respect to how we use the term 'pain': in other words with respect to our knowledge of, or acquaintance with, what we mean by that term.

Using an analogous argument, we arrive at the following more general conclusion about knowledge. In a definite sense, competence in using a term coincides with knowledge about what we mean by the term. Because linguistic competence is a product of socialization, it follows that knowledge about what is intended with language, is itself a product of socialization. In this sense, knowledge is not determined by a correspondence with some reality that exists independently of our awareness of it, but by its conformity with certain social norms. This is not synonymous with the reductionist approach favoured by certain sociologists of knowledge who define knowledge in non-epistemic terms such as socialization. Rather it serves to remind us that we cannot speak of knowledge without taking into account both the fact that we are the beings that we are and the fact that we live and learn together the way we do.

According to Elgin, it is possible to distinguish two lines of argument in Wittgenstein which support this view of knowledge. First of all, there is his criticism of the idea that knowledge considered as a true understanding of how things are, consists in a correspondence between understanding and reality. Secondly he draws our attention to the way in which we actually interact with the world around us and thereby acquire knowledge.

The first line of argument criticizing the notion of a correspondence between understanding and reality consists of three parts. First of all, it is noted that the relationship which ties knowledge as true description to its object, is – to put it mildly – highly elusive. We have no criteria which would allow us to specify correctly the relation in question and thereby discard those cases where correspondence does not exist. In order to have such criteria, we would need to have access to the object corresponding to our knowledge before we have knowledge about it.

Secondly, correspondence in itself does not amount to knowledge. The fact that p is the case naturally justifies us in believing that p is the case. However it is not simply a question of a correspondence between thought and object. We require a cognitive norm which says that we *ought to* believe that p is the case when there is a correspondence. If now one requires – as indeed one does require – that this norm is true, the question arises about what it is in the correspondence that justifies us in saying that we know that this norm is true. Let us consider various alternatives. We could argue, for example, that the norm is true because it would be unreasonable not to believe that p is the case when there is a correspondence. However, this merely refers us to another norm and not to the correspondence which is meant to clarify why the original cognitive norm is true. We might therefore instead wish to maintain that the norm is true because the truth that p is the case becomes knowledge when we believe that p is the case. In this case, we run into the first difficulty, namely that we have no criteria which would allow us to specify the correspondence relationship between the supposed knowledge that p is the case and the fact that p is the case, and thus reject those cases where there is no correspondence.

Our awareness that there is something problematic with the idea of knowledge as a correspondence between our understanding and the object of this understanding, arises from the radical way in which the learning process itself is kept distinct from its product i.e. knowledge. We learn to think as our teachers do. A pupil is considered to have learned geography if his understanding of geographical questions agrees with the corresponding views of respected experts. Because knowledge consists of such a correspondence, it is a direct product of learning. If we were now to add that it is a matter of knowledge because knowledge means correspondence with a reality which is independent of us, we find ourselves confronted once more with the two earlier difficulties.

It is worth reminding ourselves that the critique levelled against this view of correspondence does not entail giving up the distinction between considering that something is true and the fact that it is true. Putnam accurately succeeds in bringing out the point that Wittgenstein is making.

> That being true is not the same as merely being accepted as true is a picture that is firmly rooted in us if anything is, and it is the root of all our thinking, as Dummett very well reminds us. We can, from within our thinking and our lives, refuse to treat it as a superstition without thinking that we must provide the guarantee from outside that metaphysical realism seeks. And this is what I think Wittgenstein was trying to tell us (Putnam 1994b, 262).

I shall return to this question later in Part IV where I present in some detail my approach of pragmatic (or internal) realism and show how it is possible to speak of objectivity and truth while at the same time rejecting metaphysical realism.

The second line of argument which, according to Elgin, supports the view that there is a connection between competence in using a given term and knowledge of the object denoted by the term, can be summed up in the slogan: pay attention to what we do and not to what we say! As far as the actual proclamation of correspondence as a guarantee of truth and knowledge is concerned, we can do nothing with it unless we relate it to the cognitive criteria of everyday life and the scientific community. The quest for knowledge gives rise to cognitive demands which conversely in turn help to structure the quest by determining what is proof, relevance, and sound argument. It is also by the use of such criteria that it becomes apparent when agreement has been reached. Note that this is not a definition of knowledge in terms of consensus. Such a definition would trivialize the complex process involved in the acquisition and accumulation of knowledge. It would overlook the fact that the knowledge criteria both of everyday life and the scientific community are many-faceted and on countless occasions difficult to satisfy. Knowledge is not attained by learning in each specific case one truth after the other, but by learning to manipulate complex networks of cognitive involvement and obligations (Elgin 1996, 81f.).

Such communicational, conceptual and epistemic limitations help to underline the problem of realism in the following sense. Evidence becomes evidence only after the experiences which we have had as the creatures we are, have been placed within a context of cognitive involvement and obligations. Nevertheless it would be wrong to say that through our experiences we cause the evidence. On the one hand, we take it for granted that there is a reality which is independent of us and we acknowledge that we cannot say whatever we like about it, since not every action based on our suppositions about what is correct, is necessarily successful. If, for example, I were to open the window, assert that I can fly and hop out, it does not take very long before reality offers resistance. On the other hand, whenever we speak about reality, we are speaking of something that is conceptualized and comprehended by us. It is in this sense, and only in this sense, that reality is not independent of us, but is our own creation. I thus reject certain postmodernist views that there is nothing more than text or narrative, and that truth, therefore, is no more than consensus about the respective text or narrative. One person who defines truth in this way, is the radical anti-realist, Don Cupitt. In his view, truth is only attained in language and culture. We have no access to some objective universe which is, so to speak, prior to language, and which we could use to examine the agreement between our linguistic representations and that reality (Cupitt 1991, 143–145). I am quite prepared to accept this point. It is less plausible, however, when Cupitt looks upon reality exclusively as a battlefield for rival narratives about what is going on. Truth is therefore a state of argument. At best it is the narrative which at present tops the list of narratives. It is a continuously fluid consensus that is forever shifting (Cupitt 1991, 20). Let me give four reasons which would seem to speak against such anti-realist theses and in support of realism.

Reasons for realism

The first reason consists of a kind of *reductio-ad-absurdum* argument. Suppose, as is the case in certain forms of anti-realism, that we were to deny that there is a reality which is independent of us. Such a denial would have absurd consequences. If there is no independent reality, the expression *experience of reality* becomes meaningless. Given our denial, such an experience can only be *an experience of another experience*. In addition, if it is meaningless to speak of the experience of reality, it ultimately becomes also meaningless to speak of concepts. Experience of reality namely presupposes concepts without which we would be unable to identify what we experience. If there is no reality which is independent of us and offers resistance, but at the same time different conscious minds apparently have experiences, and are able to communicate with one another, it follows that possible similarities between their experiences are not what these experiences are said to be about. After all, one has denied the existence of a reality which is independent of us and which offers resistance. This entails that we cannot discuss whether a conscious mind is filled with sick fantasies or whether an experience is illusory. However the fact of the matter is that there are clear cases where we are able to discuss such matters, and it is therefore pointless to deny, as some anti-realists do, that there is a reality which is independent of us. Because we can speak in a reasonable way about concepts, consciousness, experience, and how reality, so to speak, offers resistance, anti-realism must be rejected as unsustainable.

Another argument which speaks against anti-realism and supports realism is the following. Sometimes we require to go beyond the ideas that we happen to have. This comes about because of a special feature connected with the circumstance that we base our actions *inter alia* on our knowledge claims and truth claims. These claims can turn out to be incompatible with one another, and because of the actions which they inspire, can lead to practical conflicts. If for example we are convinced that courts of law are infallible, we will hardly be interested in refining the methods of judicial proof. On the hand, if we suspect that innocent people have been sentenced, it becomes important to be able successfully to establish who is guilty and who is innocent. In such cases, it is thus extremely important to investigate the statements we are justified in making. This requires that we, so to speak, go outside the knowledge claims themselves and ask for relevant evidence. Different methods have been developed in different circumstances; in forensic science for example, there is DNA testing which is designed to help us to determine the perpetrator. The fact that we can both successfully apply methods but also modify them as well, when they are not working satisfactorily, justifies us in the realist assumption that there is a reality which is independent of us.

The third argument consists in noting that the realist assumption of an external reality which is independent of us is supported by our experience that with respect to our actions e.g. hopping out of the window, we cannot assert anything we like about the nature of reality e.g. that we human beings are capable of flying unaided. Reality offers resistance and it is this experience of resistance which speaks in favour of realism. As I shall show in Part IV, this argument has an important role in my own thinking. The assertion that reality offers resistance is not a philosophical thesis, but simply indicates what we in practice link our views about reality and the actions associated with these views, to.

By taking this argument somewhat further, we arrive at a fourth reason which speaks in favour of realism. Although in certain cases we may have difficulty in understanding and communicating with one another, we nevertheless for the most part manage to do so. It is therefore imprudent to deny that we in a definite sense are living in the same reality, which must therefore be a reality which is independent of us. Since our words and expressions refer to this independent reality, we are able to understand and communicate.

In one sense, this argument for realism is plausible. And indeed it is plausible, provided that we do not interpret the assumption that words and expressions refer to a reality which is independent of us, in too general a way. This is unproblematic, provided that we do not forget that the function of words and expressions in referring, has been preceded by the fact that in different situations we have begun to introduce certain words and expressions in order, with their help, to be able to refer to entities and things. On the other hand, problems do arise if it is maintained that words and expressions in themselves represent or refer to what they are about. They would in fact do this, even if we were brains in a vat filled with nutrients and our brains were stimulated in such a refined way that we have exactly the same experiences as we would, if we were real beings in a real world. Making use of one of Putnam's arguments, I shall show that the idea that words and expressions in themselves represent or refer to what they are about, does not hold.

Brains in a vat

As I understand him, Putnam strikes out in two directions simultaneously. In part he wants to show that the thesis of metaphysical realism, namely that there is a correspondence relationship between respectively words and mental images, on the one hand, and, on the other, a reality which is unconceptualized by us, leads consequently to our being unable to distinguish between an imagined reality and what might be called genuine reality. In order to be able to decide if there is a correspondence between language and unconceptualized reality, we have to have access to that unconceptualized reality before we have access to it via our conceptualizations. In part, he wishes to show that the anti-realist denial of a reality which is independent of us cannot be sustained either. The use of words with the meanings we attach to them, presupposes our interaction with reality. In order to reach his twin goals, he begins with a science fiction scene, "The case of brains in a vat." He invites us to imagine that a human being (you can imagine this to be yourself) has been subjected to an operation by an evil scientist. The person's brain (your brain) has been removed from the body and placed in a vat of nutrients which keeps the brain alive. The nerve endings have been connected to a super-scientific computer which causes the person whose brain it is to have the illusion that everything is perfectly normal. There seem to be people, objects, the sky, etc; but really all the person (you) is experiencing is the result of electronic impulses travelling from the computer to the nerve endings. The computer is so clever that if the person tries to raise his hand, the feedback from the computer will cause him to 'see' and 'feel' the hand being raised (Putnam 1981, 5f.).

Several details follow, but we can hop over them. Putnam then extends his example to the case of several brains involved in a though experiment.

Instead of just having one brain in a vat, we could imagine that all human beings (perhaps all sentient beings) are brains in a vat (or nervous systems in a vat in case some beings with just a minimal nervous system already count as 'sentient'). ... This time let us suppose that the automatic machinery is programmed to give us all a *collective* hallucination, rather than a number of separate unrelated hallucinations. Thus when I seem to myself to be talking to you, you seem to yourself to be hearing my words. Of course, it is not the case that my words actually reach your ears – for you don't have (real) ears, nor do I have a real mouth and tongue. Rather, when I produce my words, what happens is that the efferent impulses travel from my brain to the computer, which both causes me to 'hear' my own voice uttering those words and 'feel' my tongue moving, etc., and causes you to 'hear' my words, 'see' me speaking, etc. In this case, we are, in a sense, actually in communication. I am not mistaken about your real existence (only about the existence of your body and the 'external world', apart from brains). From a certain point of view, it doesn't even matter that 'the whole world' is a collective hallucination; for you do, after all, really hear my words when I speak to you, even if the mechanism isn't what we suppose it to be (Putnam 1981, 6f.).

Putnam then asks the critical question: suppose that the story is true. Would we in such case i.e. if we were brains in a vat, be able to maintain or think that we are in point of fact brains in a tank? Putnam's answer is 'no', because the story in one definite respect is self-contradictory (Putnam 1981, 7).

The answer is going to be (basically) this: although the people in that possible world can think and 'say' any words we can think and say, they cannot (I claim) refer to what we can refer to. In particular, they cannot think or say that they are brains in a vat (even by thinking 'we are brains in a vat') (Putnam 1981, 8).

They cannot do so, because they lack an important prerequisite for being able to refer. What causes the illusion of reference when the brains in their vat speak about apples, for example, is that we have conventions for reference. When we speak about 'apples' it is inextricably bound up with our non-verbal transactions with apples.

There are 'language entry rules' which take us from experiences to such utterances as 'I see an apple' and 'language exit rules' which take us from decisions expressed in linguistic form ('I am going to buy some apples') to actions other than speaking.

> Lacking either language entry rules or language exit rules, there is no reason to regard the conversation ... as more than syntactic play (Putnam 1981, 11).

Why, for example, should the brains not be able to refer to apples by means of the word 'apple'? The problem arises because brains would use the word 'apple', have thoughts about apples and form conceptions of apples although apples in fact did not exist. This objection can be generalized to all words including the word 'tank'.

> By the same argument, 'vat' refers to vats in the image in vat-English, or something related (electronic impulses or program features), but certainly not real vats, since the use of 'vat' in vat-English has no causal connection to real vats (apart from the connection that the brains in a vat wouldn't be able to use the word 'vat', if it were not for the presence of one particular vat – the vat they are in; but this connection obtains between the use of *every* word in vat-English and that one particular vat; it is not a special connection between the use of the particular word 'vat' and vats.) ... It follows that if their 'possible world' is really the actual one, and we are really the brains in a vat, then what we now mean by 'we are brains in a vat' is that *we are brains in a vat in the image* or something of that kind (if we mean anything at all). But part of the hypothesis that we are brains in a vat is that we aren't brains in a vat in the image (i.e. what we are 'hallucinating' isn't that we are brains in a vat.) So, if we are brains in a vat, then the sentence 'We are brains in a vat' says something false (if it says anything). In short, if we are brains in a vat, then 'We are brains in a vat' is false. So it is necessarily false (Putnam 1981, 14f.).

The argument shows clearly that Putnam does not question the realist view that reality is, in a definite sense, independent of us. His argument, in this sense, supports the realist picture. With regard to this point, it is crystal clear what Putnam's aim is. On the other hand, I agree with Crispin Wright that it is not so easy to grasp what exactly is the target for Putnam's critique of metaphysical idealism. According to Wright's proposal for a precise definition of metaphysical realism, one possibility is the following. According to the metaphysical realist, we have, on the one hand, reality or the world or whatever we want to call it, and, on the other hand, our thoughts and concepts. This division implies that it is only due to an accidental harmony, or by means of a lucky guess, that we are able to arrive at a more or less comprehensive picture which happens to be correct in its basic essentials. This compels the metaphysical realist to reckon in principle with the possibility that even something that appears to us humans as an ideal theory can in fact be false or embarrassingly incomplete. Metaphysical realism thus leads to scepticism in the sense that, in principle, we can never trust our theories.

Despite this consequence, metaphysical realism maintains that reality or the world or whatever we want to call it, has the appearance it does i.e. is divided into categories or species, and has properties, quite independently of any human classificatory activity on our part. If we conceive of reality or the world in this way, then the idea that there might be beings which are so cognitively equipped that they are unable to frame concepts which correctly reflect the real categories or species, is not an alien idea for us. The true nature and structure of reality or the world would thus lie beyond the cognitive understanding of these beings.

In Wright's view, Putnam's brains in the tank are such beings. Because of the nature of the relation which they have to their surroundings, and because of the nature of this world itself, they are doomed to lack concepts which would allow them to imagine this world's true nature and their own relation to it. The point of the tale of the brains in the tank is to show that metaphysical realism cannot rule out such a world or such beings. Putnam can, therefore, avail himself of the following argumentative strategy. Putnam shows that the idea of the brains in the tank is based on presuppositions which in turn prevent what is said in the world of this thought experiment from meaning what it is intended to mean. Because of this, he can maintain that every such thought experiment is self-contradictory and thereby false.

What is characteristic for metaphysical realism is that it is based on the assumption that it is in principle possible to have an unbridgeable gap between reality and our cognitive capacity. It is thus theoretically possible that something like the tale of the brains in the tank might be true. The consequence is that despite the fact that our lives are characterized by a wealth of cognitive abilities, we cannot rule out that, in some sense, we find ourselves in a reality, but we are unable to say anything about the nature of this reality and our relation to it (Wright 1994, 238).

Putnam's reasoning demonstrates where the problem arises in defending metaphysical realism. Simultaneously, his argument is a support for realism which has not always been noted when he is dismissed as an anti-realist. He also shows a way to argue against the anti-realist view that reality is merely a construction. Such a view cannot explain the fact that the development and application of concepts is a capacity we ultimately derive in a very bodily fashion through a causal relationship to reality. The brains in the tank can certainly experience the illusion of carrying out certain actions, but certain actions e.g. physical love, require real bodies. Putnam's reasoning can thus function as a support for realism, but a realism that is quite different from metaphysical realism. This has failed to be noticed, not only by those who dismiss Putnam as an anti-realist, but also by those anti-realists I wish to describe as metaphysical anti-realists.

Anti-realist objections

Let me repeat the three main theses of metaphysical realism:
(1) Real objects exist.

(2) These objects exist independently of our experience of them or our knowledge about them.

(3) These objects have quite determinate properties and have quite determinate relations to one another, independently of the concepts which allow us to understand them, and independently of the language we use to describe them.

According to Michael Devitt, it is a matter of a minimal realism which merely asserts that there are objects which exist independently of minds. Devitt holds that such a minimal realism is sufficient to allow us to deal with every form of anti-realist objection (Devitt 1991, 45). Let us investigate whether minimal realism is adequate when it comes to developing a satisfactory view of reference, truth and meaning. For it is precisely in relation to this complex, that many of the so-called anti-realist objects are put forward. Let us also examine which of the anti-realist objects are reasonable and which are not.

I shall present two types of anti-realist objection which I shall then criticise in turn. Whereas according to the first type of objection, metaphysical realism is a practical impossibility, according to the second type of objection, it is false. What is common to both objections is that an attack is made on the view of metaphysical realism that real objects exist, in the sense of unconceptualized objects, no matter how they actually are, and that truth consists in a correspondence between words and statements on the one hand, and on the other hand, unconceptualized objects and facts, irrespective of how they actually are.

The first sort of objection maintains that metaphysical realism with its correspondence theory of truth is a practical impossibility since we cannot prove, and consequently cannot know, that there really are real objects which are independent of our experiences, our concepts, and our language. Douglas McDermid calls this objection "the comparison objection":

> If truth were a correspondence with the facts, then we could verify our belief that *p* only if we could somehow confront *p* with the relevant portion(s) of reality and confirm that the two "fit" or "agree." Since we cannot possibly perform such a comparison, the intuitively appealing idea that truth is correspondence with reality ironically results in something virtually no one wants to accept – namely, skepticism. Unless we are prepared to concede that knowledge of the external world is an impossibility we must give up the correspondence theory in favor of some conception of truth that can do justice to our claims to know (McDermid 1998, 776).

Thus according to the anti-realist, we should refrain from asserting that objects exist independently of us, and instead maintain that reality is merely linguistic in character as the aforementioned Cupitt does. Given the way McDermid formulates "the comparison objection", and the formulation of anti-realism that Cupitt adopts, namely that it is a matter of practical impossibility, it is assumed, however, that the metaphysical realist picture of truth and reality is a comprehensible one. The question is whether it is. I shall return to this question.

The second type of anti-realist objection is to the effect that metaphysical realism is false because all objects are constituted by our consciousness, and are therefore not independent of us. Everything we conceive or encounter in perception, belongs to our mental images, and is therefore in a very definite sense created by us. For us, there can be no reality which is independent of us. If we were to object that these images are produced causally by an external reality, we would find ourselves confronted with the first anti-realist objection, namely that we cannot show, and therefore cannot know, that the objects which cause our mental images, really exist outside of the mental images themselves.

Both types of objection are, however, deeply problematic. In the case of the first type of objection, a general doubt is expressed about whether we can demonstrate, and therefore know, that there are real objects. The doubt becomes a doubt about whether there can exist in any sense real objects. If we argue anti-realistically in this way, we are apt to forget that doubt too can be justified. Obviously in certain situations, it can be justified in doubting whether there exists definite objects, but what reasons can be adduced for doubting, as a general principle, that real objects exist? Our experiences from everyday life that reality offers resistance, teaches us to decide when it is reasonable, and when it is unreasonable to doubt the existence of objects. Reasonable doubt about objects presupposes that there are unproblematic cases of real objects.

In the second type of objection, namely that metaphysical realism is false because all objects are objects which are constituted by us and are not independent of us, it is certainly reasonable to point out that we cannot in a definite sense argue about what lies beyond our conceptualizations. We can only argue about what we have conceptualized. The subsequent reasoning is, however, fallacious. Just because within a conceptual framework we have to reckon with objects which are constituted by us, it does not follow that there are no objects which are independent of us. In my view, this sort of anti-realist reasoning comes about because one objects, not only to metaphysical realism, but also to the epistemological realism which is sometimes associated with it. The epistemological realism criticized by the anti-realists maintains that there are truths which are transcendent in the sense that they are true, irrespective of our capacity to understand and formulate them (Dancy 1985, 19). The epistemological realist, who in this case is also a metaphysical realist, thus maintains that there are truths, which transcend the evidence, about objects which are independent of our experiences, concepts and our language, and are such that their properties and relations are independent of our capacity to understand and formulate them. Since the epistemological anti-realist denies as a matter of principle that there can be any truths, whatsoever, which transcend all evidence, it follows that there cannot be such truths about objects which are independent of our experiences, concepts and language. Given that metaphysical realism asserts that there are objects which have definite properties and stand in certain definite relations independently of our concepts – in other words, they assert that there are truths which transcend all evidence – in the eyes of the metaphysical anti-realist, metaphysical realism must be false.

This kind of anti-realist reasoning, however, does not observe that this talk about transcending evidence is ambiguous because the word truth is employed in two distinct senses. Sometimes, 'truth' means fact and on other occasions it means true statement. Correspondingly, the expression 'a truth transcending all evidence' can have two distinct meanings, namely a fact which transcends all evidence and a true statement that transcends all evidence. The anti-realist strategy under discussion denies both that there are facts which transcend all evidence and true statements which transcend all evidence. To deny that there are facts which transcend all evidence would be the same as to deny that something can be the case without our knowing it. Our experience that reality offers resistance which we had not expected, is in itself sufficient reason for accepting that there exist facts which transcend all evidence, and which we can know something about only after we have experienced and conceptualized reality's resistance.

This circumstance certainly suggests that the anti-realist is correct in the sense that the realist thesis about true statements which transcend all evidence is, at the very least, problematic. If we begin with the statements themselves, they are either written or spoken. As such, they are available to us. They do not transcend all evidence. However most often, statement is taken to mean the content of a statement about which a judgement is possible. To speak of true statements which transcend all evidence, is problematic for the following reason. As the content about which a judgement is possible, it is certainly not identical with the statement of which it is the logical content. Neither is it identical with the fact to which it refers. What is it then that transcends all evidence? I am unable to see how the question could be answered. If it is the case that no answer exists, then it follows that it is literally meaningless to deny that there are true statements which transcend all evidence. This step serves no function. Nevertheless if one takes it, one ends up sharing in this matter the same problematic presupposition on which the epistemological realist bases his case, namely, that the idea of true statements transcending all evidence is meaningful, because the meaning of the words which make it up is to be found in that which they refer to. Whereas the epistemological realist maintains that true statements transcending all evidence exist, the anti-realist maintains that they do not.

In this case, yet another difficulty arises. If we maintain (or respectively deny) that there are true statements transcending all evidence, it is reasonable that we also ought to maintain (or respectively deny) that there are false statements which transcend all evidence. In this case, for the realist, there are many such statements, whereas for the anti-realist it is difficult to explain what we are to mean by denying that there are false statements which transcend all evidence.

An idea which plays an important role in this matter, in the epistemological realist's assertion, and the epistemological anti-realist's denial, that there are truths which transcend all evidence, is the semantic realist idea that the meaning of statements consists in the conditions which make the statements true or false. The question of whether the conditions are fulfilled or not, does not depend on whether we have knowledge of this or not. For the realist, this is more or less self-evident. On the other hand, the anti-realist questions it. Let me critically analyze this idea of semantic realism by drawing on the work of Michael Dummett.

2 Critique of semantic realism

Semantic realism, according to Dummett who has frequently criticized it in many of his writings[13], contains the following three theses:
(1) a thesis on objectivity,
(2) a thesis on truth conditions,
(3) a thesis on realism.
The thesis on objectivity maintains that a sentence must in principle be accessible to anyone i.e. it can be translated in principle to any language whatsoever, since otherwise communication would be impossible. The sentences are in principle accessible to anyone, inasmuch as they are related to matters of fact which constitute the truth conditions of the sentences. It is clear that in the case of semantic theory, we are dealing with what is sometimes called the 'mapping view of language' and sometimes the 'picture view of language' in contrast to e.g. 'reality constructing views of language'.[14] The ontological thesis behind the mapping view and picture view is that there is a reality which is independent of our language, but which, in one way or another, can be described and rendered by means of our language. It follows from this view of the relationship between lan-

---

[13] See e.g. Dummett 178 and 1993.

[14] For this distinction, see e.g. Grace 1987.

guage and reality that anything that can be described and rendered, can be described and rendered in any language whatsoever. The linkage between languages comes about via reality and the entities to which the expressions of language refer. We thereby obtain both the thesis on truth conditions which holds that the meaning of a sentence consists in its truth conditions, and the thesis on realism, which asserts that every statement is either true or false, irrespective not only of our factual knowledge but also of our ability to know which of these two properties – true or false – a given statement has.

What is of central importance to semantic realism is that a statement's meaning is defined exclusively in terms of its truth conditions. In this way, it is hoped to be able to avoid relativizing the meaning of a statement by making it dependent on our always temporary and incomplete understanding and knowledge. It is questionable, however, if this idea about the complete independence of a statement's meaning in relation to knowledge and understanding, is a reasonable one. I shall try to indicate the difficulties involved by giving two examples of statements which in certain respects are similar to one another, but which belong to two fundamentally different types. The statement 'My desk weighs 20 kilograms' is an example of a statement which fulfils the semantic realist requirement that the meaning of a statements consists in its truth conditions. It is a statement, the meaning of which really does consist in its truth conditions, and which, in fact, is either true or false. We can conceive in the substantial sense in which this statement is either factually true or factually false because in this particular case, we know precisely what the truth conditions are, and what means we have at our disposal for deciding whether these truth conditions are fulfilled or not. It is precisely this linkage to our knowledge and skill i.e. how we have learned what it means to know in concrete cases, that allows us to assert that the type of statement exemplified by our example, is either factually true or factually false.

When applied to another example, it is this linkage to our knowledge and skill which entails that a statement such as 'My neighbour's dog looks forward to next midsummer with pleasure' is not to be construed as a statement, that is to say a sentence which is either true or false. The negation of this statement would be 'It is not the case that my neighbour's dog looks forward with pleasure to next midsummer'. What we know and can humanly know about dogs does not allow us to assert or deny meaningfully that my neighbour's dog looks forward to next midsummer with pleasure. It is true that we have concepts which allow us to speak of a dog's pleasure. It is also true that we know on the basis of similarities between a dog's life and a human being's life, when for example a dog is in pain. On the other hand, a dog's life and a human being's life are so very different when there is talk of such things as midsummer that the above sentence cannot be included among the set of statements.

In discussing anti-realism, Dummett speaks exclusively about it in relation to the problem associated with what he calls semantic realism. According to Dummett, there is

> a cluster of problems traditionally classified as typically metaphysical, problems bearing a structural similarity to one another but differing in subject matter. These are problems about whether or not we should take a realist attitude to this or that class of entity. In any one instance, realism is a definite doctrine. Its denial, by contrast may take any one of numerous possible forms, each of which is a variety of anti-realism concerning the given subject matter: the colourless term 'anti-realism' is apt as a signal that it denotes not a specific philosophical doctrine but a rejection of doctrine (Dummett 1991, 4).

In Dummett's interpretation, anti-realism is thus itself not a defined philosophical position, but rather a rejection of a philosophical position. According to his reconstruction of what he wishes to call semantic realism, the meaning of a statement consists, as noted, of its truth conditions. Every statement is either true or false, irrespective of any capacity we might have for deciding its truth or falsity. Dummett, therefore, characterizes the dispute between realists and anti-realists, not as one about entities, but as a dispute about classes of statements. These can be statements about the physical world, mental events, processes, states, mathematical statements, statements about the past or the future etc. The areas determine which sentences belong to the set of disputed statements. Dummett defines realism in accordance with this

> knowing it: they are true or false in virtue of a reality existing independently of us. The anti-realist opposes to this the view that statements of the disputed class are to be understood only by reference to the sort of thing, which we count as evidence for a statement of that class. That is, the realist holds that the meanings of as the belief that statements of the disputed class possess an objective truth-value, independently of our means of statements of the disputed class are not directly tied to the kind of evidence for them that we can have, but consist in their manner of their determination as true or false by states of affairs whose existence is not dependent on our possession of evidence for them. The anti-realist insists, on the contrary, that the meanings of these statements are tied directly to what we count as evidence for them, in such a way that a statement of the disputed class, if true at all, can be true only in virtue of something of which we could know and which we should count as evidence for its truth (Dummett 1978, 146).

> The very minimum that realism can be held to involve is that statements in the given class relate to some reality that exists independently of our knowledge of it, in such a way that that reality renders each statement in the class determinately true or false, again independently of whether we know, or even are able to discover, its truth value. Thus reality involves acceptance, for statements for the given class, of the principle of bivalence, the principle that every statement is determinately true or false (Dummett 1993, 230).

I would like pause to consider the question of how Dummett looks upon the relationship between realism and the acceptance of the principle of bivalence, and anti-realism and the rejection of this principle. Dummett distinguishes between logic's *tertium non datur* '*A* or not-*A*' (the law of the excluded middle) and the semantical principle which corresponds to it, namely the principle of bivalence, which asserts that every statement is either true or false. The reason why it is important to distinguish between the semantic and logical principles is the following. Whereas an acceptance of the semantic principle of bivalence normally entails an acceptance of the law of the excluded middle, the converse is not valid (Dummett 1978, xix). The anti-realist cannot allow that the principle of bivalence holds in general because anti-realists do not wish to discard the link with our ability to determine a statement's truth or falsity. The realist on the other hand normally maintains that the bivalence principle holds in general, since realists look upon the question of a statement's meaning exclusively in terms of its truth conditions, irrespective of any capacity we might have, for determining its truth or falsity.

This sounds as though there was a necessary connection between, on the one hand, being a realist and accepting the bivalence principle, and, on the other hand, being an anti-realist, and rejecting the bivalence principle. In a later work, Dummett is doubtful about this. Taking into account how a given species of statements are to be understood, he writes that

> it is not the mere adherence to or rejection of the principle of bivalence that marks the difference between a realistic and anti-realistic interpretation. Impressed by the fact that many philosophical views which involved rejecting some form of realism turned on, or at least naturally led, to a repudiation of bivalence, I have been guilty in the past, of speaking as though what characterizes anti-realism is the rejection of bivalence, so that, provided one accepts bivalence, one is a realist (Dummett 1993, 269).

It follows that a denial of the bivalence principle need not be immediately considered synonymous with being an anti-realist. It is possible to advocate one kind of realism while at the same time querying the range of the principle of bivalence. Dummett proposes therefore a weaker principle as a characterization of a realist. It applies, not to every statement, but more restrictedly, and holds that "every unambiguous statement must be determinately either true or not true" (Dummett 1993, 467). Let us see what it entails for how we make use of the principle of bivalence.

The scope of the principle of bivalence

Dummett illustrates his worry about generally accepting the principle of bivalence, by posing the following two questions about future events and mental dispositions. Is it really true or false now what determinate event is going to occur next year, if the causal chain leading to the event has not yet begun? Is it really true or false that everyone is brave or cowardly, if many people are in fact never exposed to dangers which would put them to the test? This is not to question the validity of the law of the excluded middle. On the other hand, it does call into doubt the corresponding semantic principle, namely the principle of bivalence, which was intended to do justice to questions relating to truth and falsity with respect to each specific domain.

When Dummett speaks of semantic realism, there are two levels which are involved. He distinguishes between semantic theories and theories of meaning. A semantic theory includes principles for deciding what kind of semantic value an expression can be assigned (Dummett 1991, 139). If you are a realist, you require with respect to a definite class of statements that the statements in the class have one of the semantic values true or false. A theory of meaning consists of a theory of reference, a theory of meaning or sense, and a theory of force (Dummett 1993, 84) and presupposes a semantic theory as its foundation (Dummett 1991, 138). A realist theory of meaning maintains that the meaning of statements consists in their truth conditions which are either satisfied or not. Reference is determined in terms depending on the existence of truth conditions and force with reference to the fact that a statement is made into a true statement by its truth conditions being fulfilled. For simplicity's sake, I shall in the future make use of the term 'semantic realism' to cover what Dummett calls realist semantic theories and realist meaning theories respectively.

The first thing I want to discuss is semantic realism's idea that a statement is either true or false so that its meaning consists in its truth conditions, irrespective of whether we have knowledge of them or not. For semantic realism, it is of fundamental importance that truth does not run the risk of being relativized by being linked to our ability to determine the truth value of statements. If truth is defined in terms of such an ability, the semantic realist argues, then changes in this ability would entail changes in what is true. The semantic realist wishes to emphasize that what is true, is true both now and for always, and therefore does not change.

There is obviously something in this. But where does the feared relativization of the concept of truth occur, leading one to believe that there can be no linkage with our ability to decide which sentences are true? This question is not easy to answer because it is also a truism that we are already dependent on our epistemic capacities in being able to understand what is meant by saying that something is true or false. This we do by having learned the following circumstance. How we decide whether statements are true or false is connected in one way or another with our knowledge of the procedures for deciding matters and with our knowledge of what these various procedures can be applied to. We know, for example, how to proceed in practice in deciding whether or not my desk weighs 20 kilograms. Namely we have access to procedures which enable us to decide if the unambiguous statement 'My desk weighs 20 kilograms' is true or not. We know what it means when we maintain with respect to such a sentence that it is true or false depending on whether its truth conditions are satisfied or not, precisely because we have procedures to decide whether these truth conditions are satisfied or not.

> We are entitled to say that a statement *P* must be either true or false, that there must be something in virtue of which either it is true or it is false, only when *P* is a statement of such a kind that we could in a finite time bring ourselves into a position in which we are justified either in asserting or in denying *P*; that is when *P* is an effectively decidable statement (Dummett 1978, 16f.).

I cannot see how this linkage to our capacity to decide the truth of statements could run the risk of entailing that truth becomes relativized. The target of my criticism is thus not the objectivity of truth; nor do I doubt that the meaning of unambiguous statements consists in their truth conditions nor that they are always either true or false. It is reasonable to say this simply because we have access to procedures which enable us to decide if the truth conditions are satisfied or not. On the other hand, I do question the generalisation from what holds for unambiguous statements to *all* meaningful statements. I shall explain what I mean a little further on when I come to discuss the range of the principle of bivalence.

The question of whether truth conditions are independent of our ability to decide the truth of statements is closely linked to the question of the applicability of the bivalence principle. I shall give three different senses in the word 'statement' is used. For safety's sake, I would stress that these meanings refer to differing philosophical characterizations, and not to the performance itself when, for example, in everyday life we say that someone asserts something or other. Not every statement constitutes a statement in one of the three following senses.

The first philosophical sense of the word 'statement' is when in relation to a given conceptual system we lay down what can be asserted in the system. Thus for example the constitutive rules for the system of arithmetical concepts determines what it is meaningful to assert i.e. what statements are statements in the system and moreover which of these statements are true. Thus it is not meaningful to assert that prime numbers are slow, but it is meaningful to say the number 5 is a prime number. Moreover, it is a true statement. To say that a statement is always either true or false means, in this particular case, that the statement is true or false according to the constitutive rules for the conceptual system in question. In another philosophical sense, the word 'statement' is used with respect to how particular words are used. Thus normally the green traffic light means 'go' while the red traffic light means 'stop'. There are no epistemic problems involved here. The statement that the green traffic light means 'go', is simply true, and the statement that the red traffic light means that it is forbidden to stop, is false. To ask what the statements mean in themselves devoid of any linkage with our actual lives is meaningless. Finally we have the most common philosophical use of the word 'statement' when we assert that some factual state of affairs holds or does not hold.

On occasion, there are reasons for doubting if a statement really is a statement of fact. Let me illustrate this problem by citing the following two statements which the theistic philosopher Richard Swinburne considers to be factual statements but which I, for reasons that I shall shortly present, do not consider to be factual statements.

p_1. There is a being like men in his behaviour, physiology, and history who nevertheless has no thoughts, feelings, or sensations.

p_2. Some of the toys which to all appearances stay in the toy cupboard while people are asleep and no one is watching, actually get up and dance in the middle of the night and then go back to the cupboard, leaving no traces of their activity (Swinburne 1993, 28).

I hold that these are not factual statements. As soon as we have to deal with the question of which sentences can be considered factual statements, we find ourselves taking account of observational evidence. We require to ask ourselves what observational evidence would be relevant in deciding if a particular sentence is to be considered a statement. Thereafter we decide once more with the help of observational evidence which statements are true or false. But why specifically observational evidence?

Observational evidence

I do not deny that there are exceptions. The truth or falsity of the statement that I just now, that is to say on Wednesday 17 October 2001 at 12.47, am considering whether to take a walk after lunch, along the bank of the River Fyris, instead of going back to write this book, can only be decided by introspection. In spite of such exceptions, we are required in the majority of cases when we assert that something is the case, to refer to observational evidence in order to decide whether the statement in question is true or false. In a continuously occurring interaction, this is in turn a precondition for being able to decide if it is a matter involving a factual statement. A common objection to this way of looking at things is that it is not really a matter of evidence, but rather the following. Because of the way in which the three following examples are formulated, it is either the case or not the case, in other words either true or false, that God is a person without a body, that my neighbour's dog looks forward with pleasure to next midsummer, and that the toys in the toybox get up and dance in the middle of the night when everyone is sleeping and is not in a position to observe them, and thereafter return to the toybox without leaving any trail behind them. They are meaningful statements since they are grammatically correct and it is possible to understand the words which make them up. Therefore what they say is either the case or is not the case.

My criticism is not that we do not know or cannot know what is the case. It is rather that there is no point in thinking about such things. In the case of the toy example, it is explicitly said that the toys are unobserved and that no trail or hint of their movements is left. The illustration says nothing about how in such circumstances we observationally experience reality's resistance and consequently nothing about how we in this respect would be able to interact with it. In my view, what is crucial is the possibility or lack of possibility to interact with the reality mentioned in a supposed statement, as it is observed to offer resistance. For this reason, I hold that in the case of such supposed statements, it would be better if we did not interpret our ability to understand such sentences as a ground for claiming that we are dealing with factual statements. Just because we can understand something, it does not follow that it is a factual possibility, nor that we are able to speak of it being either the case or not the case. However, it is precisely such a conclusion that Swinburne would seem to draw when he maintains that belief statements are also statements of fact because we understand the words which make them up, and can also grasp both the belief statements and their negations. It is true that the negation of the sentence that God is a person without a body, is that it is not the case that God is a person without a body. In contrast to Swinburne and others who have no problem in speaking about God as a person without a body in the supposed statement about the nature of reality, I cannot see how I could reasonably conceive that the belief statement that God is a person without a body, could be true; nor how its negation, that God is not a person without a body, could be true in the sense of being in agreement with how reality, as conceptualized by us, is observed to offer resistance.

I have the same difficulty with regard to the other examples which have been given. However, I do not conclude as the positivist critics of religion have done, that statements of belief are nothing more than an expression of feelings and therefore completely non-cognitive. A third alternative exists, namely to abstain from treating the above examples as factual statements, and instead determine the cognitive aspect of religious statements, in some fashion, other than in terms of factual statements. In Part III, I shall develop just such an alternative by showing that truth in the case of religions and their secular counterparts means being in agreement with the reality, conceptualized by us, and offering resistance in our existential experiences of what it means to be a human being. Since I assign the existential aspect an important role, as far as our conception of reality is concerned, I have no difficulty with the view that religious statements, from my own philosophical perspective, are not statements of fact. It is certainly true that being religious or being a believer means more than limiting oneself to the existential aspects. I would, however, remind the reader that religious expressions originate and develop in a religious context where people look at life from a religious angle. Taking this into account and given the view of philosophy I present in Part I, I wish to point out that when religious claims to knowledge are raised as general claims to knowledge, our communicative, conceptual, and epistemic limitations ought reasonably to apply here too.

Another objection to my emphasis on observational evidence comes from those who wonder what I have made of the generally accepted insight that our observations are theory-laden. Because this influence can be strong enough for scientific theories to alter our observations, critics hold that observational evidence cannot have the decisive importance that I ascribe to it. I would like to answer this objection in two parts.

First of all, I want to examine what is justified in the remark about the theory-laden nature of observations and what is not. To this end, I consider it fruitful to follow in the footsteps of Evandro Agazzi in distinguishing between perception and observation and taking note of how this distinction explains the theory-laden nature of observations and the conclusions which according to Agazzi can or cannot be drawn on the basis of this explanation. Observation differs from perception inasmuch as whereas perception does not entail judgements

> observation implies judgements, and these in turn presuppose the possession of *concepts*, and the ability to connect them. Concepts and judgements grow up in a nest of correlations of increasing complexity, and all this means again a modification of the cognitive apparatus, that may affect the formation of new observations (the same perceptions may lead to different observations according to the observational experience already stored by the observer). However, observation is not the highest level of cognitive activity. The connection of judgements of which we have spoken includes *intellectual* operations such as inferences, deductions, formation of global representation, construction of new intellectual tools. Taking all this into account, we can say that the cognitive apparatus includes a whole of elements that we can call *cognitive background* (Agazzi 2000, 54).

A further difference between perception and observation is that perceptions *can be* influenced by this background whereas our observations *are* influenced by it

> in the sense that the judgements we attain in the process of observation cannot fall outside the framework of our cognitive apparatus such as it concretely is (that is, including its cognitive background). This fact has been stressed, but also partially been misunderstood, by the advocates of the so-called theory-ladenness of observation. The

misunderstanding consists in the fact that they usually mean that an observation is *determined* or at least influenced by the *theory* in which it is allegedly situated, so that it cannot provide the independent criterion for evaluating the soundness of this theory, or for comparing different theories. The mistake in this position resides in the fact that (except in very special cases), observations can actually arise independently of the theory *in which* they are performed, though they depend on the general cognitive background that, as an overall framework, includes both the observation and the theory concerned (Agazzi 2000, 54).

My second point takes up the criticism that observational evidence cannot be of the decisive importance I hold it to be. Here I shall make use of the distinction noted above between theory and background. As far as I can see, given such a distinction, theories can be thought of as functioning as explicitly structured views about how we can understand reality, and as such are neither true nor false statements. This does not entail instrumentalism which holds that theories are simply more or less well-functioning tools which allow us to make predictions; if the tools do not work, the theories are eventually discarded. On the other hand if they do work, the theories are considered to have demonstrated their viability by their results. Even if theories can be thought of as explicitly structured views about how we can understand reality, and in this sense have a definite function, they are not ultimately merely tools. Insofar as they allow us to say something true about what is observable and not about something unobservable which is behind or beyond the phenomenon, they say something – admittedly indirectly – about reality (van Fraassen 1980, 18). Let me develop this idea with the help of van Fraassen's account of the nature and function of theories.

I have earlier argued that it is pointless maintaining that sentences are factual statements if we cannot even imagine what observational evidence would count for or against them. It is not enough to say that the sentence 'My neighbour's dog looks forward with pleasure to next midsummer' is true if and only if my neighbour's dog looks forward with pleasure to next midsummer while it is false if and only if it is not the case that my neighbour's dog looks forward with pleasure to next midsummer. We also need to be able at least to imagine the kind of observational evidence which would allow us to decide the sentence's truth-conditions, and to determine if they are satisfied or not. Not even introspective statements constitute in certain circumstances an exception to this requirement. When I say that at a given moment I felt a desire to pitch in and help my pressurized neighbours by dropping off their daughter at her nursery school despite some discord between us, I am making an introspective statement. Now let us suppose that the child on the way to the nursery slips on the footbridge, bangs her head on a stone and dies. The parents are distraught and seek to channel their grief by accusing me of causing another's death on the grounds that I pushed the child off the footbridge out of a spirit of revenge. Let us assume further that the police and the prosecutor believe the parents. In such a situation, it is important that I make it plausible that I had good intentions, and that what happened was an accident. I must be able to support my introspective statement that, at the actual time, I did indeed feel a sense of benevolence and was driven by a desire to help, by pointing to behaviour and pronouncements made by me which according to others signify that I did indeed mean well.

Bringing in observational evidence in this way also plays an important role in the function of theories. I believe that there is an important kernel of truth in van Fraassen's contention that while the aim of science is to seek the truth, it is truth about observable phenomena and not truth concerning things behind or beyond the phenomena.[15] The search for truth about observable phenomena naturally also covers the task of rendering what could not previously be observed, observable, but this is something which is quite different from trying to find the truth behind or beyond the phenomena. In the latter case, it is impossible to determine if we have found what lies behind or beyond the phenomena. In my view, therefore, we are no longer involved in a scientific enterprise when we look for the truth behind or beyond the phenomena. In saying this, I do not mean that such an enterprise is illegitimate. I mean simply that it is not a *scientific* enterprise. A scientific enterprise does not aim at making discoveries about the unobservable (van Fraassen 1980, 5). As I have said, this must not be confused with discovering something which is observable: this is something quite different. van Fraassen therefore regards his view about the function of theories as

> a resolute rejection of the demand for an explanation of the regularities in the observable course of nature, by means of truths concerning a reality beyond what is actual and observable, as a demand which plays no role in the scientific enterprise (van Fraassen 1980, 203).

The function of theories is to enable us to provide satisfactory descriptions of what is observable. If a need arises to postulate structures which are not observable – which occurs most often when we are unable to proceed further with our scientific explanations – these structures are to be seen as theoretical tools for obtaining satisfactory descriptions of what is observable. In order for scientists to be able to generate empirically testable hypotheses on the basis of such postulated structures i.e. theories, it is not necessary for them to assert that they are true (van Fraassen 1980, 3). The acceptance of a theory is equivalent to a belief that the theory is empirically adequate; in other words that what can be said with the help of the

---

[15] See van Fraassen 1980, 61, 70 and 203.

theory about what is observable to us, is true.[16] This is quite different from scientific realism which holds that theories are descriptions of reality and that postulates are truths. As the realist Brian Ellis, for example, formulates it, scientific realism is the view "that the theoretical statements of science are, or purport to be, true generalized descriptions of reality" (Ellis 1979, 28).

But what do we accomplish with such a claim? Does being a realist have any significance for scientific work? I cannot resist drawing attention to Arthur Fine's characterization of the realist. To the question what the realist can add when the confirmed results of science have been accepted, Fine's answer is: "a desk-thumping, foot-stamping shout of 'Really!'." The realist is not content to accept that the theories are empirically adequate: "what the realist wants to add is the emphasis that all this is really so" (Fine 1984, 97). Given the previously discussed communicational, conceptual and epistemic limitations, it seems to me most reasonable to content oneself with empirical adequacy, in other words with what can be said to be true about observable phenomena with the help of hypotheses generated from the theories, and to reserve the term 'factual statement' only for those statements made about phenomena which are observable, at least in principle, to human beings.

Let me now come back once more to the question of the scope of the principle of bivalence. In the light of the foregoing line of argument, I would question the idea concerning the general scope of the principle of bivalence that all meaningful sentences, even where we neither have access to observational evidence nor even *can* have it, are always true or false.

Critique of the general application of the principle of bivalence

A first step towards questioning the general application of the principle of bivalence in the above sense consists in accepting two distinctions:
(1) the previously mentioned distinction between the semantic principle of bivalence and the logical law of the excluded middle and
(2) the distinction between, on the one hand, sentences expressing statements and, on the other hand, what the statements are statements about.
I shall give two examples to illustrate these distinctions but first I would like to emphasize that the second distinction is not quite as trivial as it may seem. In fact, not even as penetrating a defender of the realist viewpoint as William Alston has really dealt with it adequately. This is apparent for example when he defines 'proposition' as the actual content of a statement, a content which is the bearer of a truth value and which is rendered true by facts (Alston 1996, 22ff.), and demands "that there is an identity of content

---

[16] See van Fraassen 1980, 18 and 64.

between proposition and fact" (Alston 1996, 33). If we start by assuming that a definite statement and a definite fact are linked to each other by having the same content, it is then tempting to say the statement is either true or false since it has the same content as the corresponding fact which either exists or does not exist. Let me give two examples to show how problematic this link is.

The first example is the following: 'Caesar woke up on his right side on his first birthday.' Given that Caesar is a real historical person and our knowledge of what it means to celebrate a birthday as a one year old and to waken on our right hand side, it is reasonable to maintain that either it was or wasn't the case that Caesar woke up on his right side on his first birthday. On the other hand, we cannot in terms of evidence and substance maintain that the sentence is true. We know how we would proceed if it was a matter of people around us. But in the case of Caesar, there is nothing which would enable us to decide the question. In all this, there is no difference between the semantic realists and their critics.

Let us now distinguish between the predicates 'is true' and 'is false', on the one hand, and the predicate 'is either true or false', on the other. Undoubtedly we can assign to the sentence 'Caesar woke up on his right side on his first birthday' the predicate 'is either true or false' since we know that Caesar was a real historical person, and moreover, we know what it is to celebrate one's birthday as a one year old and to wake on one's right hand side. However, we cannot decide if the sentence is true or false. Although we can assign to the sentence the predicate 'is either true or false', we thereby give no information at all about facts. In order to be able to point to the relevance of this remark for my ensuing critique of the view that the principle of bivalence has an unlimited range of application, I would like to mention another way of dealing with 'true' and 'false' which also plays a role in the discussion.

This approach consists in speaking of 'true' and 'false' solely in the strict logical sense, namely as the truth values 'true' and 'false' and not in a substantial, contentual sense as the predicates 'true' and 'false'. Irrespective of what a sentence says and more generally, irrespective of what kind of sentence it is, a sentence is assigned the value T and F in order, for example, to test whether it follows from certain other sentences. Such an emphasis on the logical aspect of the notion of either true or false entails naturally that one completely ignores whether the sentences express factual statements or not. Such a use of the principle of bivalence – if indeed such a use occurs – would not however seem to be that which the realist has in mind. Nevertheless in bringing up the logical perspective, I want to draw attention to the fact that it is one thing to view the distinction between true and false in terms of the truth values T and F respectively: it is quite another to interpret the distinction between true and false in terms of the predicates 'true' and 'false'. It seems to me that this distinction is not always noted when the categorical aspect which characterizes both truth values T and F in the logical perspective, is transferred to talk about the predicates 'true' or 'false' in a substantial sense. Whereas the distinction between T and F is valid generally in the sense that it can be applied to all sorts of sentences, the distinction between the predicate 'true' and the predicate 'false' cannot be applied to all kinds of (meaningful) sentences. Let me show why this is not the case.

The semantic realist is obviously not interested in only working with the two truth values T and F with regard to arbitrary sentences. Neither does the semantic realist simply maintain that the predicate 'is either true or false' applies to the sentence 'Caesar woke up on his right side on his first birthday'. For safety's sake, let me reiterate that to assign a statement the predicate 'is true or false' is quite different from assigning it the predicate 'is true' or the predicate 'is false'. In his use of the principle of bivalence, the semantic realist wants above all to assert that a definite sentence can be assigned in an objective, substantial sense the predicate 'is true', or can be assigned the predicate 'is false' in an objective, substantial sense. However, it is precisely through maintaining the latter that the semantic realist's application of the principle of bivalence becomes problematic. We are able to assign the sentence the predicate 'is true' or 'is false' in an objective, substantial sense only if we can reasonably – that is, with some sort of evidential support – assert, for example, that Caesar woke up on his right side on his first birthday or if we can reasonably deny that Caesar woke up on his right side on his first birthday. The sentence certainly belongs to those which express a factual statement about something being the case or not being the case. The logical law of the excluded middle holds. The sentence, however, provides no information at all about facts, and is therefore uninteresting for us. I cannot resist the following impression. When it is asserted that the principle of bivalence is also valid for sentences such as certain religious ones where there is no evidence for or against them, one of the underlying motives would seem to be to preserve them as something interesting or significant, or to confer on them such a status. Sentences which cannot be characterized as factual statements do not seem to satisfy the requirements for being really interesting or significant. As I shall show in Part IV and subsequently, there are better philosophical ways of showing why religious expressions are significant for us human beings.

I shall apply the distinction between a sentence considered as an expression for an assertion or statement, and what the statement is a statement about, to a further example, namely the sentence mentioned earlier, namely 'My neighbour's dog looks forward with pleasure to midsummer.' Because we know too little about dogs to be able to know something about a possible connection between the tail-wagging of the dog and midsummer, it is unreasonable to assert or deny that my neighbour's dog looks forward with pleasure to midsummer. We know what it means in the case of human beings when we speak of looking forward to midsummer because we understand what constitutes a fulfilling human life. This is not so in the case of a dog: we do not know what for a dog constitutes a fulfilling life. For this reason it is pointless to assign even the predicate 'is either true or false' to the sentence 'My neighbour's dog looks forward with pleasure to midsummer'.

The sentence in this particular example differs in this respect from that in the first example. Whereas the sentence 'Caesar awoke on his right side on his first birthday' can be assigned the predicate 'is either true or false', this is ruled out in the case of the sentence about my neighbour's dog. Semantic realists treat even this latter indicative sentence as a statement which is either substantially true or substantially false because they pay no attention whatsoever in their application of the principle of bivalence to our ability to determine the statement's truth or falsity. The critic of semantic realism does not even consider the sentence about my neighbour's dog as a statement at all. The reasons why we are unable, in any substantial sense, to assign the sentence about my neighbour's dog and the sentence about Caesar the predicate 'is true' or the predicate 'is false', are therefore completely different. In the case of the neighbour's dog example, it is because we do not in general know what would constitute the fact that would render the sentence 'My neighbour's dog looks forward with pleasure to midsummer' true: in other words, a fact which would constitute observational evidence allowing us to decide that the tail-wagging is linked to midsummer and not to some interesting passing smell. In the case of the Caesar example, the reason is another. Even if it is either the case or not the case that Caesar awoke on his right side on his first birthday, we have no access to observational evidence which would allow us to maintain that the sentence about Caesar is true, or maintain that the sentence is false. On the other hand, we do know how to proceed in identifying observational evidence, if such existed. As a result, the sentence about Caesar can at least be assigned the predicate 'is either true or false'.

For the semantic realist, it is important not to link the question of a statement's truth to our capacity to decide its truth or falsity. For anti-realists, on the other hand, this linkage is crucial and because of this, they prefer to speak of 'statements'. I adopt this latter approach inter alia, for reasons adduced by Putnam.

> Even if we (*with* our language in place) must say that the sky is blue, and even if we must allow that that fact is (causally and logically) independent of how we talk, we do

not have to concede that there would be a thing called "the proposition that the sky is blue" even if we did not talk that way. It is statements (not abstract entities called "propositions") that are true or false, and while it is true that the sky would still have been blue even if language users had not evolved, it is not true that *true propositions* would still have existed. If language users had not evolved, there would still have been a world, but there would not have been any *truths*. But recognizing that fact – and it is an important one – does not require us to say that the sky is not blue independently of the way we speak. What it does require us to do ... is to give up the picture of Nature as having its own language which is waiting for us to discover and use (Putnam 1994a, 302).

As I have said, in my critique of this viewpoint I am not in principle opposed to the idea of linking a sentence's meaning to its truth-conditions. The meaning of certain sentences does in fact consist in their truth-conditions. Even a critic of semantic realism can, therefore, distinguish between truth and meaning. On the other hand, I am critical of the generalization that a definite property of certain sentences, namely the property of having truth-conditions, is a necessary precondition for its meaningfulness.

An extreme anti-realist thinker like Cupitt, whom I mentioned earlier, wants to go as far as denying the possibility, even in certain cases, of speaking of truth-conditions, since he holds that the only things that are given to us, are texts and narratives.[17] In this case, we find ourselves back with the assumption which Cupitt and other anti-realists share with the metaphysical and semantic realist. It is the idea of an ontological division between us and our notions on the one hand and reality as it exists in its unconceptualized form on the other, so that we and our notions constitute one pole corresponding to the other pole consisting of reality which is unconceptualized and independent of us. The metaphysical and semantic realist proceed from this idea of a relationship to an unconceptualized reality as such, and affirm both poles of the relationship. The metaphysical anti-realist proceeds from the same idea but denies one pole in the relationship, namely that there is a reality which is independent of us. I would like to explain why I do not consider that this is a plausible way of dealing with the question of existence by discussing the question of when and how it is reasonable to speak of existence.

Existence

One of those who has given some thought to this question in Sweden is Sören Stenlund (Stenlund 1987). He chooses as his starting point an example from the history of science, when there was a discussion about whether there was another planet in addition to those already known. I shall hop over the details, and concentrate on what is relevant here, namely the

---

[17] See e.g. Cupitt 1991.

problematic nature of the common assumption shared by metaphysical and semantic realists on the one hand and metaphysical anti-realists on the other. The debate about an additional planet arose because of changes in current theories about the universe. Obviously it was not the attempt to arrive at a new theory which caused the existence of another planet. On the other hand, it is a question of an internal relation between the theoretically anticipated, that is intentional planet, and the real one, that is the planet actually observed. With respect to the observations expected on the basis of the chosen theory, the intentional planet is so to speak the logical prerequisite for talk about the real planet. If then on the basis of theories which allow us to put forward testable hypotheses which, moreover, have been confirmed, and apparent counterexamples have been shown not to falsify the hypotheses, we have no alternative but to maintain that there is another planet. This is not a proof of the existence of this planet. Given the prevailing theoretical and empirical situation, however, it would not be particularly wise to deny the existence of a further planet.

Let us raise the question about what the metaphysical and semantic realists might add. The requirement that the object is independent of us, would entail that the truth about the new planet's existence or non-existence is independent of any relationship with the scientific context, by means of which knowledge about a further additional planet was obtained. This metaphysical realistic requirement attributes nothing to the following crucial questions relating to actual knowledge:

(1) When is it reasonable to begin discussing whether there is possibly a further planet?

(2) When is it justified in accepting and thereafter asserting that there is another planet?

I cannot see in what way we would be able to speak about the real planet, its existence, properties and its relation to other planets, other than in terms of existing theories. Nor can I see why this would be insufficient.

The next step in my critique of the common picture shared by metaphysical realism, semantic realism, and metaphysical anti-realism, concerns the concept of existence which forms the basis of this picture. I shall reject the view criticized by Putnam among others, that the word 'existence' is uniquely defined:

> that is, that I am saying the same sort of thing when I say that the brick houses on Elm Street exist and when I say that prime numbers greater than a million exist, notwithstanding the enormous differences between the uses of words (in the case of this example, between the use of words in empirical description and in mathematics). Of course, it would be wrong to register that difference by saying flat-footedly, that exist has several different meanings, in the sense of deserving several different dictionary entries. But the assumption that the meaning of words, in any conventional sense of that phrase, determines exactly what is *said* on each occasion of the use of words re-

flects a picture of how language functions that I would argue is deeply misguided (Putnam 1999, 179, footnote 12).

Drawing on the work of Uskali Mäki, let me try to show that the word 'exist' is neither uniquely defined nor has different meanings, in the sense that one of these meanings would refer to real existence, as the metaphysical realist maintains it must, in order for something to be considered as existing, but which the metaphysical anti-realist denies by reference to the fact that everything is only language, text or narrative. Mäki distinguishes three different uses of the word 'existence'. According to Mäki, existence can mean

(1) independent existence,

(2) external existence,

(3) objective existence (Mäki 1996, 432f.).

Independent existence (1) means that X exists independently if and only if X exists independently of human consciousness. Material objects have, for example, independent existence. (2) External existence means that X exists externally if and only if X exists outside human consciousness. It is not merely material objects which have an external existence: social phenomena, for example, also have an external existence. We live in different societies which, so to speak, really exist, but these are not independent of our social utopias for one thing. (3) Objective existence means that X exists objectively if and only if we can, thanks to an individuating description or some theory in general, identify X, but X is not caused by this individuating description or theory. Material objects, social phenomena such as money or economic markets as well as priorities, intentions and expectations can exist objectively i.e. they are logically independent of their descriptions or explanations. For example, it is not the case that consumer priorities first come into existence when they have been identified and explained in a particular economic theory. Consumer priorities already exist in the form of concrete purchases before we have produced a theory about them. What the theory then explains is, however, neither some view embraced by the consumers, nor their physical activity which consists in buying, but rather their priorities. In this sense, consumer priorities exist objectively. In other words, they are independent of any descriptions which may occur although they exist neither independently or externally like certain forms of object.

It is typical of metaphysical and semantic realism that objective existence is equated with independent and external existence. It is typical of metaphysical anti-realism that one retains this view but denies objectivity because one denies that there can be anything that exists independently of and external to us and our language. As I have shown, independent and external existence is not a prerequisite for being able to speak of objective existence. This brings me to the last step in my critique of the idea which is common to both metaphysical and semantic realism and metaphysical anti-realism. Once again, I shall base my criticism on Putnam's critique of metaphysical realism. The aim of his critique is to show why metaphysical realism, although superficially plausible, is in the end a fundamentally unsustainable position. Given that metaphysical anti-realism categorically denies metaphysical realism, Putnam's critique of metaphysical realism also entails the fundamental non-sustainability of that position as well.

3 Pragmatic realism: realism from an internal perspective

Putnam is at pains to point out that his critique is aimed at metaphysical realism and not commonsense realism. He points out the enormous difference between

> commonsense realism and the elaborate metaphysical fantasy that is traditional realism – the fantasy of imagining that the form of all knowledge claims is fixed once and for all in advance. That fantasy goes with the equally fantastic idea that there must be just one *way* in which a knowledge claim can be responsible to reality – by 'corresponding' to it, where 'correspondence' is thought to be a mysterious relation that somehow underwrites the very possibility of there being knowledge claims (Putnam 1999, 68).

Thus Putnam rejects the idea

> that we can speak once and for all of 'all propositions' as if these constituted a determinate and surveyable totality, and of one single 'truth predicate' whose meaning is fixed once and for all (Putnam 1999, 68).

I shall examine exactly what it is that Putnam rejects. I begin by repeating the three basic theses of metaphysical realism:
(1) real objects exist,
(2) these objects exist independently of our experience of them or our knowledge about them and
(3) these objects have quite determinate properties and have quite determinate relations to one another, independently of the concepts which allow us to understand them, and independently of the language we use to describe them.

According to Putnam, the problem is what exactly is meant by saying that the object and its properties and relations are independent of concepts and language. It sounds as though everything is unambiguous and he therefore characterizes metaphysical realism by the following three theses:
(4) "[T]he world consists of some fixed totality of mind-independent objects."

(5) "There is exactly one true and complete description of 'the way the
    world is'."
(6) "Truth involves some kind of correspondence relation between words
    or thought-signs and external things or sets of things (Putnam 1981,
    49)."

Putnam's theses (4)–(6) can be seen as a consequence of theses (1)–(3), if
thesis (3) is taken as a statement about the nature of reality, as is the case
in metaphysical realism.

Putnam encourages us to consider the following kind of questions: when
we try to decide how many objects or things there are in a room, should we
only reckon the matchbox or also include the matches in it? Are we to
count only the books or also the pages in them? Are the same things and
the same number of things involved when the botanist, carpenter or dealer
speaks of timber? With regard to the question of how many objects there
are, there is not simply one answer since we seldom are dealing with one
well-defined kind of set of objects. The way in which we answer the question about the number of objects depends on what we mean by such words
as 'object', 'thing', 'entity', 'magnitude' etc. The variation depends on
what we for the moment are interested in (Putnam 1988, 110–114).

The word 'object'

The reason why words such as 'thing' or 'object' can refer to different
things and objects is not because such words are ambiguous, but because
depending on the circumstance, they are part of differing individuating descriptions. Seen from our human perspective – and what other perspective
could we have? – it means that we are dealing with different descriptions
of reality, because individuating descriptions vary according to particular
interests. Seen from our human perspective, it is therefore pointless in
maintaining that there is exactly one complete true description of reality.

One of those who criticizes Putnam on this point is Risto Hilpinen (Hilpinen 1996). According to Hilpinen's reading of Putnam, the latter is simply asserting a triviality, namely that the word 'object' does not stand for a
contentually differentiated object but can be used in different ways on different occasions. Putnam then uses this to assert that the metaphysical realist's requirement of independently existing objects as a guarantee for the
one true description of reality is meaningless. Hilpinen raises the following
objection to this line of thought. The number of alligators in the world, for
example, is not dependent on our different descriptions of reality. The
trivial fact that some people from ignorance call alligators crocodiles, is
irrelevant. According to Hilpinen, there is, therefore, a true description of
reality with respect to the number of alligators and other specified objects.

Hilpinen, however, misses an important point. In the example he presents, it is a matter of a correspondence, not between word and objects which are independent of our conceptualization of reality, but of a correspondence between words, on the one hand, and objects which are conceptualized by us, on the other. This is precisely Putnam's point. Putnam's objection to metaphysical realism is directed precisely at the referential relationship between words and objects. The idea which he rejects is the idea of a direct access to objects which are independent of conceptual structuring. He is also opposed, however, to the relativistic view that this implies that anything whatsoever can be asserted, and that there are no restrictions to what constitutes knowledge for us humans. Knowledge is based on empirical assumptions in the sense that reality, through our experiences, limits what we human beings can reasonably assert about it. The way in which our experiences are presented is, however, to some extent dependent on the concepts which we ourselves or earlier generations have created. For this reason, it is impossible to rule out in advance the existence of alternative ways of describing reality, depending on the conceptual structures being used. For this reason, Putnam also can say:

> 'Truth', in an internalist view, is some sort of (idealized) rational acceptability – some sort of ideal coherence of our beliefs with each other and with our experiences *as those experiences are themselves represented in our belief system* – and not correspondence with mind-independent or discourse-independent 'states of affairs'. There is no God's eye point of view that we can know or usefully imagine; there are only the various points of view of actual persons reflecting various interests and purposes that their descriptions and theories subserve (Putnam 1981, 49f.).

As regards the idea of truth as idealized rational acceptability, Putnam himself holds that he has been misinterpreted. People have ascribed to him

> the idea that we can sensibly imagine conditions which are *simultaneously ideal* for the ascertainment of any truth whatsoever, or simultaneously ideal for answering any question whatsoever (Putnam 1990, viii).

Because of this, he makes clear how the expression is to be understood:

> According to my conception, to claim of any statement that it is true, that is, that it is true in its place, in its context, in its conceptual scheme, is, roughly, to claim that *it could be justified were epistemic conditions good enough* (Putnam 1990, vii).

This does not coincide with some God's eye point of view since the sufficiently good epistemic conditions are sufficiently good epistemic conditions for us humans, as the beings we in fact are. What is characteristic of a God's eye point of view is that it is supposed to be possible to go beyond the limitations which are imposed by our human situation. A true statement is thus a statement which we human beings are able to justify, or would be in a position to justify if the epistemic conditions to do so were sufficiently favourable. It is exactly this which Hilpinen misses in his criticism of Putnam's critique of metaphysical realism. Appelros points out the problematic assumption which Hilpinen's criticism is based upon:

> [the] realist assumption that once an object referred to has been identified by means of a referring expression, the act of reference has no more part to play for the referent. The act of reference is seen only as providing a means to identify the referent, which is then treated as if unconceptualized, or as an independently existing object conceptualized in a certain way which is thought to have absolute priority. It is believed that the general and specific context of utterance, including the conceptualization of the referent, can be discarded once the referring expression has done its job to connect us with a language and mind-independent object. ... [I]t is problematic to claim of an object that it is independent from, or something else than, the contextually constituted referent to the referring expression that was used when talking about the object in question. Even in order to make the above claim the object needs to be referred to again, and is thus not unconceptualized. In every act of reference the object is again conceptualized with a certain dependence on physical characteristics, and involving certain conceptual relations and functions.
>
> Of course there are cars, toy cars, fathers and mothers [and alligators] and all sorts of things that we talk about and refer to. We handle them and rely on them as physically existing independently of ourselves and our minds. ... However, the fact that we can identify an object by means of referring to it does not warrant the further step of claiming that we unproblematically can go from this referent to the object as unconceptualized (Appelros 2002, 65f.).

Appelros' critical examination of the realist assumption which forms the basis of Hilpinen's critique shows in what senses the idea of truth as correspondence is and is not excluded from Putnam's internal (or pragmatic) perspective. I shall return to this, and will be content for the moment to make the following observation. The idea of truth as correspondence is not ruled out if what is intended is (1) the minimal formal Aristotelian definition of truth according to which a statement is true if and only if what the statement says, is the case. The idea of truth as correspondence is on the other hand ruled out if what is meant is (2) a correspondence between words and unconceptualized objects. Even the assumption of such a correspondence takes place within the framework of a conceptualization, and can obviously be understood as far as the meaning of the words that make it up are concerned. On the other hand, the distinction between conceptualized and unconceptualized objects does not help us in understanding the concept of truth with respect to being able to distinguish two statements from false ones. If this linkage is lacking, I cannot see the point of having a truth concept at all.

It is clear that two completely different philosophical perspectives are expressed in metaphysical realism and in the critique of this position. (1) Metaphysical realism sees no difficulties in speaking about real things and about reality with the help of the linguistic means which are at our disposal, as though they are unconceptualized things. It can speak as if the conceptualization employed is definitely the correct one. Or again, as if the reality which is independent of our concepts is a criterion, and the supposed correct conceptualization is a measure of what is real or not. (2) In the alternative viewpoint, attention is drawn, by contrast, to the fact that irrespective of how we speak about the reality which is independent of experience and knowledge, we cannot but employ the concepts which have been developed by us human beings and refer to our human experience which has been conceptualized precisely with the help of human concepts. The reality which is independent of our concepts does not become in this instance a criterion for what is real or not. Instead the distinction between 'real' and 'not real' becomes simply a further example of conceptual development. When metaphysical realism claims to be able to say something about an unconceptualized reality, it forgets that reality for us human beings is always reality which is conceptualized and understood by us. To emphasize this is certainly the same as taking a stand against metaphysical realism, but it does not entail metaphysical anti-realism. A realistic perspective, more specifically one which is pragmatic (or internal) realist with respect to our conceptualization, is still a possibility.

The constitution of reality

I want to make clarify what is involved in the pragmatic (or internal) realist perspective by pointing out the important conceptual difference between 'conceptualized', 'constructed' and 'constituted'. It is due to this division that we can understand what is involved in the distinction between 'real' and 'not real' in an internal perspective. I shall follow Appelros in her presentation of the threefold division involving 'conceptualized', 'constructed' and 'constituted' (Appelros 2002, 22–33). She emphasizes that conceptualization is a prerequisite for all our talk about reality in all its aspects. We need concepts to be able to communicate and to survive in both our physical and non-physical environments. Different environments lead to different conceptual structures in different cultures. The magnitude of these variations does not, however, rule out conceptualizations. Without presupposing concepts (or whatever we wish to call them) such as substance, time, space, person, body, gender and identity, reality remains incomprehensible to us.

Because of this, some wish to say that reality is a social construction, and that it is we who in fact create it. Reality would not exist if we had not constructed it through agreement and convention. In certain senses, this is naturally correct. Thus money, for example, is a socially constructed reality which consists in an agreement between men to confer on certain notes which are used as money, a specific function. The situation is quite different when we are dealing, for example, with a mountain. In the case of a mountain, it is its physical existence which is the key to our conceptualization with respect to mountains. We cannot alter the mountain's physical reality by altering our conceptualization of it. On the other hand, our view of physical reality is altered when we alter our conceptualizations of it. In the case of money, the physical reality aspect is of subsidiary importance. We can alter the physical embodiment of the monetary function, without altering the reality of money itself. Its reality is to be found primarily in the social conventions which steer the way we handle what we have learned to call money. In the case of mountains, the physical aspect of reality is of significantly greater importance. But even in this case, the way in which the mountain's physical properties are conceptualized in a specific situation is what constitutes the mountain's reality for us.

Appelros introduces a third type of example which lies somewhere between the almost exclusively physical character of the mountain and the almost exclusively socially constructed concept of money. In one respect, a professor belongs to the socially constructed reality. A professor is a person with certain duties and certain rights. A professor's reality, however, is not solely determined by social convention. We cannot, as in the case of money, ignore the physical properties underpinning the professor's function. In other words, we cannot alter this and at the same time, preserve the professor's reality intact. Conversely, it is not merely a professor's physical qualities which constitute a professor's reality. A real professor is characterized by the fact that he or she is authorized to be a professor: a false professor pretends to possess such authorization when in fact it is lacking. Common to both real and false professors is that they must be human beings: they cannot be fish or stones. In addition, they have to be adults or at any rate, they cannot be infants in arms. Moreover they ought preferably to have functioning brains.

Appelros now reckons up three factors with the help of which we can specify what for us constitutes some kind of reality. In principle, these factors are applicable to everything when it is a question about the constitution of something's reality. The relative importance ascribed to each of the three factors varies, however, depending on the issue in question. Appelros illustrates these three factors with the professor example. First of all, we need to be part of a linguistic community with an agreed conceptualization of physical objects and their properties, in order to be able to conceptualize the physical characteristics which are needed for someone to be taken as a professor. Something similar also applies to mountains. In this case, too, we need to be part of a language community with an agreed conceptualization in the case of physical objects and their properties, in order to be able to conceptualize the physical properties needed for something to be considered as a mountain. Secondly to be able to speak about a professor, we require also to conceptualize the non-physical circumstances which must be fulfilled before we are ready to assign to some person the status of professor. It requires for example a social institution such as a university which is created to look after and disseminate information that is important for society. With reference to this institution, certain people are by agreement assigned certain rights and duties. Something similar holds also for mountains. In order for us to be able to speak about a mountain, it is necessary to conceptualize the non-physical circumstances which must hold for us to be able to call something a mountain rather than a hill. In the case of the tourist industry, where we draw the line is not un-interesting, depending on the target group involved. Thirdly in order to be able to speak about a professor or a mountain and to be able to identify them correctly, we need finally to combine our conceptualizations about physical aspects of reality with our conceptualizations concerning the non-physical aspects of reality which are socially constituted by us, in the concepts of professor and mountain respectively.

> This is accomplished by being part of a linguistic community sharing the same conceptual structures, in which conceptualizations (and whole conceptual structures) are related not only on a physical basis but also functionally to each other. The reason why our conceptual structures are such complex systems, with indispensable non-physical aspects, is that our social, physical, and existential needs, in our interactions with our surroundings, prompt not only physical, but also social and existential responses from us. Thus there exists a basic human need for conceptualizations that are not solely based on physical characteristics and relations (Appelros 2002, 27).

Behind this way of reasoning, there is a view of philosophy which is essentially different from the view which lies behind metaphysical realism. The fundamental idea in metaphysical realism i.e. the idea of an unconceptualized universe which is independent of us, to which our views about reality must correspond in order to be considered true, constitutes a sort of representationalism. Human consciousness and our language exist, so to speak, to represent or reproduce reality. In the second view of philosophy which is expressed in the quotation above and which also forms the basis of the present work, we human beings, participate in a decisive way with the help of concepts developed by us to constitute reality which we ourselves are a part of and to which we must simultaneously and consciously relate to and interact with. It is not the case that with the help of concepts we have developed, we cause the objects which exist outside our consciousness. But because of this, it does not follow that the only conceivable alternative would be metaphysical realism's idea of truth as correspondence, that is to say, as a form of pictorial similarity between statement and an unconceptualized reality. I shall first of all criticize the traditional view of truth as correspondence, a view which presupposes metaphysical realism, and thereafter in Part IV go on to present a more reasonable, view about truth as correspondence which rests on an internal, or as I prefer to call it, a pragmatic realist standpoint.

Critique of the correspondence theory

It is not entirely easy to specify exactly where the problem arises with the view of truth as correspondence. I shall begin by saying what is *not* problematic. The problem does not consist in the minimal formal Aristotelian definition of truth, according to which a statement is true if and only if what is asserted in the statement, is actually the case. Some philosophers prefer at this point not to speak of a definition at all, and regard it more as a formal condition which every claim to constitute a definition of truth must satisfy. In my view this distinction between a definition of truth and a formal condition which every definition of truth must satisfy, has the advantage that it does not at any rate exclude the idea of different material definitions of truth. I shall return to what is involved in this issue later.

The idea of truth as correspondence, on the other hand, causes problems when it is not simply talk about correspondence in an utterly minimal and formal sense, but when instead correspondence is thought of as a criterion of truth. The problem consists then in the following. Suppose we accept the idea of a correspondence between statements and factual situations in themselves, that is to say, as they really are independently and unconceptualized by us, or between words and things in themselves. Suppose further that we hold that this relation can be discovered. But these assumptions presuppose that we have access to these unconceptualized things and factual situations, already before we are in a position to express them. As we all know, it is not unusual for us to have different views about reality and to present, so to speak, different suggestions about correspondence in these different views of ours. In order to be able to decide which of these linguistically formulated suggestions really do express a correspondence, we ought to have access to the corresponding things and factual situations in an unconceptualized form. But this would mean that we have access to the corresponding things and factual situations already before we have access to them. The problem with correspondence, according to Putnam, is

> not that correspondences between words or concepts and other entities don't exist, but that *too many* correspondences exist. To pick out just *one* correspondence between words or mental signs and mind-independent things we would have already to have referential access to the mind-independent things. You can't single out a correspondence between two things by just squeezing *one* of them hard (or doing anything else to just *one* of them); you cannot single out a correspondence between our concepts and the supposed noumenal objects without access to the noumenal objects (Putnam 1981, 72f.).

This does not mean, however, that truth only consists in coherence.

Internalism does not deny that there are experiential *inputs* to knowledge; knowledge is not a story with no constraints except *internal* coherence; but it does deny that there are any *inputs which are not themselves to some extent shaped by our concepts*, by the vocabulary we use to report and describe them, or any inputs *which admit of only one description, independent of all conceptual choices.* Even our description of our own sensations, so dear a starting point for knowledge to generations of epistemologists, is heavily affected (as are the sensations themselves, for that matter) by a host of conceptual choices. The very inputs upon which our knowledge is based are conceptually contaminated; but contaminated inputs are better than none (Putnam 1981, 54).

This, however, does not mean in any way that with the assistance of language and our thoughts, we would not be able to describe something which lies outside language and thoughts themselves, even if something can be described by us only by describing it i.e. by using thoughts and language. In itself, there is nothing here which a metaphysical realist could not subscribe to. The difference lies in the fact that the metaphysical realist asserts that the description refers to something as if it were independent of how we formulate it. If the metaphysical realist wishes to avoid ending up with a trivial minimal realism, namely that there exist things and objects which exist independently of us, he or she is compelled to maintain something similar. The pragmatic or internal realist's arguments, as we have said, are intended to show that the view of the metaphysical realists, given that they are not prepared to content themselves with an empty, minimal realism, entails something that is unreasonable. In order to be able to describe what is asserted to exist and to possess properties independently of how we conceptualize it, we ought in such a case to have access to it before – thanks to our descriptions – we do, in fact, have access to it. I prefer therefore the pragmatic realist view that something can be described only by making use of thoughts, concepts and language since this circumstance "plays an essential role within language and thought themselves and, more important, within our lives" (Putnam 1994a, 297). What I propose to show in this book, is that this is also true with respect to the phenomenon of religion.

In this second part, I have discussed some aspects of the problem of realism in general and have presented my arguments against metaphysical realism. In the next part, I shall deal with the problem of religious realism and apply the consequences of my critique of metaphysical realism, to the case of metaphysical realism in the religious domain.

Part III

The problem of religious realism

There is a good deal of overlap between the various discussions about realism, but in one specific respect, the discussion about religious and scientific realism differs from the discussions of semantic and epistemological realism. In the discussions of semantic realism, realism is classified as semantic inasmuch as it has to do with a semantic determination of sentences, namely that their meaning consists of their truth conditions. In the discussion of epistemological realism, realism is classified as epistemological because it has to do with the possibility of truths which transcend the evidence, and with the question of the limits of knowledge. The two adjectives 'semantic' and 'epistemological' indicate that we find ourselves at a philosophical meta-level. But in the case of the adjectives 'scientific' and 'religious', this is no longer quite so clear. In the discussions about scientific realism, the main issue is not in what sense realism is scientific or non-scientific. The discussions are instead about the view of reality which is involved, or ought to be involved, when one is dealing with scientific theories. The tone of the discussion become significantly more polarized when for example someone with a scientific viewpoint maintains that the only legitimate view of what is real, is that which is presented by the natural sciences.

The discussions about religious realism also deal, to a large degree, with what view of reality is required or ought to be required in the case of religion. Those in particular on the religious end of the spectrum are concerned to elucidate the essential meaning of the epithet 'religious' and it is this question which tends to dominate the debate. For not a few participants in the discussion of religious realism, the adjective 'religious' is used not merely to distinguish religious realism from other forms of realism, but to declare a certain religious standpoint. Views about what is considered to be genuinely religious is allowed to steer the treatment of the philosophical question about religious realism. In this case, we are faced with the following problem which I shall formulate with the help of Keith Ward's presentation of the issue. It is true certainly that he formulates it in relation to religious pluralism, but it is also an excellent example of the situation which a person who defends religious realism at a religious object level, finds himself in.

The problem is this: many religions claim to state truths about the nature of the universe and human destiny, which are important or even necessary for human salvation and ultimate well-being. Many of these truths seem to be incompatible; yet there is no agreed method for deciding which are to be accepted; and equally intelligent, informed, virtuous and holy people belong to different faiths. It seems, therefore, that a believing member of any one tradition is compelled to regard all other traditions as holding false beliefs and therefore as not leading to salvation. Since each faith forms a minority of the world's population, all religious believers thus seem committed to saying that most intelligent, virtuous and spiritually devoted people cannot know the truth or attain salvation. This is a problem, because it is in tension with the belief, held by many traditions, that the supremely real being is concerned for the salvation of all rational creatures. How can this be so if, through no fault of their own, most creatures cannot come to know the truth and thereby attain salvation (Ward 1990, 1)?

Although the formulation of the problem that Ward gives, is linked to a religious perspective, I do not intend to embark on a deeper study of the religious theological arguments since they are not part of my philosophically external position, it can, nevertheless, be useful to bear Ward's presentation of the issue in mind when we now go on to deal with some of the discussions about religious realism.

1 Religious metaphysical realism

One proposed definition of realism is as follows. Although the definition speaks of theological realism and not religious realism, there is no essential difference involved.

Theological realism is the theory that there is a transcendent divine reality, the principal object of religious belief and language, the existence of which is not contingent upon (or, positively, is independent of) our thoughts, actions and attitudes. Theological non-realists maintain that meaningful religious faith and language are possible without there being any such independently existing reality Scott and Moore 1997, 402).

I shall shortly return to the fact that in this quotation, one talks primarily of existence in the case of realism, but in the case of non-realism one speaks primarily of meaning. Let us begin with the definition of theological realism – or in my terminology – religious realism. The advantage with this type of definition is twofold. The question of whether religious belief or religious language is about an independent divine reality, and therefore also the question of whether religious belief of religious language is meaningful, can be discussed irrespective of whether one is religious or not. Whether this is so, is, however, a debated issue and forms part of the multilevel discussions of religious realism. It is a matter of controversy what is meant by existence and how in such a case, existence and meaning are to be thought of as linked with one another. If we are not prepared to accept the view that there is such a link between existence and meaning, as the religious realist wishes to maintain, it also becomes a matter of controversy whether religious faith and religious language can be detached from the religious person's experience and practice in the way the religious realist wishes to do. Another difficulty is that the characterization of the non-realists is carried out so to speak, on the realist's terms. Some of those who have been characterized by realists as anti-realists or non-realists, would certainly have preferred another formulation than the one contained in the last sentence of the passage from Scott and Moore just quoted. Certainly there are anti-realists like Don Cupitt who deny the existence of an independent divine reality. I shall return to examine his anti-realism. On the other hand, the arguments of the non-realists are more concerned to show that an explanation of the meaning of religious belief and religious language does not presuppose the metaphysical realist assertion about an unconceptualized divine reality which exists independently of us. For that reason, there is no need to enter into a discussion about a divine reality, whether in the form of assertions or denials.

When I read the various contributions to the discussion of religious realism, I get the definite impression that believers as well as critics of religion, with very few exceptions. make use of the following assumption which is taken more or less for granted, namely that to be a true believer entails, from a philosophical point of view, that one is also a metaphysical realist. The believer who is a metaphysical realist then tries to argue that there is a transcendent divine reality, whereas the atheistic metaphysical realist tries correspondingly to refute these arguments, or to argue directly that such a transcendent divine reality cannot exist because of various logical reasons, or that it is utterly improbable that such a reality can exist. In Part II, I gave a critical account of metaphysical realism in general. What consequences does this critical analysis have for both religious realists and their metaphysical realist critics?

It is in no way surprising that we also encounter the problems of realism in the domain of religion. Here, too, the fundamental problem is that, on the one hand, we can say nothing meaningful about a supposed unconceptualized reality, while on the other hand we cannot meaningfully assert that language and thought do not describe something which lies outside of them, even if this something can only be described by using language and thought in the process of description. There is nothing to prevent metaphysical realists accepting this. The difference is that the metaphysical realist asserts that the descriptions relate to something as though it were independent of how we formulate it. If metaphysical realists do not wish to end up with a trivial minimal realism, namely that there are objects and things which exist independently of us, they are compelled to maintain something like this. The pragmatic or internal realist's arguments set out to show that the metaphysical realist standpoint, inasmuch as it goes beyond a minimal realism which says nothing, is unreasonable. In order to be able to describe what is said to exist and to possess properties independently of how we conceptualize it, we ought namely to have access to it before we – thanks to our descriptions – have access to it. The fact that something can be described only by employing our thoughts, concepts, and language, does not rule out the claim that we are making assertions about a reality in itself, irrespectively of whether this reality as such can be comprehended as divine or not. It is not that we cannot have knowledge about reality in itself. The question is instead whether the idea of a reality in itself is unreasonable. The whole problem is intensified in the religious domain by the fact that religious realists do not simply assume an unconceptualized transcendent divine reality and make assertions about it. In addition they emphasize the hidden, the mysterious and the radical otherness of this reality.

The problem with religious metaphysical realism

The problem with religious metaphysical realism can, therefore, be formulated in the following way, where I shall restrict myself to Christianity and above all to how its theistic aspects are presented in the Christian theistic philosophy of religion. Christianity is the religion in which I was brought up; it is also the one I know best. As far as other religions are concerned, my knowledge is derived entirely from my general reading. In Christianity, God is completely transcendent in relation to the world that we live in, which means that we in fact know nothing about God, and can, therefore, make no assertion about God. As my critique of semantic realism has shown, statements about factual matters presuppose knowledge of procedures, which enable us to decide the truth of the statements. As I see it, this linkage to observational evidence must be present in order for us to have any reasonable possibility at all to pick out among all the statements, those which claim to be statements about matters of fact. There are certainly cases where we cannot decide whether a particular sentence constitutes a statement about a matter of fact or not. In such a case, one should refrain from altering this to maintaining the possibility that the sentence is a statement about a matter of fact, and then in the next step maintaining that the statement is either true or false. I shall argue that this restriction should also be applied to statements about God.

It follows then that, on the one hand, as regards the question of God who is said completely different, we cannot grasp how there could be procedures which allowed us to makes statements about God. On the other hand, believers claim to know a great deal about God, which they then use as the basis for statements about God, the world, history, and humanity.

This is possible, according to some, because the gap between God and human beings has been bridged through revelation.

This is a very simplified account but it makes clear how this way of thinking follows the conceptual model of traditional epistemology. On the one hand, we have the knowledge subject with his or her consciousness and knowledge claims. On the other hand, we have reality which, so to speak, confronts the knowledge subject. The main epistemological question is then obviously how the gap between the knowledge subject and the knowledge object can be bridged. In the religious context, reference is most often made to revelation as the means by which an active divinity bridges the gap.

This kind of epistemology presupposes, however, a questionable assumption, namely that we are able to adopt a position where we regard things completely from the outside; in short, we presuppose a kind of God's eye point of view because we would otherwise not be able to speak about a relationship between the knowledge subject and reality, which as the object of knowledge, confronts the subject. What is problematic with this assumption, is that we human beings, given that we are the beings and organisms that we are, cannot place ourselves in such a position. For this reason, I prefer another epistemological perspective: given the condition under which we live, that is to say given that we are the beings we are, with all our limitations and possibilities, it seems to me more appropriate to consider the following question as chiefly an epistemological question. The question is namely what we human beings can reasonably assert or doubt with respect to the reality which is conceptualized by us, which we form part of and which we consciously need to relate to and interact with, in order to survive and live a fulfilling life.

What do these two mutually incompatible views of philosophy have to say about religious realism and religious anti-realism? Because of the limits of my own knowledge, I shall confine myself to the philosophy of religion as practised in the English speaking countries and in Scandinavia. Here the situation appears roughly as follows. As an example of someone who is a pronounced religious metaphysical realist, I shall choose Roger Trigg. He emphasizes that

> [w]hat reality is like and how we conceive it are always separate questions ... What is real is independent of our conceptions of it. This, at least, is what the realist would maintain. ... Realists about the existence of God will typically regard the question of whether God exists as genuine and would assert that such existence is in no way logically dependent on our understanding. Indeed, they would claim, God's existence must be wholly independent of the nature of contingent beings like ourselves. Atheists, however, would also agree with this. They might accept that there could be a God, but hold that there is not. This is an argument about what is in fact the case. Atheism holds that that reality does not in fact include God, but its readiness to talk of

falsity suggests that it concedes the possibility of truth in this area (Trigg 1997, 213f.).

Take note of the introductory words of this passage: "What reality is like and how we conceive it are always separate questions." The rest of the quotation should be read from this perspective. Reality's existence which is independent of us, as well as its unconceptualized nature which is also independent of us, are one thing: our conceptions are something quite distinct. I have already raised objections in Part II to this assumption and I shall return to it in Part IV. Here I would like instead to continue with my somewhat summary account of how religious realists and their critics react to one another.

Religious anti-realists such as Cupitt confront this metaphysical view with an alternative by pointing out the paradoxical character of religious language. The anti-realists hold that it is right that religious language also has an indicative form and contains statements which appear to be statements of fact. In the main, however, it is suggested that religious language expresses a view of life by basing it upon a view of what human life consists of when it is at its best, namely upon a view of what people take to be valuable, but which they find wanting in their lives, and long for. It is because of this that such expressions as 'grace', 'salvation', 'perfection', and 'holiness' are considered to be of central importance.

Dewi Philips is also a critic of religious realism. Now it is certainly the case that Phillips holds that the whole discussion of religious realism and anti-realism is based on a conceptual misunderstanding which is expressed in the assumption that God is an object among others, an object that does or does not exist (Phillips 1993, 85ff.). It is certainly the case that Phillips has a point; nevertheless, I am inclined to agree with Appelros' observation that Phillips, by opposing the realist view of God as an entity which either exists or does not exist, plays a part in the non-realist reaction against religious realism (Appelros 2002, 13). He does so, for example, by questioning in many of his writings, whether it is reasonable to cite evidence for God's existence.[18] According to Phillips, evidential arguments for God's existence lead simply to God's reality being reduced to be a reality derived from this evidence. In this way, religious realists transform God into an inferred entity which rules out the possibility of a firm and unshakeable belief in God, since belief in the existence of inferred entities cannot be other than hypothetical belief, that is to say, belief which only possesses a certain degree of probability. Religious realists such as Basil Mitchell[19] and Richard Swinburne[20] do not, however, agree that arguments

---

[18] E.g. Phillips 1988, 9f.
[19] See e.g. Mitchell 1973.
[20] See e.g. Swinburne 1981.

for God's existence would thereby transform God into an inferred entity of only hypothetical character. Mitchell and Swinburne set out to develop the best philosophical explanation of belief in the reality of God. For them, there is no contradiction involved in maintaining (1) that God is an experienced reality for believers, (2) that belief is trust and devotion *and* (3) that belief can be affected by intellectual doubt which is why belief in the reality of God can also require philosophical support. They cannot see that a substantial difference between God as an inferred entity and God as an experienced reality would thereby have been introduced.

On this topic, Phillips and his realist discussion partner completely miss each other's points, which is made quite clear in Joseph Runzo's discussion volume, *Is God Real*? (Runzo (ed.) 1993). Here can be found quite different views about what philosophy is. The religious realists treat the criticism which Phillips levels at them as a critique of their arguments which, as they concede, could certainly be sharpened in certain respects. For Phillips, however, it is not a matter of the arguments themselves and their possible strength, but rather a matter of the philosophical presuppositions for these arguments. Taking as his starting point Wittgenstein's later philosophy, Phillips' critique is mainly directed at the type of metaphysical realism which forms the basis of the arguments of religious realists for God's existence or reality. On the other hand, what Phillips shares with the religious realists, is concern for the good which, they both agree, religion brings with it. Thereafter they go their separate ways as regards their views of religion and about what its goodness consists in.

It is thus a combination of a particular view of philosophy and a particular view of religion which explains why Phillips argues for his type of philosophy of religion, and rejects a realist philosophy of religion. I agree, therefore, with Ulf Zackariasson's observation that

> Phillips rejects the idea that determining the likelihood of God's existence is the central task of the philosophy of religion. In my terms, we can understand Phillips as saying that this idea is based on a mistaken conception of religion. If we attend more carefully to religious practice, we would see that a religion is not at all like what analytical philosophers of religion think that it is. Therefore the problem with mainstream philosophy of religion is not that attempts to justify belief in God's existence are unconvincing; the problem is that the wrong problem was instituted from the beginning. Nevertheless, I think … that Phillips' work is also a response to the problems, which motivated philosophers to formulate philosophical arguments for the existence of God. His work too, can be understood as concerned about the preservation of the goods of religion. Accordingly, we can say that he shares an extra-philosophical problem with the philosophers he criticizes, but they hold different views of what philosophical problems the philosophy of religion should deal with (Zackariasson 2002, 70f.).

More exactly, one could – putting it in somewhat simplified terms – say that Phillips with his view of religion and with the help of Wittgenstein's later philosophy, sets out to dissolve such philosophical problems as pseudo-problems which have arisen, according to Phillips, due to an unreasonable view of religion.

Despite the fact that Phillips has a view of philosophy and, therefore, of the philosophy of religion which is quite different from that of the realist philosophers of religion whom he criticizes, he maintains, as little as they do, that belief causes what is true. On the other hand, he rejects metaphysical realism's idea that our statements are representations of an intrinsically unconceptualized reality. Instead Phillips stresses the following. When we make a statement about reality, we always do so on the basis of a particular practice and its associated language. Even if Phillips himself means that the whole discussion of religious realism and anti-realism is based on a conceptual confusion, it is, nonetheless, the attention paid to practice and the language associated with it which he shares with the anti-realist.

This is roughly speaking the essence of the discussion concerning religious realism and what the realists call anti-realism. It is not unusual in the philosophy of religion, in particular, that realists consider themselves to have the right to set the interpretational agenda. As I have already remarked, I am not primarily interested in developing an anti-realist position, whether in general, or in relation to the religious domain in particular. Rather, I would like to offer a critique of metaphysical realism, and hopefully replace it with a more philosophically defensible form of realism. This modest aim is, however, frequently classified in the context of the philosophy of religion by metaphysical realists as an expression of a pronounced anti-realist position, implying the denial of God, sacrilege or the disparagement of religion in general. The reader should bear in mind that this need not at all be the case when subsequently, I present a more philosophically adequate account of how we can deal with the problem of realism in the religious domain. Therefore when I come shortly to summarize religious metaphysical realism, it is not to deny it, and present the negation as an anti-realist position. I do it quite simply to be able to introduce my critique of religious metaphysical realism.

I would like to summarize religious metaphysical realism in analogy with the summary of metaphysical realism in general, in terms of the following six points. Observe first, however, that for the metaphysical realist, these points also include God which means that since 'God' is a religious term, religious metaphysical realism Is not a purely philosophical position, but a religious one which makes use of metaphysical realism as a support for its religious position. On the other hand, atheistic metaphysical realism is a philosophical position since one either argues against the argument for the existence of God, or else tries to show that the God as defined by the religious realist does not exist, or cannot exist. As different versions of metaphysical realism, atheistic and religious metaphysical realism share the same problems.

As far as religious metaphysical realism is concerned, a further specific problem occurs. The atheistic metaphysical realist asserts that there is a reality which is independent of us, but that this reality does not contain a God, as an entity independent of us. As the quotation from Moore and Scott shows, the religious metaphysical realist, on the other hand, does not assert that God is an entity in a reality which is independent of us, but rather that God *is* a reality which is independent of us. The theologically much discussed question of the relationship between God as a reality which is independent of us, and the world or universe as a reality independent of us, can be left aside since it lies outside the limits of the present enquiry. The assumption that there is a transcendent divine reality which is independent of us is, in fact, the fundamental assumption of the religious metaphysical realist, not that there exist real entities in a reality which is independent of us. It follows that the critique of religious metaphysical realism has in part a different formulation from the critique of metaphysical realism in general. The six points which sum up religious metaphysical realism are as follows:

(1) There is a transcendent, divine reality. Just as the general metaphysical realists feel unable to deny that there are real objects, so religious metaphysical realists feel unable to deny that there is a transcendent, divine reality. This is the religious dimension which is not shared by the atheistic metaphysical realist.

(2) This transcendent, divine reality exists quite independently of our experience and our knowledge of it.

(3) Independent of our concepts with the help of which we comprehend it, and independent of our language which helps us to describe it, the divine reality has quite definite properties and has quite definite relations to our reality. It is here that things become problematic if it is meant that it is possible to say something about "what reality is like" to borrow Trigg's formulation, without perceiving that reality for us is always a reality which is understood and conceptualized by us. If we fail to take note of this and hold that it is possible to make statements about what makes up this transcendent, divine reality then the following three theses are also implied.

(4) The transcendent, divine reality consists of a definite number of beings, powers, forces or whatever, which exist quite independently of our human consciousness.

(5) There is exactly one complete description of the transcendent, divine reality since it is this which decides which knowledge claims about it, are justified.

(6) Truth is therefore a sort of correspondence between religious statements, on the one hand, and supernatural, intrinsically unconceptualized,
factual states, on the other.

Since the transcendent, divine reality is unique, it is the genuine reality,
and therefore is identical with *The Truth*. And since The Truth is unique,
there can only be one true belief, that is to say, one representation of The
Truth. Although it is possible to conceive of several incomplete and partly
true representations, religious metaphysical realism tends, nevertheless, to
have exclusivist consequences. When one looks at things from the other
end, the situation is quite different. As I shall show, other positions e.g.
some forms of pluralism, can also be associated with metaphysical realism.

There are certainly exclusivists who accept the theoretical possibility
that their own belief can be false. Exclusivists of this type, whom I have
met personally and spoken with, have always, nevertheless, a habit of
adding that no philosophical or scientific arguments have hitherto convinced them that this is the case. This inspires in me a certain scepticism:
if we ignore e.g. moral considerations or that our own religious expressions are no longer felt to be existentially adequate, what would constitute
convincing epistemic, logical, or other rational reasons for getting exclusivists to admit that their own beliefs are false? In practice, it would seem
that our own beliefs are not considered to be false. Precisely because we
are certain, we believe. If, therefore, for various reasons, we do not in
practice reckon with our own belief being false, it tends in practice to be
the case that every belief which cannot be understood as being part of, or a
variant of, our own belief, is rejected as false. In addition, it is also the
case in practice that every argument that can be directed against another
belief, is automatically taken to be an argument on behalf of our own belief. Conversely every argument which can be adduced for our belief, is
automatically taken to be an argument against every other belief. Because
of the exclusivist's certainty of belief, the notion that our beliefs, and not
just those of someone else, might be false, has no place in practice.

Inclusivism and pluralism, in contrast to exclusivism, seem more reasonable standpoints. I shall show that neither exclusivism, inclusivism or
pluralism solve the problems which are inherent in metaphysical realism.

Exclusivism, inclusivism and pluralism

An exclusivist position of the above kind immediately encounters both
theoretical and practical difficulties. Note that I speak of exclusivism as an
expression for religious metaphysical realism, in other words, of the sort of
exclusivist view which holds that there is only one representation of the
Truth. I am not speaking about exclusivism in the weaker sense, namely,
that if a belief is not compatible with our own belief, they exclude one an-

other. It is certainly the case that they can exclude each other for reasons which are not metaphysical. For example, there can be psychological reasons such as when we are suffering from an emotional blockage, we cannot encounter people who hold another belief; or it can be legal reasons such as when a certain public office requires that the person holding the office is a member of a given religion. An initial problem which arises in connection with exclusivism in the stronger sense, is that the dividing line between exclusivism, on the one hand, and inclusivism and pluralism respectively, on the other hand, does not run between religions but cuts straight through every world religion. Since this is, above all, an internal problem for the religions concerned, I shall not deal with it here, but instead I shall consider another problem which arises from the fact that every world religion seems to have its representatives with exclusivist claims which entail total incompatibility between religions. References to revelation are certainly rather common, but they are of no assistance since ideas about revelation also form part of the religious ideas, and can also themselves be incompatible with the ideas about revelation which are entertained by other religions. In the comparison with other religions, using ideas about revelation which are intended to function primarily as reasons in one's own religion, is to argue in a circle. If these reasons cannot be transformed into relevant reasons in other religions as well, the ideas of one's own religion about revelation remain part of what are quite specific religious views with a quite specific content, and cannot be understood without these views and content. As a result they cannot be used as arguments for the truth of just these specific religious views and content. In other words, they cannot be used as arguments which are also acceptable to the followers of other religions.

Similarly, references to examples of morally superior lives and explanations of these examples on the basis of one's own belief system do not help in the choice between different exclusivist claims.

> We cannot decide on the basis of the moral lives prescribed or lived, for the virtues and acts encouraged often are not that different, while adherents of all faiths seem capable of living morally praiseworthy lives (Peterson, Hasker, Reichenbach and Basinger 1991, 223).

If exclusivism is not a viable approach, then what about an inclusivist position? Common to both is that even inclusivists base their case on their own religion which represents the truth. Like the exclusivists, they assert that there is only one absolute truth, and that this truth has been revealed to the full in only one religion, namely their own religion. In contrast to exclusivists, however, inclusivists recognize that the divine being can also be encountered in other religions and divine grace can be obtained. Inclusivists certainly make exclusivist claims as regards the complete truth of their own religion. At the same time, followers of other religions have the possibility of being saved by virtue of the salvation which is offered by these other religions. The complete explanation of these offers of salvation is available, however, only in the one true religion.

The selfsame criticism which can directed against the exclusivists immediately arises here as well. Let us suppose that we have a multiplicity of religions, all of which assert that they themselves constitute the genuine and complete religion. It is worth recalling that there are religious people who do not make any such claims on behalf of their own religions. On the other hand, if such claims are made by the various religions, is there any room for arguments which are neutral with respect to the various religions, and which can decide which of the religions is making a justified claim? I would like to stress that I am not speaking about radically neutral arguments from a God's Eye point of view, but only about arguments which are neutral with respect to the religions involved. In Parts IV and V, I shall show how arguments which refer to religions and their secular counterparts, despite the fact that they are not formulated in vacuum devoid of a view of life, can, nevertheless, be neutral in the sense that they do not presuppose a specific religion or specific view of life. Even if philosophical perspectives rest on certain presuppositions about views of life, they are, nonetheless, as I have shown in Part I, different from religious or other kinds of view of life presuppositions. References to revelation cannot, therefore, form a part of philosophical arguments since ideas about revelation are also religious ideas, and can therefore be intrinsically incompatible with ideas about revelation in other religions. As I have said, we become involved in a vicious circle when, in making a comparison with other religions, we make use of ideas about revelation which are part and parcel of a particular religious conceptual world, as an argument for the truth of just this conceptual world.

Because of such difficulties, John Hick is equally opposed to exclusivism and inclusivism. For this reason, he advocates in many of his writings a pluralistic position. Let us see if Hick manages to avoid the problems which beset both exclusivism and inclusivism, and which arise from their foundation in metaphysical realism.

Like every other truth claim, each religious truth claim is an expression of our human efforts to relate to reality. In the religious context, it is more specifically related to the transcendent divine reality. But because this divine reality is transcendent – by definition outside our human reality – and therefore completely different in character, human religious truth claims cannot be treated as a description, in the usual meaning of the term, of this transcendent divine reality which they, nonetheless, refer to as the source and basis of our own reality. Since religious truth claims are not descriptions in the usual sense of the word, there is therefore room for more than one true belief. Hick illustrates the situation with the tale of the blind men and the elephant, a tale which is ascribed to Buddha:

> An elephant was brought to a group of blind men who have never encountered such an animal before. One felt a leg and reported that an elephant is a great snake. Another felt a tusk and reported that an elephant is like a sharp ploughshare. And so on. And then they all quarrelled together, each claiming that his own account was the truth and therefore all the others false. In fact of course they were all true, but each referring to one aspect of the total reality and all expressed in very imperfect analogies (Hick 1993, 140).

Many consider this an illuminating picture. However, when seen in relation to the discussions about religious realism, it is afflicted with a troubling presupposition. Who in fact is the narrator? It is clearly someone who knows what an elephant is. If the tale is intended to illustrate the situation in the world of religions, the following question arises: who is the narrator who knows how incomplete all the different religions are in their representations of the transcendent divine reality? Obviously it is someone who knows what is really the case. As the tale of the elephant is concerned, it can be anyone who knows what an elephant is. In the case of religions, no human being can assume an analogous position. The problem with the story is that in order to be comprehensible, it presupposes an external perspective on the part of the narrator who knows that all the blind men are really referring to the same thing, namely the elephant. At the same time, it is precisely the narrator's external perspective which undermines the very point of the story, namely that every position is only one perspective among others. It then follows that the narrator's position also merely reflects one perspective among others which, according to the story, it is not meant to be.

In spite of this difficulty, Hick holds that the different religions are not only different views of reality but interpretations of the same thing, namely the ultimate, indescribable, transcendent, divine reality. In this respect, Hick's pluralism also entails metaphysical realism. A common way of arguing philosophically for the realist basis of such a pluralism is by appealing to the philosophy of Immanuel Kant. As I shall show, a Kantian inspired religious realism is also incapable of solving the problem of metaphysical realism in the world of religions.

Kantian inspired religious realism

Hick and various other people try a philosophical foundation for the realist obligations which their pluralistic position involves, by making use of Kant's distinction between things-in-themselves and the phenomena in which we encounter reality as it manifests itself to us. Hick refers to Kant as the person

> who has argued most influentially that perception is not a passive registering of what is there but is always an active process of selecting, grouping, relating, extrapolating, and endowing with meaning by means of our human concepts. This led him to distinguish between the noumenal world, the world as it exists unperceived, and the phenomenal world, that same world as humanly perceived, with all the differences that the act of perception makes. I am suggesting applying this insight to our awareness of the Real, by distinguishing between the noumenal Real, the Real *an sich* and the Real as humanly perceived in different ways as a range of divine phenomena (Hick 1995, 29).

Let us see what precisely this sort of Kantian inspired philosophy of religion rests upon when we follow in Kant's footsteps and distinguish between, on the one hand, things-in-themselves, about which we know nothing apart from assuming that they give rise to things in our reality, and, on the other hand, phenomena i.e. reality as it manifests itself to us. Kant's idea that sensory experience is necessary, but insufficient for knowledge plays an important role. Sensory experience which has not been ordered in terms of the categories of reason such as cause and substance or in terms of the forms of human intuition such as space and time, does not constitute knowledge. Nevertheless, it is not the categories of reason and the forms of intuition which cause the existence of that which we have knowledge about. The assumption that the existence of reality is not dependent on us, would seem to presuppose the assumption about things-in-themselves.

In Part II, I have already shown how the very idea of things-in-themselves in some unconceptualized form is open to doubt. In Part IV, I shall argue for what I consider to be a superior assumption about the presupposition which is needed to be able to maintain that the existence of reality is not dependent on us. For the moment, however, in criticizing the Kantian influenced argument used to support realist religious pluralism, I would like to focus instead on something else.

When in the context of the philosophy of religion, I read how Kant's distinction between things-in-themselves and phenomena can be applied in the religious domain, I cannot resist the impression that there is a confusion between epistemology and ontology. It is one thing to assume things-in-themselves as a presupposition for being able to say that the world is the same, even if it manifests itself to us in different ways. One example would be to assume a divinity-in-itself in order to be able to assert that all religions ultimately deal with the same thing, even although the divinity-in-itself manifests or reveals itself to us in different ways in the different, historically given religions. It is, however, quite another thing to glide from talk about things-in-themselves to talk about reality-in-itself, ascribing to this reality not only a completely independent existence i.e. complete transcendence, but also definite properties which, for example, manifest themselves to us human beings, even although these properties are assumed in fact to lie beyond our possibilities for conceptualization since they belong to a reality which is transcendent for us. I shall illustrate this apparent confusion of ontology and epistemology with the help of a contribution by Joseph Runzo to the discussion of religious realism and anti-realism in his published anthology *Is God Real?* (Runzo 1993).

Runzo distinguishes between God-in-Godself or the noumenal God and God as manifested to us through our experience. Belief in God is a complex which involves three dimensions. First of all there is (1) belief in God-in-Godself. However, since we would have no access to God-in-Godself without God's manifestation, belief in God, seen from our human perspective, is simultaneously (2) belief in God as the God of history i.e. God as he manifests himself in historical experiences. These experiences vary depending on the specific religions involved. Within a particular religious framework, in which God's own manifestations are considered to be expressed, belief in God is moreover (3) belief in God as the God we confront as individual human beings. According to Runzo, there are three reasons for such a division between God-in-Godself, God as the God of history, and God as the God we confront as human individual human beings. First of all, thanks to this tripartite division, we can still talk about one and the same God, although there is a host of religions with different historically and culturally influenced religious ideas. Secondly, despite the fact that that there is a great variety of religious belief with differing claims about God, the threefold division does not mean that only one belief in God can be true. Since manifestations of God are many, it would be strange if only one manifestation in this multiplicity were the one true manifestation of God. Thirdly and finally, Runzo holds, with respect to the theologies which have arisen in the different religions, that even the God which the different theologies talk about, can be ascribed reality. This is so because there are many manifestations of God-in-Godself, and the God of the theologians is the result of theological reflections about the personal experience of God as well as about how God is manifested within one's own particular religious tradition.

This, roughly speaking, is how Runzo looks upon the connection between God-in-Godself, the God of history and the God we confront as individual human beings. Let us examine more closely one of several reasons which according to Runzo, speak in favour of religious – or as he calls it – theological realism.

> Given a Kantian perspective, God in Godself, the noumenal God, is not directly accessible to human perception or understanding. But if a realist follows out Kant's metaphysics, then God appears to us *qua* phenomenal. Though there is only one real, noumenal God 'behind', so to speak, phenomenal divine reality, this does *not* mean

that God of whom theology speaks is somehow unreal or less real than the noumenal. If the God we confront, the God of history, is God *qua* phenomenal, it does not follow that this God is just a product of our needs or imagination or is a mere metaphysical shadow. Noumenal reality and phenomenal reality are two different categories of reality, and the terms denote two different senses of 'reality'. There is nothing less real about war and human kindness, tomatoes and tornadoes, because *they* are part of phenomenal reality and not noumenal reality. Likewise the God of history, the God one confronts, is no less real for not being in the category of the noumenal. Like wars and tomatoes and human kindness, the God of history, the God a monotheist confronts, *is* part of reality – for what could be *more* real than that which we do experience? To try to escape the reality of our experience for something putatively 'purer' is to fall prey to the worst element of a degenerate Platonism. For this is to turn away from the only means we *do* have for understanding the divine and our humanity in relation to the divine (Runzo 1993, 166f.).

I find two oddities in Runzo's way of arguing. The first oddity is when he exclaims rhetorically "what could be *more* real than that which we do experience?". This may be so, and it would also be imprudent to ignore our experiences, but it in no way follows from this that what is experienced as being real, is thereby, simply for this reason, evidence that things are as they are asserted to be, in our truth claim about reality. Observe that Runzo means by reality that which is not dependent upon our experiences. The second oddity concerns Runzo's observation that "[t]o try to escape the reality of our experience ... is to turn away from the only means we *do* have for understanding the divine and our humanity in relation to the divine." If Runzo means, what he says, namely that the reality of our experience is the only means we have for understanding the divine and our humanity in relation to it, I cannot see how this fits in with what Runzo says initially in the quotation, namely that "God in Godself, the noumenal God, is not directly accessible to human perception or understanding." The idea is naturally that we have indirect access to the divine. But such a thought becomes vacuous if we link it to "[n]oumenal reality and phenomenal reality are two different categories of reality, and the term denotes two different senses of 'reality'." We can then never decide if a supposed indirect access to the divine reality is genuine or not.

I recall that an utterance, according to the formal, minimal Aristotelian definition of truth, is true if and only if what is asserted really is the case. This definition by itself does not allow us to determine which utterances are really true because for this, we must have criteria for truth. For something which we hold to be true to be really true, then what we hold to be true, must obviously be the case. But from our mere conviction that something is true, no matter how strong that conviction may be, it does not follow that it really is the case. The metaphysical realism which forms the basis of Runzo's Kantian inspired formulation of belief in a transcendent divine reality which is independent of us, leaves us in the lurch as far as the question of truth criteria is concerned. This vacuum requires to be filled, partly because of the following reason which emerges from Runzo's own way of thinking. Even if more than one belief can be true, it does not follow that every belief is true. Indeed every belief might be false. These and other difficulties help to produce the opposing position to metaphysical religious realism, namely religious metaphysical anti-realism.

2 Religious metaphysical anti-realism

I shall begin by giving a brief account of religious metaphysical anti-realism and then offer some criticism. As already noted, Cupitt is one of the most radical religious anti-realists. He leaves us in no doubt that what he considers most objectionable, is the claim to absolute religious truth. On the other hand, it is not always clear what Cupitt exactly denies. It is one thing to deny that religious ideas are descriptions of an unconceptualized, transcendent, divine reality which is independent of us; it is quite another to deny that there is a transcendent, divine reality at all. I shall return to this distinction. Cupitt makes no bones about claiming that religious ideas are symbols for human hopes, efforts, ideas and human longing. For this reason, we ourselves are totally responsible for these symbols and the use we make of them. It will not do, for example, in Christianity to retain antisemitic and sexist symbols simply on the grounds that they are to be found in the Bible or in the Christian tradition. I would agree with Cupitt, but I reject the anti-realist philosophical underpinning he gives to this view.

The following three objections arise. The first concerns a certain lack of clarity about the logical order between the denial that there is a transcendent, divine reality i.e. the denial of R1, on the one hand, and the view that religious ideas are nothing more than expressions of human hopes, efforts, ideals and human longing, on the other. It is one thing for the anti-realist to deny that there is a transcendent, divine reality because religious ideas are nothing more than expressions of human hopes, efforts, ideals and human longing. Here the assertion about the nature of religious ideas precedes the denial of a transcendent reality. It is another matter when the anti-realist conversely begins by denying the existence of a transcendent, divine reality, and thereafter draws the conclusion. that religious ideas are nothing more than an expression of human hopes, efforts, ideals and human longing. The choice of relative order gives rise to different types of difficulty.

In the first case, the difficulty consists in showing that religious ideas in reductionist terms are literally nothing more than an expression of human hopes, efforts, ideals and human longing. It is obviously possible to give examples of religious ideas where different theories or explanatory models are needed to be able to show that they are merely expressions of wishful thinking, neuroses, or certain socio-economic conditions of life. On the other hand, it is impossible to show that these examples of religious ideas cannot be anything other than just such expressions. Scientific explanation does not allow this sort of generalization.

In the second case, the difficulty consists in either showing that there cannot be any transcendent, divine reality at all, or in showing that such a reality does not exist. With respect to the former, I cannot see why there cannot be a transcendent, divine reality. With respect to the latter, we have an example of the general difficulty which is associated with showing that something does not exist. One can point to something which exists, but not to something which no longer exists, or which does not exist in the immediate neighbourhood. Clearly, reasons have to be given for why it is considered that a definite object such as the transcendent, divine reality does not exist. If we show that the idea itself of a transcendent, divine reality is in fact an expression of something else, we find ourselves once more face to face with the difficulty involved in the first case.

A second conceivable objection to religious, metaphysical anti-realism is as follows. Let us suppose that the anti-realist, in his criticism, maintains that the religious realist's idea of a transcendent, divine reality which is independent of us, is incomprehensible, not linguistically, but philosophically incomprehensible, in the sense that certain components in the idea are incompatible with each other. In such a case, the anti-realist places himself in a difficult position. If he denies that there is a transcendent, divine reality, it also means that the anti-realist's denial is equally incomprehensible philosophically. One cannot reasonably deny something which one has initially dismissed as incomprehensible.

A third objection is finally that the statement that religious ideas are nothing more than expressions for human hopes, efforts, ideals, and human longing implies that religious language is superfluous. The religious realist holds that if religious ideas are not ideas about a transcendent, divine reality, because according to the religious anti-realist such a reality does not exist, they really are superfluous. If religious ideas are nothing but an expression of human hopes, efforts, ideals and human longing, we would be able to content ourselves with the non-religious ideas which we already have at our disposal. Why then, in this case, have religious ideas not ceased to exert their influence? Is it because they supply something which the non-religious ideas lack? For the religious realist, the following explanation seems the simplest: religious ideas are not superfluous because, if they were, they would have ceased to exist. In other words there must be a substantial difference between them and their non-religious counterparts.

The best explanation for this is to assume that religious ideas, in contrast to the non-religious ones, are about a transcendent, divine reality which is independent of us.

I have already set out my reasons criticizing this kind of metaphysical realism. One of them is aimed at the metaphysical realist's assumption that reality consists of a determinate number of objects which exist independently of our human consciousness. This entails that there is an exact and complete description of reality since it is the unconceptualized, independent reality which decides which statements about it are true. Even this thesis runs the risk of being vacuous if no epistemological implications attributed to it. If we do not have any ideas about how this decision procedure would actually be carried out, there is no reason to maintain that it is the unconceptualized reality which decides which statements are true. If we do have ideas about this, we end up with the following problem. When we want to test statements against reality, we ought to have access to the reality which exists outside of our statements about it, before we present our statements about it. But this we cannot do because our reality is always a conceptualized one.

For this reason, I would like to propose the following alternative to the metaphysical realist explanation of religious language. It is an alternative which instead is based upon internal realism – or as I shall often call it in the present work, pragmatic realism – and upon an outside perspective in relation to religions and their secular counterparts. The alternative which I propose, fixes upon two features. Firstly, the possibility of understanding reality in religious terms would appear to be part and parcel of our human existence, something given with this existence. Secondly, religious language in the eyes of many people provides, when compared with its secular counterparts, a more adequate means of expression for articulating our responses to life's inevitabilities, namely love, joy, happiness, suffering, guilt, and death. For them, religious language is a language which allows us more adequately to express the experience, in confronting life's inevitabilities, of reaching a limit, not because they have attained superior understanding, but because it is psychologically and logically impossible for them to question what is constituted as real. Analogously, many other people look upon non-religious language as a more adequate means of expressing this experience of encountering a limit, in confronting life's inevitabilities, not because in contrast to religious people they are more enlightened and therefore know better, but because it is psychologically and logically impossible for them to question what is constituted as real. I shall return to examine the nature of this disagreement in Part IV.

People recognize their lives in these religious and non-religious expressions, and also allow their lives to be shaped by them. When people reflect about love, for example, they try to form some idea of it with the help of literature, theatre, film, art, and religion. They may also compare their own shortcomings and disappointments, and try to form an idea of what pure love might be. In this way, love becomes a limit concept. For believers, it seems natural to call this pure love God. What is said about God is then not true or false because it agrees or does not agree with the reality conceptualized by us which offers resistance to us in our *observational* experiences. Instead, it is true or false depending upon whether it agrees or does not agree with the reality conceptualized by us which offers resistance to us in our *existential* experiences. As I shall formulate it in the book's conclusion, in the case of observational experience, it is a question of empirical adequacy, whereas in the case of existential experience, it is a question of existential adequacy. Both kinds of adequacy are required if we are to be able to relate to, and interact with reality as conceptualized by us in all the respects that we experience it as offering resistance.

Such a view presupposes neither that we add a statement about an unconceptualized reality which is independent of us, or that we deny this statement. The problem with the anti-realist denial is that this denial – exactly like the assertion made by the anti-realist's opponent, the religious realist – is based upon the ontological division between unconceptualized reality on the one hand, and our views on the other. The difference between realist and anti-realist consists then in the fact that the latter eliminates one half of the division, while the former makes use of the reference to the unconceptualized reality in itself, as that which decides which views about it are true. As I have already shown, the idea that it is the unconceptualized reality which we make statements about, is untenable since reality for us is always a reality which is understood and conceptualized by us. In order to allow the unconceptualized reality in itself to decide which of our conceptualizations are correct, we would have to have access to the unconceptualized reality prior to having conceptualized it.

As I shall show in the next section, I share the type of anti-realist critical view which holds that religious truth claims cannot be understood as statements in the usual sense, namely as we employ them in everyday life and in the sciences, since we cannot specify how we could test them. The fact that religious utterances cannot be tested i.e. can neither be falsified nor confirmed, has in the logical positivist critique of religion been construed to mean that religious utterances are cognitively meaningless i.e. are neither true nor false. I share the view that religious utterances are not statements because we do not even know how we would test them. I would not agree, however, with the conclusion which is drawn by the logical positivists that religious views are nothing more than an expression of diffuse emotions. In Part IV, I shall show how both these aspects can be linked to one another to yield a third way between religious, metaphysical realism and non-cognitivism. As a prelude to that, I shall now explain why I hold that religious utterances are not statements. I do this by taking up an earlier critique of semantic realism.

3 Religious statements as purported assertions

Let us recall how Dummett defines semantic realism. According to him, it embraces the following three theses:
(1) a thesis about objectivity,
(2) a thesis about truth conditions,
(3) a thesis about realism.
The thesis about objectivity maintains that a sentence must in principle be available to anyone. In other words, it must in principle be translatable into any language whatsoever, since otherwise communication would be impossible. This is an ontological thesis inasmuch as it posits a reality which is independent of our language, but one which, nevertheless, can in some sense be described and represented by means of our language. It is this view of the relationship between language and reality from which it follows that whatever can be described and represented, can in principle be described and represented in any language whatsoever. The linkage between languages goes via reality and its entities, to which expressions of language refer. Thus apart from the thesis about truth conditions, namely that the meaning of a statement consists in its truth conditions which are, or are not satisfied, independently of whether we have knowledge of it or not, we obtain also the thesis on realism which holds that every statement by virtue of the nature of reality, is either true or false independently, not only of whether we actually know this or not, but also of our capacity to know which of these two properties a particular statement possesses. What characterizes semantic realism is its claim that the meaning of a sentence is defined purely in terms of its truth conditions. In this way, it is held that we can avoid the meaning of a sentence being relativized by a reference to our incomplete understanding and knowledge at a particular moment.

Let us apply this view to the religious domain, reminding ourselves of what the religious realist, Roger Trigg, whom we have already mentioned, maintains, namely:

> Realists about the existence of God will typically regard the question of whether God exists as genuine and would assert that such existence is in no way logically dependent on our understanding. Indeed, they would claim, God's existence must be wholly independent of the nature of contingent beings like ourselves. Atheists, however, would also agree with this. They might accept that there could be a God, but hold that there is not. This is an argument about what is in fact the case. Atheism holds that re-

ality does not in fact include God, but its readiness to talk of falsity suggests that it concedes the possibility of truth in this area (Trigg 1997, 214).

On the basis of this, we can define semantic realism in the domain of religion with the help of the following four theses:

(1) Religious statements are descriptions of a transcendent, divine reality.

(2) The meaning of these statements consists in their truth conditions which are satisfied or not, irrespectively of whether we have knowledge of them or not.

Thereafter, the atheistic and religious semantic realists go their different ways. The atheist believes that a successful case has been made for the non-existence of a transcendent divine reality. In other words,

(3) Religious statements are indubitably statements, but they are false.

In contrast to the atheist, the religious semantic realist holds that there is a proof of the existence of God, and that in one way or another e.g. by divine revelation, we know that the truth conditions are satisfied. In other words,

(4) Religious statements are not simply statements: they are, moreover, true statements.

The essential problem is not in talking of statements also in the religious domain. It is not unusual that we employ the same linguistic expression in different contexts with different meanings. However, a problem arises if it is asserted that these religious statements are the same sort of statements which are to be found in ordinary life and in the sciences, in other words statements which allow us to make assertions about what is true or false with regard to what is observable. In the case of ordinary life and science, talk about statements concerning reality, therefore normally presupposes

(1) that one reckons with true as well as false statements and

(2) that one requires reference to empirical evidence as soon as we have to decide which utterances can be reasonably considered as statements, and which not.

Even if believers consider that certain religious statements are false – frequently those which occur in *other* religions – the majority of believers rule out, for religious reasons, the possibility that their own religious truth claims are false. When in the religious domain empirical evidence is adduced, it is most often employed for the purpose of confirmation rather than for possible falsification. Allusions to revelation, as noted, do not work since there are mutually inconsistent views about what revelation is and we possess no criteria which do not themselves presuppose revelation, to allow us to decide which revelation is actually true.

I would like to ponder this question and discuss in some detail how far religious utterances are statements. As far as I can see, the thesis that religious sentences are statements presupposes two fundamental assumptions of semantic realism, namely

(1) a statement's meaning consists of its truth conditions so that a statement is always true or false,

(2) the idea of truth conditions can be made comprehensible without linking it to our epistemic capacity.

Such is the meaning of what many religious, metaphysical realists in particular assert, namely that religious statements say something about what is, or is not the case e.g. that God exists or does not exist, even if we human beings had never existed.

I shall show why the thesis that religious sentences are statements can find no support in these two assumptions. Even if both assumptions express different requirements, they are linked inasmuch that a critique of the first requirement presupposes a critique of the second. The result of this twofold critique will turn out to be that the purported statements in the domain of religion should not be classified as statements.

Logical positivist critique of religion

The conclusion that religious utterances are not statements is also a conclusion drawn in various formulations of the positivist critique of religion. Although the positivist critics of religion themselves have in turn been greatly criticized, I hold that the idea that religious utterances are statements still gives rise to a number of serious philosophical problems.

My own critique of the view that religious utterances are statements, will not be a repetition of the positivist one. I hold, for example, that the positivists are wrong when they draw the conclusion that religious utterances are cognitively meaningless. Their view of meaning is too closely tied to statements and the idea that the meaning of a sentence consists in its verifiability or falsifiability in an exclusively empirical sense. Instead, I shall develop my critique of understanding religious utterances in terms of statements, by referring to parts of my earlier criticism of metaphysical realism. I begin by giving an example of a positivist critique of religion, and discuss some of the objections which have been raised to it.

Perhaps the most influential positivist critic of religion is Antony Flew. In his tale of the invisible gardener, he sets out to show that religious sentences which are asserted to be statements, are not really statements at all. I have no idea how often this tale has been quoted in the philosophical literature, but I would guess that it must occurred a great number of times. Nonetheless I want to quote it here, not simply because some readers may not be acquainted with it, but above all because it makes a point which is still worth discussing,

> Once upon a time two explorers came upon a clearing in the jungle. In the clearing were growing many flowers and many weeds. One explorer says, 'Some gardener must tend this plot'. The other disagrees. 'There is no gardener'. So they pitch their tents and set a watch. No gardener is ever seen. 'But perhaps he is an invisible gardener.' So they set up a barbed-wire fence. They electrify it. They patrol with bloodhounds. ... But no shrieks ever suggest that some intruder has received a shock. No movements of the wire ever betray an invisible climber. The bloodhounds never give cry. Yet still the Believer is not convinced. 'But there is a gardener, invisible, intangible, insensible to electric shocks, a gardener who has no scent and makes no sound, a gardener who comes secretly to look after the garden which he loves.' At last the Sceptic despairs, 'But what remains of your original assertion? Just how does what you call an invisible, intangible, eternally elusive gardener differ from an imaginary gardener or even from no gardener at all (Flew 1955, 96)?'

What seems to happen when the believer is confronted with empirical data which threatens to falsify the religious claim, is that empirical data no longer have any crucial significance for the claim. The religious claim which initially appeared to be a conceivable hypothesis dies "the death of a thousand qualifications" (Flew 1955, 97).

Counterarguments

This type of criticism has itself in turn become a target of counterarguments. I shall give two examples. The first is Reaburne S. Heimbeck's criticism; the second is that put forward by Richard Swinburne. After a brief presentation of their criticism, I shall explain my own doubts about their way of arguing in order to make clear that the thesis that religious utterances are statements, is still a controversial one.

Heimbeck wants to show that purported religious statements really are statements, by arguing that they imply ordinary empirical statements which are open to falsification. Heimbeck's example of a religious assertion is: "God has provided all men, through the life, death and resurrection of Jesus of Nazareth, the grace sufficient for eternal salvation." According to Heimbeck, this religious statement implies the empirical statement; "Jesus of Nazareth was alive at time t_1, dead both clinically and biologically at t_2 and alive again in bodily form at t_3" (Heimbeck 1969, 95). Since the implied statement is empirically falsifiable, it follows that the original statement which implies it, is also indirectly, empirically falsifiable.

I shall query this mode of reasoning by looking more closely, first of all, at the interplay between conceptual considerations, in our case concerning life and death, and at the view of what is involved in falsifiability. Secondly I shall examine the role which the concept of resurrection plays in Heimbeck's argument. Heimbeck maintains that the statement "Jesus of Nazareth was alive at time t_1, dead both clinically and biologically at t_2 and alive again in bodily form at t_3" is an empirically falsifiable assertion. It is made up of three constituent statements:

(1) Jesus of Nazareth lived at time t_1 – empirically falsifiable.
(2) He was dead both clinically and biologically at time t_2 – empirically falsifiable.
(3) He was alive again in bodily form at time t_3.

It may be asked whether (3) is an empirically falsifiable statement since it is a question of being "alive *again* in bodily form" (my italics) and not simply "alive in bodily form." A statement that a given person is alive at a given moment is empirically verifiable. The statement that a given person is both clinically and biologically dead a given time is also empirically verifiable. Both statements together about the same person, who after being clinically and biologically dead, is alive again, however, rule out each other, if we accept the conceptual means which we usually employ when it is a matter of clinical and biological life or death. One or other of the statements must therefore be false. The reason is perhaps that something has been overlooked. As long as there is no indication that this is indeed the case, we ought not to use this possibility as a reason for using the concepts of life and death in a way different from the one we actually employ.

For Heimbeck, these two statements do not rule each out in the particular case of Jesus. One possibility is naturally to say that a conceptualization which contains views about resurrection, are – at least to some extent – of a different character than an empirical conceptualization. However, it is precisely the empirical which is important for Heimbeck. When he, therefore, holds that both statements do not rule each other out with regard to Jesus' resurrection, as far as I can see, it depends on the prior acceptance of Jesus' resurrection. Jesus who was dead both clinically and biologically, is said to be living again, given the assumption that he has risen from the dead. The concept of resurrection is, however, not an empirical concept, since we cannot decide on the basis of what, for human beings, are epistemologically good grounds, whether the fact that a previously dead man can, so to speak, regain life is due to resurrection or something else. I am not against the concept of revelation being used as religious concept. However, speaking for myself, I cannot see how, given the acceptance of the previously mentioned communicational, conceptual, and epistemic limitations which characterize our lives as human beings, a view about resurrection can belong to the same logical and conceptual level as the view of clinical and biological death. In other words, I cannot see how an idea of resurrection could be represented with the help of clinical and biological concepts. It is exactly this that is needed in order to be able to talk of empirical falsifiability. Resurrection does not seem to be something which could be understood in isolation from the believer's religiously coloured conceptual identification of the event.

As I shall argue in Part IV, this does not make religious views cognitively speaking meaningless. In the case of religions and their secular counterparts, it is not a question of conceptualizations of how our conceptualized reality offers resistance in our observational experiences, but rather of how our conceptualized reality offers resistance in our existential experiences of what it means to be a human being, namely to live with life's inevitabilities. Given the different functions which religions, their secular counterparts and the sciences have in our lives, and given my earlier criticism of both metaphysical and semantic realism, I cannot accept the third part of Heimbeck's supposed statement as empirically falsifiable. For that reason, I cannot see either how the implication which Heimbeck claims to exist between "God has provided all men, through the life, death and resurrection of Jesus of Nazareth, the grace sufficient for eternal salvation" and "Jesus of Nazareth was alive at time t_1, dead both clinically and biologically at t_2 and alive again in bodily form at t_3", could be a valid one. Since the latter statement is not empirically falsifiable, it follows that the former is not indirectly falsifiable either. Heimbeck's criticism of the positivist critique of religion has thus failed to show that the purported religious statements are indeed statements.

Let us see if Swinburne's criticism of the positivist critique of religion is any more successful. I shall present parts of Swinburne's argument in some depth for the following reasons. First of all, my critique of Swinburne's position plays an important role in the elaboration of my own pragmatic realist position with regard to religion. Secondly, Swinburne is one of the most influential theist philosophers of religion. Finally I wish to avoid the misunderstanding that my critique is merely directed at a mere man of straw.

Like Heimbeck, Swinburne also wants to defend the statement character of religious utterances. While Heimbeck adopts the view that certain religious statements imply normal empirical statements and thereby can themselves be classified as statements, Swinburne, without beating about the bush, claims that such religious statements are factual statements. He does this, for example, by arguing in his book *The Coherence of Theism* for the coherence that exists between different types of belief statement,

> which purport to affirm the existence of a being with one or more of the following properties: being a person without a body (i.e. a spirit), present everywhere, the creator and sustainer of the universe, a free agent, able to do everything (i.e. omnipotent), knowing all things, perfectly good, a source of moral obligation, immutable, eternal, a necessary being, holy, and worthy of worship (Swinburne 1993, 2).

Among other things, he wishes to reject the view that a sentence must be verifiable or falsifiable in order to qualify as a factual statement. Instead he wants to investigate the conditions which need to be satisfied for a sentence to make a coherent statement and in particular a factual statement (one which it is coherent to suppose to be true and coherent to suppose to be false) (Swinburne 1993, 3).

Swinburne uses the word 'coherent', first about factual statements, and secondly about assumptions relating, in particular, to the truth or falsity of factual statements. These belong to two quite different levels. Swinburne's use of the word 'coherent' in both cases is perhaps to be explained as follows. The word 'coherence' is ambiguous. It can refer first of all to the logical aspect of judgement. When we judge how statements relate to one another, our view is influenced by what we consider to be relevant or not. Swinburne would appear not to notice this ambiguity, with the result that he hovers between the logical aspect of coherence and the judgement and relevance aspect of coherence. My reason for immediately drawing attention to this oddity in Swinburne's use of the word coherence, is that it allows us to understand how Swinburne treats what he labels the weak verificationist principle. According to Swinburne's version of this principle, a statement is a factual statement if and only if it itself describes a factual state which is observable, or would be confirmed or refuted by some other statement which describes a state of fact (Swinburne 1993, 26).

Swinburne has various kinds of objection to the weak verificationist principle. For my purposes, it will, however, suffice to concentrate on the following two objections which are directed at the truth of the weak verificationist principle. The first objection arises from something which, in itself, might be considered to the principle's advantage, namely, that one usually argues for the weak verificationist principle by pointing out examples. The usual way of exemplifying a factual statement is to say how a statement could be confirmed or refuted by some actual or conceivable observation or experience (Swinburne 1993, 27). The connection between factual statements and actual or conceivable observations or experiences in the various examples would seem to be obvious. Swinburne gives two counterexamples to this argument:

p_1. There is a being like men in his behaviour, physiology, and history who nevertheless has no thoughts, feelings or sensations.

p_1. Some of the toys which to all appearance stay in the toy cupboard while people are asleep and no one is watching actually get up and dance in the middle of the night and then go back to the cupboard, leaving no traces of their activity (Swinburne 1993, 28).

Swinburne accepts that such statements can neither be confirmed or refuted by observation. His point, however, is that this circumstance is not sufficient to maintain the truth of the weak verificationist principle. The examples merely show that they do not satisfy the weak verificationist principle. They say nothing about whether it is justified to set up the weak verificationist principle as a criterion for factual statements. In order to show that the examples adduced are not factual statements, we need to be able to prove with the help of some principle *other than* the weak verificationist principle that the statements in the above examples are not factual statements. Only if one is able to do this, can such examples be used as an indirect support for truth of the weak verificationist principle. As long as this has not been done, the examples serve rather as counterexamples to the weak verificationist principle (Swinburne 1993, 28).

In his second objection with regard to the veracity of the weak verificationist principle, Swinburne attacks another argument which also, in itself, could be cited to the principle's advantage. I feel obliged to quote Swinburne at some length, not simply to be able to present his reasoning, but also because I have the distinct feeling that there is something here that does not add up:

> It is claimed that a man could not understand a factual claim unless he knew what it would be like to observe it to hold or knew which observations would count for or against it; from which it follows that a statement could not *be* factually meaningful unless there could be observational evidence which would count for or against it. But then the premiss of this argument seems clearly false. A man can understand the statement 'once upon a time, before there were men or any other rational creatures, the earth was covered by sea', without his having any idea of what geological evidence would count for or against the proposition. Surely we understand a factual claim if we understand the words which occur in the sentence which expresses it, and if they are combined in a grammatical pattern of which we understand the significance (Swinburne 1993, 28f.).

It is claimed that in order for someone to understand a factual statement, it is presupposed that the person knows what it means to observe what the statement claims, or knows which observations would count for or against it. According to Swinburne, it follows from that – and for safety's sake I shall quote him again "that a statement would not be factually meaningful unless there could be observational evidence which could count for or against it." In the quotation above, Swinburne then proceeds to maintain that it is possible to understand the statement 'once upon a time, before there were men or any other rational creatures, the earth was covered by sea' without having any idea about what geological evidence would speak for or against this statement, or how such evidence could be identified. If Swinburne had said that we understand, for example, a poetic picture or a mythological view of a time before there were human beings or other rational creatures and when the earth was covered by sea, I would have agreed. I would also have agreed if he had said that we can understand the statement without ourselves having any idea about the evidence which speaks for or against it, or how this evidence can be identified. Someone, however, must be able to do so in order that the rest of us can understand what the question is about. It is not the case, as Swinburne suggests, that we understand the statement, despite the fact that no-one has any geological evidence for it, provided that we understand the words which occur in the sentence which expresses it, and moreover are combined in a grammatical pattern the meaning of which we understand. It is instead the case that we understand the statement provided we want to understand it as a statement, because we know which observations *could be* taken as evidence for or against the part-statement that human beings have not always existed or the part-statement that the earth was covered by water.

Let me continue with the reconstruction of Swinburne's way of reasoning. The point that Swinburne wants to make, is that

> even if it could be shown that credal statements did not make observation-statements or statements which evidence of observation could count for or against (and I do not wish to suggest that this could be shown), that would not show – without further argument – that they did not make factual statements (Swinburne 1993, 29).

Let us examine more closely what, according to Swinburne, makes a sentence a statement. According to him, it is obvious

> that if a sentence is to express a coherent statement, the words which occur in it must be meaningful. The claim here is if words are to have meaning either they must be ordinary words used with their ordinary meaning or they must be words whose meaning is explained by means of ordinary words or observable phenomena; the words must be empirically grounded (Swinburne 1993, 36).

With this qualification in mind, Swinburne can then say:

> Normally ... a meaningful indicative sentence makes a statement, that is a claim about how things are. It makes a statement if it is coherent to suppose that what it says is either true or false, if it makes a claim about how things are (Swinburne 1993, 37).

As we have seen, Swinburne considers that the sentence that God is a person without a body, is an example of a belief statement. I would like to make two criticisms of Swinburne's way of determining what constitutes a statement. The first objection is based on the following train of thought. If we apply Swinburne's own criterion of what constitutes a statement to the sentence that God is a person without a body, the purported statement turns out not to satisfy the demands of the criterion. The second objection is the following. If in the criterion of what is a statement, we ignore the question of the evidence which speaks, or can be thought to speak, for or against the statement, we would probably be obliged to permit far too much when it comes to what can reasonably be approved as a statement i.e. a knowledge claim about the nature of reality.

I shall begin by showing what happens when one applies Swinburne's own criterion to the purported statement that God is a person without a body. We recollect that for Swinburne, a statement must be a meaningful sentence, that a sentence is meaningful if its consituent words are meaningful, and that the words are meaningful if they are empirically grounded i.e. they are either ordinary words used with their ordinary meanings or words whose meaning is explained by means of ordinary words or observable phenomena. It is obvious that the word 'God' is not a word which can be said to be empirically grounded, even if it is to be found in the Bible, and is associated with empirical, historical events. The word 'God' is certainly a common word which does not need to be explained with the help of other words. This, however, does not depend on the fact that it is empirically grounded, but is connected with the fact that 'God' is a religious term with a religious function. According to my view of the function of views of life, including religious views of life, the word God is used in expressions, images and narratives for the tension that is experienced between how life could be at its best and how it actually is. I shall return to this alternative view, when later I critically examine Swinburne's arguments for insisting that theism is more probable than naturalism.

Since God is defined to be a person without a body, let us also take a look at the phrase 'person without a body'. The word 'body' is empirically grounded, and this is also true of the word 'person'. The phrase 'person without a body', on the other hand, is not empirically grounded, if we leave aside legal persons. (In the case of legal persons, the empirical ground is an organization, company, association, or similar). If we leave aside the legal sense of the word 'person' then the usual meaning of 'person' – as opposed to the meaning philosophers speak about – refers to a human being with a body. We can certainly speak about God as a person without a body; but I cannot in that case see why one speaks of this as empirically grounded. To begin with the word 'body' which refers to something observable, and then to set a negation before it, is a process which, in my view, does not entitle us to speak of an explanation in empirical or observational terms. The words 'body' and 'person' are certainly empirically grounded but the phrase 'person without a body' is not. Thus the phrase according to Swinburne's own criterion of meaning, has no meaning. The sentence 'God is a person without a body' is thus not a meaningful sentence. It is, therefore, not a statement about which it would be coherent to assume that what the sentence says, is either true or false, relative to how things actually are.

In addition to the difficulty that Swinburne's own criterion for statements cannot be applied to the purported statement 'God is a person without a body', there is also something else which needs to be considered. For Swinburne, the sentence 'God is a person without a body' is a statement, even if no evidence can be adduced for or against it. I personally find it hard to accept the idea that a sentence can be a statement without some possibility of falsifying or justifying it, in relation to circumstances which from an epistemic viewpoint are sufficiently good, not in the greatest gen-

erality, but – to borrow a formulation of Putnam which we discussed earlier – sufficiently good for us human beings. The purported statement 'God
is a person without a body' would seem to be a sentence where there are
no epistemically sufficiently good circumstances to allow us, as human
beings, to confirm or falsify it. To refer to the possibility of eschatological
verification *à la* Hick, namely that if there is an afterlife, we would be able
to meet God as a person without a body, and thus verify the statement that
'God is a person without a body', is akin to ignoring the fact that epistemically sufficiently good circumstances apply to us in this life. Our epistemic
limitations do not allow us to make testable claims about what happens in
an afterlife.

I suppose that the basic difference between Swinburne and me has to do
with the fact that he employs an exclusively non-epistemic view of truth
which allows him to maintain that there are factual statements such that we
cannot imagine what observational evidence, for or against them, would
look like. Think of the toys which get up in the middle of the night, dance
without anyone seeing them, and then return to the box without leaving
any trace. To say this is, however, epistemically devoid of interest. But is
this not exactly what Swinburne asserts? He certainly does so, insofar as
he places epistemology and ontology in separate watertight compartments,
thereby completely ignoring a linkage to us human beings, as the creatures
we are. By contrast, I hold that although epistemology, ontology, and for
that matter semantics, form different perspectives, each with its own characteristic set of questions, we cannot ignore the semantic and epistemological issues when we wish to concentrate on the ontological one. To
maintain that a sentence is a factual statement although we do not even
know how we could verify or falsify it i.e. maintain that the sentence is
either true or false irrespective of whether we know or not what constitutes
the truth-conditions, is to speak about truth exclusively in ontological and
more precisely, metaphysical realist terms. Note that I do not deny that
there are things which we do not know, and even that we cannot know.
Acceptance of our limitations is one of my philosophical ground rules.

In Part IV, I shall show that a reasonable view of truth also requires
linkage to epistemic matters. I shall also show that this is not the same as
defining truth in epistemic terms. Thus I do not deny that a great many
things can be the case where we have no evidence for, or against them. On
the other hand, I am not prepared, because of this, to maintain that what is
expressed in such sentences as (a) 'God is a person without a body' or (b)
'Some of the toys which to all appearance stay in the toy cupboard while
people are asleep and no one is watching actually get up and dance in the
middle of the night and then go back to the cupboard, leaving no traces of
their activity', is either factually true or factually false. The kind of posi-

tion I adopt has certainly been criticized for unjustifiably making one into some kind of thought police, and for ungenerously dismissing the fact that people actually put forward such statements as knowledge statements and thus as knowledge claims. This criticism goes on to state that the issue is whether these claims to knowledge are justified. I do not dispute that people actually put forward such statements as knowledge claims, and I respect their right to do so. Given our previously mentioned communicational, conceptual and epistemic limitations, and particular in the case of epistemic ones, given what constitutes epistemically sufficiently good circumstances for us human beings, I hold that the question of whether such statements are justified knowledge claims cannot even be raised. Since there is no possibility of referring them to observational evidence, such statements cannot be treated as knowledge claims at all, and the question whether they are justified or not becomes superfluous.

My reason for not classifying these purported statements as statements of fact requires an explanation of the fundamental difference between Swinburne's way of philosophizing and mine. Swinburne fails to note the following circumstance which, in my opinion, cannot be ignored. In order to clarify what I mean, I prefer to quote Appelros at some length where she draws attention to the fact

> that certain ways of thinking are in fact unavoidable, that we do conceptualize the world by way of substance, time, space, person, identity, and so forth, is not likely to change. Cultural and geographical differences around the world make for slighter differences in conceptual structure; if you are surrounded by snow you have to relate to snow in order to survive, and if you live in the equatorial area there is no need for any concept of snow. Differences in long-time evolved organisms may of course allow for greater differences in conceptual structures; we might, who knows, develop wings and acquire a new set of concepts having to with flying and flapping wings. But even so, a human race cannot evolve uncorporality and over time drop having any concept of substance. Thus, an Eskimo people may move to Africa and over time drop the concept of snow; but the whole human race can never grow into one single organism and thus dispense with all concepts having to do with person. ...
>
> [We] are as human beings biological organisms with a certain sensory apparatus, relating to certain physical, biological, social and existential surroundings. In conceptualizing and in making use of language we presuppose this very setting that we are part of. Doing that is a prerequisite for conceptualizing in the first place; you cannot have one without the other. The prerequisites for our conceptual structures are what they are since we are what we are. They are not absolute in that they constitute what conceptualization of reality is *per se*, but they do constitute what conceptualization of reality is for us, what we can say and think. To us there is only one alternative (Appelros 2002, 38f.).

I hold that this limitation on how we can reasonably conceptualize, also applies to our views of God. It is one thing to say that presuppositions for our conceptualizations, such as substance, time, space, person, identity etc., cannot be applied to God in the same way as to us human beings.

Such categorial presuppositions are, nonetheless, still presuppositions for all our ideas. We cannot, therefore, as Swinburne does, maintain that God is a person without a body, but one with the possibility of acting by other means than bodily actions. The category of person, in this case, no longer functions as an unavoidable prerequisite for our conceptualizations. Even when it is a matter of our ideas of God, we are dependent upon our preconditions for conceptualizations. These preconditions are what they are, because we are the beings we are. This naturally influences and colours the religious experiences which religious people have. Ideas about a divine Thou are essentially linked to ideas of a person. Talk about God as a Thou, however, is part of a religious conceptualization of how reality as conceptualized by us offers resistance in our existential experiences of what it means to be a human being, that is say, to live with life's inevitabilities. Given that God occurs as a person in existentially adequate ideas, images and narratives, the use of the word 'person' in a religious context cannot be completely arbitrary. By contrast, to place ourselves outside the religious context and suggest the sentence 'God is a person without a body' as a claim to knowledge, entails abstracting from all the particular aspects that we associate with the word 'person' and which are directly or indirectly associated with identifiable bodies. I believe that this is to empty the word 'person' of all significance. It is true that we can assign the word person a completely new meaning, but in that case we should not simultaneously make free use of the established definition which has been removed by abstraction.

Many believers have been impressed and are pleased with this type of objection to the positivist critique of religion which I have illustrated with the help of the counterarguments due to Heimbeck and Swinburne. I do not deny that Swinburne's critical analysis, in particular, has helped to show the serious flaws in the positivists' way of reasoning in their critique of religion. But this is not where the problem arises. The problem is that Swinburne – and many other who agree with him – do not see the serious philosophical difficulties which are inherent in the thesis that belief statements are factual statements, because as philosophers of religion they make use of a problematic view about what constitutes a factual statement. I wish to expose some of these by applying pragmatic (or internal) realism also in the domain of religion.

In order to avoid my philosophical goal being misconstrued, I reiterate for safety's sake the view of philosophy which I have defended in Part I, and which has led me to see philosophical problems, where other philosophers, with a quite different view of philosophy, have perhaps seen none at all. As I have said, my philosophical remarks are not claims to knowledge; instead they are intended both as a contribution to the critique of problematic concepts in philosophical doctrines which otherwise seem superficially obvious and clear. They are a way of devising conceptual tools which allow us to deal more adequately with our various views of reality. A characteristic feature of my philosophical approach has been consistently to avoid a God's Eye point of view, and instead to keep to a perspective that is accessible to us as human beings: in other words a pragmatic (or internal) perspective.

Part IV

Pragmatic realism with respect to religion

According to Putnam's critics, internal realism – what I shall call pragmatic realism – is synonymous with anti-realism. Putnam, on the other hand, although he does not equate it with metaphysical realism, nonetheless looks upon it as some kind of realism. It is namely an internalism which still draws a distinction between the concept of truth and the concept of justification. Putnam illustrates how we can accept the distinction between the concept of truth and the concept of justification, while simultaneously accepting the connection between them by reminding us how we understand statements, namely

> by grasping their *justification* conditions. This does not mean that the 'internal' realist *abandons* the distinction between truth and justification, but that truth (*idealized* justification) is something we grasp as we grasp any other concept, via a (largely implicit) understanding of the factors that make it rationally acceptable to say something is true (Putnam 1981, 122f.).

I have mentioned earlier that the phrase 'idealized justification' has been misconstrued and for this reason, Putnam prefers to speak about 'epistemic conditions good enough' where the last two words are taken to mean implicitly 'good enough *for us human beings*' (Putnam 1990, vii). It is not a question of ideal conditions for justification in the sense that there are justification conditions which are common to all truth claims. Inversely, it is not a question of relativism in the sense that truth is defined in terms of conditions for justification. Although the concepts of truth and justification are related to each other, there is a difference between them. While there are degrees of justification, the word 'truth' stands for something which does not admit degrees. Thus Putnam distinguishes between truth and justification but he does not draw the conclusion of the metaphysical realist, namely that truth is independent of every conceptual schema and every justification (Putnam 1981, 55). He sums up his view of truth in the following two conditions which, according to him, must be satisfied, namely

> (1) that truth is independent of justification here and now, but not independent of *all* possibility of justification. To claim that a statement is true is to claim it could be justified; (2) that truth is expected to be stable, or 'convergent'; if either a statement or its negation could be justified, even if conditions were as ideal one could hope to make them, there is no sense in thinking of the statement of *having* a truth-value (Putnam 1983, 85).

For safety's sake, I would like to make clear that 'one' in the phrase 'as one could hope to make them' refers to us human beings with all the communicational, conceptual and epistemic limitations noted in Part I.

I have made use of Putnam's internal realism since the internal (or pragmatic realist) perspective seems to me more reasonable than both metaphysical realism and metaphysical anti-realism. It also allows me to understand better what sort of statement could be reasonably accepted as a factual statement i.e. can reasonably be assigned the predicate 'to be true or false' in the sense of agreeing or not agreeing with reality as conceptualized by us, as it offers resistance in our observational experiences. If we can specify and apply criteria which are epistemically good enough for us human beings, or in other words which are as ideal as we can hope to make them, in order to specify what it means for a sentence to be true or false, then we are dealing with a statement which has the property of being true or false. If, moreover, we have criteria which are epistemically good enough for us human beings (or in other words, criteria which are as ideal as we human beings can hope to make them) to decide whether the statements are true or false, then we are dealing with statements which are actually true or are actually false.

The kind of argument which Putnam adduces for his internal realism has therefore persuaded me that Dummett's criticism of semantic realism's unrestricted use of the bivalence principle – a criticism which I have further developed – is to some extent justified. That there are clear differences between Putnam's philosophical position and Dummett's is another issue which I need not go into here. I shall content myself with making the following remark. Whereas Dummett wishes to replace talk about truth conditions by talk about conditions which allow us to assert reasonably that something is the case (assertibility conditions) – in other words, taking the antirealist line in a verificationist sense – Putnam rejects the abandonment of the conceptual difference between truth and justification. Putnam and Dummett share the pragmatic realist perspective but in Putnam's case this implies that the concepts of truth and justification really are distinct yet nevertheless must be seen in relation to one another. I shall continue to apply this pragmatic realist perspective to religion, in particular by criticizing Christian theism and its claims that religious utterances constitute statements.

1 Christian theism

When I earlier discussed the question of what sentences could reasonably be characterized as statements, I introduced three senses in which we usually speak about statements, namely
(1) in relation to a definite conceptual system,
(2) as statements about how we make use of definite words, and
(3) as statements about matters of fact in relation to observational evidence.
Let me illustrate the first sense with a classical theistic conceptual system and discuss its relation to statements in the factual sense. According to the constitutive rules for a certain theistic conceptual system, it is not merely meaningful but indeed true that God is a person without a body, completely free, omnipotent, omniscient, infinitely good and the creator of all things. This aspect is concerned primarily with the coherence of the theistic conceptual system i.e. the connection between the role played by God as a person without a body in the theistic conceptual system and conversely the way in which the system is a precondition for understanding this notion of God.

If, moreover, the view of God as a person without a body is made into a factual statement, as we saw was the case e.g. in Swinburne, and it is claimed that it is true also outside the theistic conceptual system, the idea of God as a person without a body becomes, to say the least, hard to grasp. It is possible to describe what an acting person is and what a body is. We can also show how negation works. But in spite of the fact that we understand all the component terms in the statement, there is no conceivable way for us to be able to comprehend what this statement might imply as part of an explanation of how reality, as it is conceptualized by us, offers resistance in our observational experiences i.e. with respect to our interaction with reality. Such interaction is necessary as regards concepts which form part of sentences which reasonably i.e. in relation to observational evidence, can be classified as statements about matters of fact. There is no conceptual foundation to enable us to classify the assertion that God is a person without a body, as a statement which is either true or false. On the other hand, I do not reject the idea that conceptualizations of how reality, conceptualized by us, offers resistance in our existential experiences of what it means to be a human being i.e. to live with life's inevitabilities, are also involved in shaping how we in fact interact with reality as conceptualized by us. But in this case, it does not come about through these conceptualizations being statements about matters of fact.

The critic will perhaps object that this says more about my inability than about the impossibility of forming an idea of a person without a body. I believe that it has more to do with how religious belief is to be understood e.g. from a pragmatic realist perspective in relation to the circumstance that we are the beings that we are, or from a metaphysical realist perspective where reference to our human preconditions plays no role. With regard to the latter perspective, even the atheist Mackie denies having any problem with the idea of a person without a body. In his commentary on Swinburne's theistic description of God, he writes as follows:

> It is sometimes doubted whether such descriptions can be literally meaningful. But there is really no problem about this. We know from our acquaintance with ourselves and other human beings, what a person is ... Although all the persons we are acquainted with have bodies, there is no great difficulty in conceiving what it would be for there to be a person without a body; for example, one can imagine oneself surviving without a body, and while at present one can act and produce results only by using one's limbs or one's speech organs, one can imagine having one's intentions fulfilled directly without such physical means (Mackie 1982, 1f.).

Neither the theist Swinburne nor the atheist Mackie, despite differences in their views of life, have any trouble at all in taking utterances about God as a person without a body as statements of fact, plain and simple. I think that this is due to two views they share. As Zackariasson has formulated this double common denominator, it is partly a common propositional view of religious utterances and partly an associated view which they also share, of justification in terms of epistemic justification. Swinburne and Mackie

> agree on what kind of practice religion is, how religious belief is to be understood, and what kind of argument it is that would take us anywhere to establishing that God (probably) exists. ... The difference between Mackie and Swinburne is that they assess differently the evidence they agree is important (Zackariasson 2002, 59).

Swinburne and Mackie share the view that the theist's description are statements of fact. But their views differ about whether these descriptions are true or false.

Since in their arguments about God's existence, there is nothing to suggest that it is a question of metaphysical expression, factual statements about God e.g. as a person without a body, are interpreted literally. The question is what exactly this means. Let us see how William Alston, among others, deals with the issue. He is a Christian theist and has as little difficulty, as does Mackie, in speaking of God as a person without a body. I have chosen Alston because he has put forward certain ideas about the literal interpretation of religion. These ideas are based on metaphysical realist grounds and deserve closer scrutiny, since I have problems with metaphysical realism. I shall give a rather detailed account since I do not wish to be accused of criticizing an artificially constructed position which no one actually holds.

Religious utterances taken literally

Alston begins by reminding us that there is a difference between language and speech. A natural language is an abstract system where the systematics have both an internal and external character. The internal aspect of language refers to its phonology, morphology, and syntax i.e. the ways in which the elements of the language are combined to form larger entities. The external aspect of a language means its semantic one i.e. the way in which the elements of the language refer to things in the world and represent its nature. Given that language primarily serves as a means of communication, it is reasonable to assume that both internal structure and external reference are necessary in order for language to function as a tool for communication. In contrast to language, speech is *the use* of language in communication. It can thus refer in a wider sense both to written and oral communication. It is a question of speech when we use language systems to communicate.

One aspect of language structure, and more exactly of its semantics, is that a given word or expression has the meaning (or different meanings) that it in fact has. Thus, for example, the English word player means 1. 'an idler', 2. 'one who plays some (specified) game', 3. 'a gambler', 4. 'an actor'. The fact that a word *has* a certain meaning in a language, helps to make it useful for communication. Given the distinction between language and speech, Alston now presents his explanation of the function of the term 'literal'. When we say that an expression is literal, we mean rather that it is a matter of *using* words or expressions in a special way. The opposite of a literal use of terms is thus a pictorial use of them. There are several types of pictorial language; one of the most common is the metaphor (Alston 1996, 368f.).

Alston explains the difference between a literal use of terms or expressions and a metaphorical use as follows. For the sake of simplicity, he restricts himself to predicate terms in subject-predicate statements. When we use some meaning of a predicate term in a literal sense, we hold that the property which is designated by the predicate term belongs to the referent of the subject term, or if the predicate term represents a relation, that the relation denoted by the predicate term exists between the referent of the subject term and the other object or the other objects of the relation. When e.g. we use the word player in sense (4) above, by saying 'He is one of the players', we are maintaining that the person who is referred to, does indeed have the property which is specified in sense (4) of the word 'player'. If, moreover, our statement is true – in other words, the person referred to, really has the property alluded to – we are then able to say that it is literally true that 'he is one of the players'.

Alston now goes on to illustrate metaphorical usage. Let us suppose that I say, like Macbeth, "Life's a poor player that struts and frets his hour upon the stage and then is heard no more." Obviously life is not an actor. When I say that "Life's a poor player" the term is used metaphorically and not literally. To use a term metaphorically, means that one uses a definite meaning which a term has in a language, not in a direct sense but in an indirect one.

Instead of maintaining that the property designated by the predicate can be ascribed to the referent of the subject-term, one does something more complex. One alludes to, or hints, at the kind of thing which the term is usually applied to literally. In the example, it is the poor actor who says his lines on the stage and is promptly forgotten. At the same time, certain characteristics associated with the actor and his performance are transferred to life itself (Alston 1996, 369f.).

Alston draw attention to the fact that the term 'literal' in recent years has often been confused with such terms as 'exact', 'unambiguous', 'specific', 'empirical' and 'everyday'. It is clear that a word's meaning in a language can be more or less vague, unstructured, unspecified or otherwise indeterminate. This, however, has nothing to do with the literal use of a word. Moreover, words can be used literally, quite irrespective of whether I perform many different speech acts such as asking a question, expressing anger, or asserting that the cat is on the mat. Alston discusses in particular the confusion between 'literal' and 'empirical' since it has to do with the question of the circumstances which lead to a word acquiring a fixed, agreed meaning in a language. If this requires a linkage to empirical experience in some of the senses fixed in an empirical theory of meaning, it is self-evident that only terms with empirical meaning can be used literally. The view that only terms with empirical meaning can be used literally, stands or falls with the development of a viable empiricist theory of meaning. Alston questions if such a theory exists (Alston 1996, 370).

According to Alston there is nothing in all of this to prevent one from holding that we can talk literally about God. In order to show this, he clarifies what in his view binds meaning and concept together. As he sees it, we can associate a definite meaning with a predicate term, only if we have a concept for the property which is designated by the predicate term when it is used with exactly that particular meaning. Conversely, it is possible to use a definite term to denote this property, if one has a concept for this property. A prerequisite is naturally that sufficiently many members of our own language community share this concept. Alston sums up the relationship in the principle that a specific term in a specific language can designate a certain property *if and only if* the speaker of this language has or can have a concept for this property.

Alston then applies this argument to terms about God's properties. These can stand for properties of God *if and only* if we can form concepts of these properties of God. We can make true literal predications about God *if and only* if our language contains terms which stand for these properties. According to Alston, we can therefore speak literally about God *if and only if* we can form concepts for God's properties.

In this connection, Alston discusses the fact that the question of the extent to which certain terms can be used literally about God, is often identified with the question of the extent to which these terms are literally true about God in a sentence where the terms are used as they are used outside theology. Alston illustrates this with personalistic predicates such as saying that God has knowledge, God has intentions, God creates, God commands, and God forgives. It is sometimes maintained that the terms which stand for these properties are literally true of God in the same sense that they are literally true of human beings. Alston does not deny that we can learn the meaning of terms which stand for God's properties by learning what it means for human beings to have knowledge, to have intentions, to command and to forgive. Nor does he deny that there is no other approach. On the other hand, he wants to show that it does not follow from this that terms could be used literally about God only in the same sense they have when we use them of humans and other beings. Terms about humans and other beings can be associated at a later stage with definite technical meanings. This occurs both in natural science and theology. Even in the natural sciences, we can only learn the technical meaning of the terms, provided we have first learned their everyday meanings. Nothing prevents terms such as 'force' and 'energy' acquiring a technical meaning, and Alston asks why something similar could not happen in theology.

Alston himself takes up the objection that assumptions such as these which admit that technical meanings are developed in sciences, do not hold in theology. Theological systems do not have, for example, the same explanatory power as the theories of natural science. Alston does not deny these differences, but takes the view that he does not need to investigate them further since he wishes primarily to limit himself to personalistic predicates about God. The questions which then become of central importance are concerned firstly with the meaning of terms when they stand for personal properties in the case of human beings, and secondly with the meaning of the same terms when they denote personal properties of God.

In Alston's view, the extent to which certain predicates are literally true of God, depends both on how God is and on the content of the predicate. It would therefore in fact require not only a thorough analysis of personalistic predicates, but also an account of God's nature in order to be able to judge the extent to which personalistic predicates can be said to be literally true of God. Alston, however, refrains from doing this and takes as his point of departure one of the generally recognized properties of God, namely his incorporeality (Alston 1996, 370f.).

Some hold that incorporeality rules out personal actions. Alston sets out to examine if this is the case. In order to do this, he introduces the concept of basic action. A basic action is an action which is *not* carried out by carrying out another action at the same time. If for example, I write my name, I do it by moving my hand and guiding the pen in a special way. To write one's name is not a basic action. On the other hand, moving one's hand is a basic action provided I do not do it by doing something else. According to Alston, human basic actions involve moving some part of the body. Every action which is not a basic action, is therefore an action which is carried out simultaneously in carrying out a basic action, and which is based on some form of bodily movement in the person who acts (Alston 1996, 378). However, it does not follow from that according to Alston, that all our concepts for human action must contain references to bodily movement.

Basic actions always are based on bodily movements. The content of a basic action is a special movement of a special part of the body. It is the movement of the body which distinguishes one type of basic human action from another. Consequently, we cannot talk about a basic action without specifying some bodily movement such as kicking or raising one's arm. Obviously such action predicates cannot be used literally about a being without a body. In Alston's view, this is no loss to theology. What is interesting are the action predicates which do not refer to basic actions such as 'to do', 'to speak', 'to exhort', 'to forgive', 'to comfort' and 'to lead' and which can therefore also be used literally about a being without a body. If, for example, I say of someone that he or she has exhorted me to love my neighbour, this has nothing to do with any bodily movement in the agent. The agent's bodily movements form in no way any part of what *is meant* by 'exhort'. Hence action predicates which are not about human beings and are not basic actions need not necessarily have some reference to particular movements of the body. It is obviously a matter of a wide spectrum. A predicate such 'to kick down a door' requires naturally a special movement of the leg. On the other hand, concepts such as 'to prepare a soufflé' and 'to command' are not bound to some special kind of underlying bodily motion. Orders can be delivered by word of mouth or in writing. In principle, any bodily movement whatsoever with suitable background can serve as e.g. the giving of an order. Something similar holds in the case of preparing a soufflé. Electronics requires no bodily movements which would be unique to preparing a soufflé.

Alston's point is thus the following. Even if there is a reference to bodily movements in the case of action predicates such as preparing a soufflé
and giving an order, it is not a matter of a reference to a quite specific
bodily movements. Alston now takes the argument a step further by asking
if, in general, it is a necessary part of the meaning of such terms as 'to prepare a soufflé' and 'to give an order' – even when they are used about human beings – that external effects are caused by the agent's bodily movements. Obviously human beings cannot produce such effects without carrying out bodily movements in some form or other, but Alston means that
this is not part of the concept of human action. In his view, perhaps even
our concept of preparing a soufflé is only a way of bringing a soufflé into
existence irrespective of the way it is accomplished (Alston 1996, 378ff.).

Already here, I am compelled to point out that this is one of the points
in Alston's argument which I would like to criticize. Alston, albeit cau-
tiously, nonetheless suggests that preparing a soufflé is the same as bringing about the existence of a soufflé. I hold that it is not at all the same. If I
have the authority to demand of someone else that they should prepare a
soufflé, I have certainly brought about the existence of a soufflé, but I have
not prepared it. I may not even know what in various circumstances has to
be done for someone to be said to prepare a soufflé. Somewhere in the
chain of information, there is naturally someone who does know how in
various circumstances to prepare a soufflé. These skills can and do change,
but knowledge about the way to proceed, is – I would hold *contra* Alston –
part of the concept of preparing a soufflé. In principle, any approach whatsoever is conceivable. But such an observation says in fact virtually nothing. In the concrete situation we find ourselves in, I can only conceive of
certain ways of proceeding which in one way or another are linked to bodily movements, as forming part of the concept of preparing a soufflé. If
there are other modes of proceeding, the concept is also altered. I hold,
however, that from this possibility of an alteration in the concept, we can
draw the conclusion that reference to some bodily movement does not need
to form part of the concept of preparing a soufflé. Nor can I therefore follow Alston in the next step that he takes.

This is to link the distinction between an action which is a basic action
and an action which is not, with the distinction between general concepts
for basic actions as such and specific concepts for human basic actions.
Needless to say, the concepts for human basic actions refer to the special
movements of the body. According to Alston, this however does not apply
to general concepts for basic actions. A general concept for a basic action
is quite simply the concept for an action performed *through* or *in* (simultaneously) performing some other action. That we human beings have control only over the movements of certain of our bodily parts and must ac-

complish everything else by moving our bodies in one way or another, is one thing. According to Alston, this depends simply on our limitations, and has nothing to do with the actual definition of a basic action. According to him, we can imagine agents with and without bodies who have something other than bodily movements in their control. Alston can conceive that such agents could smash a vase, or prepare a soufflé without doing anything else at the same time to accomplish it (Alston 1996, 382f.). I cannot help wondering partly who these people are who can imagine agents with and without bodies capable of bringing about something by some means other than a movement of the body and partly how these agents can be thought to prepare a soufflé, for example, without some movement of the body being involved, since I have difficulty in seeing how we can imagine such agents at all.

Alston admits that he has little to say about the question of the extent to which it is possible for an agent, by means of his intentions or the like, to directly bring about a change outside the agent's body, if it is an agent with a body, or where no body is involved at all, in the case of an agent without a body. He concedes that it is something which lies outside of our usual experience, but he holds nonetheless that there is nothing, whether in our understanding of our cognitive limitations or in our understanding of causality, which could show that it is impossible in principle. It is therefore an open question what can cause what. If it is a question of an all powerful God, then God can obviously through his intention directly determine everything that is logically possible e.g. that the waters of the sea part. According to Alston, such action concepts can be formed in such a way that they become applicable to beings without bodies. Such action concepts differ from the concepts of human action merely by the fact that bodily movements are replaced by something else in the agent, with regard to the determination of basic actions. From Alston's point of view, there are no conceptual obstacles to agents without bodies carrying out observable actions (Alston 1996, 384).

A first question which arises, but which I shall not enter into more deeply, is the order of precedence in Alston's way of arguing. Does his view of God as an agent without a body come first or is it instead what we mean by actions? I would remind the reader of the two starting points in pursuing work in the philosophy of religion which I mentioned earlier: one can start with a definite view of religion or with a definite view of philosophy. Although I myself prefer the second approach, I have no objection in principle to choosing the first. For that reason, I see nothing odd in the fact that Alston would seem to begin with a view of God as an agent without a body and then construct a theory about what is involved in the notion of (basic) action, in accordance with his religious starting point. Thereafter, it is naturally a matter of scrutinizing the philosophical theory of the concept of basic action, so that it does not appear as a mere *ad hoc* piece of reasoning in relation to the religious starting point.

The following question, which I shall try to answer, must be raised. According to Alston there are, as has been said, no conceptual obstacles to agents without bodies carrying out observable actions. What exactly can be observed when it is supposed to be an agent without a body who carries out an alleged observable action? We can observe a definite factual state of affairs which has come about. Sometimes we can observe that the outcome is the result of an action and sometimes not. Subsidence, for example, can be observed as the outcome of an action which consists in carrying off enormous quantities of earth. However, there are other observable examples of subsidence which are not the outcome of an action. What we definitely cannot observe is that certain states of affair are the results of the actions of an agent without a body. It is certain possible if one assumes Alston's conceptual definition of a basic action, that it is the action of an agent without a body which has resulted in certain states of affair. It is, however, only these factual states of affair which can be observed. To say that they are caused by the actions of an agent without a body, is to go beyond what can be observed. For that reason, it is equally possible, even if one accepts Alston's conceptual definition of basic action, that actually it is not some being without a body which has given rise to these states of affair.

I shall not continue with this line of criticism because what is problematic in Alston's reasoning about what is possible, is precisely his use of the concept of 'possible'. I consider it odd to start out from actual human actions and then speculate about the conceptual possibilities in regard to the actions of agents without bodies. This seems like stealing a ride on the back of what is observable and factual. It is certainly true that one can take into account the possibility of the actions of agents without bodies, but I find it hard to accept that in the conceptual definition of basic action, it is thought permissible to ignore what is an observable matter of fact and maintain that something non-observable is a matter of fact, while at the same time what is an observable fact is needed as a negative point of reference: in other words, the observable matter of fact is necessary in order to be able to ignore it. The problem does not arise from linking the non-observable to the observable matter of fact. It arises because one first in the definition of basic actions ignores the observable, but then goes on to speak of the non-observable as though it were observable. It is this sort of realist thinking which I find difficult to accept and to which I have devoted the critical part of the present work, in exposing its problematic nature.

At this point, I shall leave Alston and his religious realist philosophy about how single pronouncements about the non-observable are to be linked to the observable. Instead, I shall turn to the question of how the theistic system as a whole could be based on the experience of what is observable and thereby could explain certain observed facts in the world or in human life.

Theism's relation to the observable

One thinker who links the classical theistic system to experience of the observable is Swinburne. His argument is that the available observable evidence shows that the theistic explanation of the universe is more probable than the naturalistic one, because by referring to God's intentions and actions, we can at least plausibly suggest why the natural chain of events follows in accordance with fundamental natural laws, in the way that it does. It lies outside the domain of scientific explanation to answer this question (Swinburne 1979, 140f.). In the next section, I shall examine in more detail Swinburne's arguments. For the time being, it suffices with the above short summary.

For the moment, I would like to focus on the distinction which Swinburne draws, between scientific explanations on the one hand, and explanations which explain why the natural chain of events follows the fundamental natural laws in the way that it does. Swinburne distinguishes between two types of 'why' question that arise in connection with the question why the universe is the way it actually is. It is the difference between asking a scientific 'why' question on the one hand, and asking a metaphysical 'why' question on the other. Despite this difference, Swinburne still speaks about theories and more specifically of "large-scale theories of the universe" and about "the close similarities which exist between religious theories and large-scale scientific theories" (Swinburne 1979, 2f.).

I am doubtful about this use of the word 'theory'. As I see it, in the case of scientific 'why' questions, theories are developed so that with their help we can generate testable hypotheses with the aim of being able to say something about observable phenomena. It is also sometimes said that 'why' questions in a scientific context are really 'how' questions. With regard to the second type of 'why' question, conceptualizations and sometimes also systems of a view of life kind are developed in order to allow the creation of expressions which human beings can experience as adequate in their existential reflections and their existential wonder over why we and the universe in fact exist, although it might have been otherwise. On the basis of the pragmatic realism which I argue for, so-called metaphysical theories become part of the conceptualizations of how reality as conceptualized by us offers resistance in our existential experiences of what it means to be human i.e. to live with life's inevitabilities. Our human experiences are not only of an observational character, They also have an existential character. We do not simply have experiences on the basis of observations. We also have existential experiences of what it means to be a human being. Even these latter experiences need to be conceptualized. What is meant by explanation i.e. what sort of 'why' question is involved, depends thus on the type of experience. With this in mind, I find it less appropriate to speak about religious theories in the way Swinburne does.

For Swinburne, it is not at all odd to view classical theism as being on the same logical level as "a large scale theory of the universe." As we have remarked, the question is whether this view of theory is correct. It is certainly true that the word 'theory' is used in many different ways and Swinburne certainly distinguishes between religion and scientific ones. Nevertheless he sees "close similarities between religious theories and large scale scientific theories" (Swinburne 1979, 3). Given Swinburne's underlying metaphysical realism, I interpret this to say that religious theories as well as scientific ones (including "large scale scientific theories") claim to describe how reality really is. In my critique of metaphysical and semantic realism, I have argued against the sort of radical non-epistemic perspective which Swinburne applies in order to develop what he wishes to say about statements – and by extension, as I see it – also about theories. On the basis of the pragmatic (or internal) realism which I favour, it is, however, more reasonable to retain the epistemic perspective in regard to the determination of statements and theories. If theories – leaving aside mathematical theories – are to contribute to our knowledge of reality as conceptualized by us, which offers resistance in our observational experience, then they must be empirically adequate i.e. they should enable us to generate testable hypotheses in order to be able to say what is true of what is observable.

To treat classical theism as a theory on the same level as scientific theories thus entails that classical theism must also be empirically adequate i.e. place us in a position to generate testable hypotheses to allow us to say what is true of the observable. Otherwise, I cannot understand the point of treating classical theism as a theory on the same logical level as scientific theories. However, I cannot see that classical theism has enabled us to be in a position to generate testable hypotheses. Therefore in my opinion, nothing has been gained by asserting that statements which are statements within the classical theistic system, really are statements of fact. Obviously they can be taken as either true or false within the system, but it does not follow from this, that they are either true or false outside the framework of classical theism.

In contrast to the positivist critique of religion, however, I do not draw the conclusion that religious utterances, because they are not statements outside the theistic system, are thereby meaningless. I do not rule out the possibility of talking about religious states of affair in the same way, I would contend, that we can talk about moral and aesthetic matters. In Part V, I shall return to this question when I deal with the role played by so-called thick concepts in our view of reality. I look upon statements of religion and views of life as cognitively meaningful, because they have something to say about what it means to be a human being with the experiences of suffering, guilt, love, joy and happiness, and because what they have to say is either existentially adequate, or it is not.

The role which religious expressions or other expressions linked to views of life, play in human lives i.e. what they mean, can to a certain extent – but only to a certain extent – be understood by people who, for their own part, are not prepared to accept in their lives all the associations which are linked with these expressions. Thereafter their views may diverge. Let me illustrate the issue involved with the help of the believer's perspective. Note that I speak of the believer's perspective and not of some theoretical question like that about the existence of God which has been lifted out of its religious context and discussed, ignoring the fact that reality is for us always a conceptualized reality which offers resistance in our observations and existential experiences. As long as religious expressions function in the believer's life i.e. as long as the believer bases his life on them, it is both psychologically and logically impossible for the believer to doubt them, since these expressions are precisely those in which the life of the believer finds expression.[21] When they no longer function because they have become problematic, due say to ethical reasons, they are no longer an expression of the believer's beliefs. In other words, they are no longer considered by the believer as an adequate expression of what it means to be a human being. Conversely, religious expressions when they begin to play a role in the life of a person who is initially a non-believer, can have the following effect:

> Coming to see that there is a God is not like coming to see that an additional being exists. ... Coming to see that there is a God involves seeing a new meaning in one's life, and being given a new understanding (Phillips 1970, 17f.).

There are certainly people who hold that both these aspects can be combined and that for example, an epistemic or other philosophical reason for God's existence, has led to them see God as the new meaning in their lives. This may well be so, but as far as I can see, the so-called proofs of God's existence and other similar arguments only convince those who already

---

[21] See e.g. Brümmer 1993.

believe: they convince scarcely anyone else. For this reason, I continue to hold that the two ways of speaking about God are essentially different. I cannot see how such proofs, when they are isolated from their religious context, could have religious relevance.

Other philosophers who are neither theists or atheists, refer instead to the fact that religious utterances (for example, about God) acquire their meaning from their use. Here then, we have two possibilities. In one case, the utterances become meaningful through a particular use in a particular conceptual system, the constitutive rules of which determine in general what can be said in the system. An example of such an approach is to be found in the already quoted definition of God, proposed by Swinburne:

> A person without a body (i.e. a spirit), present everywhere, the creator and sustainer of the universe, a free agent, able to do everything (i.e. omnipotent), knowing all things, perfectly good, a source of moral obligation, immutable, eternal, a necessary being, holy, and worthy of worship (Swinburne 1993, 2).

Usage is determined here in relation to what is understood to be theories or theory-type structures.

In the second case, the utterances acquire their meaning by a particular use in relation to how people concretely live their lives. Let me illustrate this second possibility with the help of Wittgenstein's famous and often cited example about belief in the Day of Judgement (Wittgenstein 1966, 55f.). According to Wittgenstein, the believer does not see his life in the perspective of the Day of Judgement: the believer lives his life in that perspective. It is not a question of referring to evidence or other reasons for and against this picture; nor is it a question of interpreting one's life with the help of this picture, conceived as some kind of theoretical model. The use of the picture of the Day of Judgement expresses an approach to living and a reaction to life's conditions. Such pictures show both the meaning of the words used and how the words used, give meaning to the believer's experience of life.

It is undoubtedly true that the empirical is in a definite sense relevant when, for example, the believer believes in Judgement Day, but only in the sense which presupposes that the believer has already accepted religious ideas and pictures. On the basis of such ideas and pictures, the believer is in a position to distinguish what of the empirical is relevant when he or she is living in the perspective of Judgement Day. It can be everything from empirical observations pertaining to the flow of money between the industrial countries and the development countries to empirical studies of the cultivation of various kinds of crops in various kinds of soil. Much that is empirical can reveal itself to be relevant in a perspective of absolute responsibility. This is, however, something quite different from taking religious utterances as statements about matters of fact in the usual meaning of the word.

Obviously one does not need to do it, but in that case we should not place so called religious statements about matters of fact and what we usually mean by statements about matters of fact on the same footing, and draw comparisons between them. If we do place them on the same footing and compare them, the customary rules for judging statements about matters of fact apply also to religious utterances. Experience has shown that the criteria used for testing what we usually mean by statements about matters of fact are more reliable than religious criteria. Bearing this in mind, I accept the norm that we require to relate ourselves to what is observationally evident for us, already when we have to decide which utterances can reasonably be treated as statements, and we also require to relate ourselves to what is observationally evident for us, when we have to decide which of the utterances, accepted as statements, are true, and which are false.

What then are we to make of the manifest occurrence of evil? Does not evil falsify as empirical fact the statement that God is love, or that an infinitely loving and omnipotent God exists? It is certainly the case that references above all to incredible suffering and evil are used as an argument against the existence of a loving and omnipotent God, and this reference has induced some people to cease to believe in God. Nevertheless, it is not a question of falsification in this instance. Observe that I am not talking about a conceptual, logical train of thought akin to the following: (1) if God is all powerful, then God is in a position to prevent incredible suffering and evil (2) if God is infinitely loving, then God will wish to prevent incredible suffering and evil (3) there is incredible suffering and evil (4) therefore God does not exist. I am speaking about people who, because of incredible suffering and evil, have ceased to believe in God. In this particular case, it is not a matter of a statement that has been refuted, but rather that a person's view of the meaning of life has undergone a change. But could we not say that this has happened just because the statement that God exists, given the existence of incredible suffering and evil, has been falsified? But then what exactly has been falsified? If we wish to refute the claim that there is water on the moon, we know what we wish to refute and what observational evidence we have to cite to settle the matter. But what are we trying to refute when we set out to falsify the claim that God exists?

As an argument for not wishing to speak about falsification, I would like to cite the fact that evil is something to which we must find a way of existentially responding, if we wish to have a fulfilling life. We do this with the help of images and expressions which we can experience as adequate i.e. in which we can existentially identify ourselves and the presuppositions of our lives. In a definite sense, these images and expressions are obviously subjective. But if we think of the beings we humans, with our various conceptualizations (including those relating to our views of life) have developed into, then the question about what images and expressions, linked to views of life, we experience as adequate, is not an arbitrary subjective matter. Discourses have been developed which allow us to determine which criteria are suitable for testing the existential adequacy of images and expressions. The pictures and expressions which in fact are found to be existentially adequate, can then be different for different people and even vary in the case of one and the same person. This is also true of pictures and expressions of what is evil. For this reason, I hold, it is not a matter of falsification in the foregoing empirical sense, according to which the emphasis is placed on evil as experienced as an empirical phenomenon. Instead, the emphasis is on the existential experience of evil. For example, certain religious pictures and expressions can cease to function in the life of the believer precisely because the believer has been face-to-face with evil. Conversely, it can also be the case that the same religious pictures and expressions can appear adequate for precisely the experience of evil so that people find themselves beginning to accept a religious belief.

Swinburne on probability

Before leaving the idea that religious expressions are statements of fact, I would like to return to Swinburne's way of dealing with the question of evidence. As has been pointed out, according to Swinburne, all available evidence demonstrates that the theistic explanation of the universe is more probable than the naturalistic one, because a reference to God's intentions and actions can make it at least plausible why the natural chain of events follows fundamental natural laws in the way that it does. Let me draw attention to some of the difficulties in some of the assumptions underpinning Swinburne's technically sophisticated reasoning. He holds

> that various occurrent phenomena are such that they are more to be expected, more probable if there is a God than if there is not. The existence of the universe, its conformity to order, the existence of animals and men, men having great opportunities for co-operation in acquiring knowledge and moulding the universe, the pattern of history and the existence of some evidence of miracles, are all such as we have reason to expect if there is a God, and less reason to expect otherwise (Swinburne 1979, 277).

In order to support this thesis, Swinburne makes use of so-called confirmation theory, more specifically an application of Bayes's theorem, which asserts that the probability of a hypothesis h is a function of empirical evidence e and background knowledge k. The crucial question is whether Swinburne uses the same concept of evidence as occurs in Bayes's theorem as he does when he applies the theorem to determine the probability of theism. For safety's sake, I would stress that I am not going to cite and critically analyse the actual arguments which Swinburne puts forward. It is rather the underlying assumptions for these arguments which is the central focus of my critical interest and, more specifically, his way of speaking about evidence.

Let me begin, first of all, by giving certain terminological definitions. Then I shall clarify how Swinburne defines the concept of evidence at the same time that he introduces the symbols of confirmation theory. Swinburne speaks of "P-inductive arguments" and "C-inductive arguments":

> Let us call an argument in which the premises make the conclusion probable a correct P-inductive argument. Let us call an argument in which the premises add to the probability of the conclusion (i.e. make the conclusion more likely or more probable than it would otherwise be) a correct C-inductive argument. In this case let us say that the premises 'confirm' the conclusion (Swinburne 1979, 7).

Swinburne also reminds us that the aim of the argument is to get other people to accept the conclusion. For this purpose, it is not enough that the premises lead necessarily to the conclusion, or render it probable. It is also necessary that the premises are accepted as true by those discussing the conclusion (Swinburne 1979, 7). In addition, we have the following:

> A hypothesis up for investigation is often represented by h. Then $P(h/e,k)$ represents the probability of a hypothesis h given evidence e and k.[Footnote omitted.] It is often useful to divide the evidence available into two parts – new evidence and background evidence; if this is done, the former is often represented by e and the latter by k. Background evidence (or background knowledge, as it is sometimes called) is the knowledge which we take for granted before new evidence turns up (Swinburne 1979, 15f.).

Swinburne then gives a concrete example of what this can imply. Suppose that some detectives are investigating a murder. Let h stand for the hypothesis that Jones has committed the murder; let e stand for the sentence which gives all the evidence which the detectives have unearthed e.g. Jones' fingerprints have been found on the murder weapon; Jones was in the vicinity of the scene of the crime at the time the murder took place etc; finally let k stand for the sentence which gives the detectives' general knowledge about how the world functions e.g. every human being has a unique set of fingerprints; people leave fingerprints when they touch metal and wood etc. The probability that Jones has committed the murder, given the accumulated evidence, is given by the formula $P(h/e,k)$. In general, we have:

> For all propositions p and q $P(p/q) = 1$ if (and only if) q makes p certain, e.g. if q entails p (that is, there is a deductively valid argument from q to p); and $P(p/q) = 0$ if (and only if) q makes $\sim p$ certain, e.g. if q entails $\sim p$. [Footnote omitted.] $P(p/q) + P(\sim p/q) = 1$. So if $P(p/q) > \frac{1}{2}$ then $P(p/q) > P(\sim p/q)$ and it is on q more probable that

p than that ~*p*. So (for background knowledge *k*) an argument from *e* to *h* will be a correct C-inductive argument if (and only if) $P(h/e.k) > P(h/k)$ and a correct P-inductive argument if (and only if) $P(h/e.k) > \frac{1}{2}$. The division between new evidence and background can be made where you like – often it is convenient to include all evidence derived from experience in *e* and to regard *k* as being what is called in confirmation theory mere 'tautological evidence', that is, in fact all our other irrelevant knowledge (Swinburne 1979, 16).

So far, no problem regarding the concept of evidence arises. It becomes problematic, however, when Swinburne begins to speak about evidence for God's existence. The point of applying Bayes's theorem is based on the pact that we can speak about probability even if we cannot give exact numerical values i.e. when for various reasons, it is asserted that something tends to support something else, and therefore numerical values are proposed which seem reasonable:

> In using the symbols of confirmation theory I do not assume that an expression of the form $P(p/q)$ always has an exact numerical value. It may merely have relations of greater or less to other probabilities, including ones with a numerical value, without itself having a numerical value – $P(h/e_1.k)$ for example, may be greater than $P(h/e_2.k)$ and less than $P(h/k)$ and less than $\frac{1}{2}$ without there being some number to which it is equal.[Footnote omitted.] Clearly, for example, we may judge one scientific theory to be more probable than another on the same evidence while denying that its probability has an exact numerical value; or we may judge a prediction to be more probable than not and so to have a probability of greater than $\frac{1}{2}$, while again denying that that probability has an exact numerical value [Footnote omitted.] (Swinburne 1979, 17).

Swinburne sees no difficulty in speaking about probability in this way even with regard to God's existence. For my own part, I find it difficult to accept the way in which Swinburne at this point not only introduces the concept of evidence in a formal sense by introducing symbols which belong to "confirmation theory", but also argues substantially with the help of this concept of evidence. Let us therefore continue to follow his reasoning.

> For the moment let *h* be our hypothesis – 'God exists'. Let e_1, e_2, e_3 be the various propositions which men bring forward as evidence for his existence. Thus let e_1 be 'there is a physical universe'. Then we have the argument from e_1 to *h* – a cosmological argument. $P(h/e_1.k)$ represents the 'probability that God exists given that there is a physical universe – and also mere tautological evidence, which latter can be ignored [']. If $P(h/e_1.k) > \frac{1}{2}$ then the argument from e_1 to *h* is a good P-inductive argument. If $P(h/e_1.k) > P(h/k)$ then the argument is a good C-inductive argument (Swinburne 1979, 16f.).

I would like to give six partly inter-related reasons for objecting to Swinburne's way of arguing. My first objection is as follows. Swinburne is naturally correct in saying that there are people who count "There is a physical universe" among what they consider to be evidence for God's existence. Certainly religious people cite many things which they take to be evidence for God's existence. But because someone considers that something is evidence for God's existence, it does not follow that it is indeed evidence. For a Christian perhaps, it is evidence and therefore convincing. If, however, as Swinburne does, we aspire to convince people other than Christians, then the supposed evidence must be of a kind that can be accepted as evidence in the intended respect also by others.

The second objection deals with a somewhat different aspect. From the fact that someone considers something as evidence for something else e.g. God's existence, it does not follow that it is also evidence in the sense that it can be cited as evidence or proof for something else. But what of the cosmological proof of God's existence, according to which everything that is contingent taken together i.e. the universe, requires a non-contingent explanation? Does this mean that conversely what is contingent becomes evidence for God's existence? Let us examine this more closely. In the cosmological proof of the existence of God, one infers from the fact that this is contingent and this is contingent ... and that the universe is contingent, that there is something which is non-contingent, namely God. The point at issue is to show that the universe could not exist or could not be explained, unless God existed. The universe functions in this case as evidence for God's existence. Do not the only fingerprints which are not the murder victim's, function similarly as evidence that they must belong to the murderer? In order to decide this question, we require additional proof which ties the murderer and no-one else to the fingerprints. I cannot see what possible evidence there is, which ties God to the fact that the universe exists, if one has not already at the outset assumed that God is the creator. The crucial question here is what is meant by saying that the universe as something contingent requires a non-contingent explanation. Obviously there are people, for whom it is important that such an explanation can be put forward, but there are also people for whom it is not important.

A third difficulty which arises from Swinburne's argument is the following. Note that Swinburne does not speak about physical objects but about the physical universe. There is nothing odd in saying that one looks upon physical objects as evidence for something. But is this also true of saying that the universe is evidence for something? If the evidence cannot in some or other way be traced to sensory experience, I for one cannot understand what is meant by evidence. In the present case, I do not see, for example, how the presumed evidence expressed by the sentence 'there is a physical universe' could be related to someone's sensory experience. The sentence, as noted, says not that 'there is this and that physical object'. Here there is a clear reference to sensory experience. By contrast 'there is a physical universe' is of a totally different character. Unless we are the type of philosopher who explicitly sets out to refute the sceptic's challenge that we cannot know if there is an external world i.e. a physical universe, we do not generally treat 'there is a physical universe' as a statement which is open to arguments for and against. The sentence 'there is a physical universe' can logically therefore not function as a statement of fact. If it has some function, it is to express – in this case in a very contrived way – a conceptual precondition for being able to make statements about physical things, no matter how big or small they may be, and about empirical matters of fact. It is thus quite pointless to maintain that the sentence 'there is a physical universe' is a statement of fact. It cannot, therefore, be considered as providing us with evidence. The reason, as we have remarked, is not that the evidence is insufficient: it is that it is not meaningful to speak about evidence at all, in the case of the sentence 'there is a physical universe'.

After this conceptual objection, let us for argument's sake return to Swinburne's view that the sentence 'there is a physical universe' constitutes evidence for God's existence. My fourth objection consists in pointing out the following difficulty, which affects Swinburne's argument: how could we show that the physical universe as a fact constitutes evidence for God's existence. Simply because something is a fact, it does not follow that just this fact constitutes evidence for a definite statement of existence. From the existence of a physical universe, it does not follow automatically that this fact constitutes evidence for the existence of God. Something is needed which determines why it is relevant to characterize just this matter of fact as evidence. When Swinburne says that the sentence 'there is a physical universe' is among "the various propositions which men bring forward as evidence for his [God's] existence" (Swinburne 1979, 16), I maintain that we are permitted here to speak of evidence if the people who put forward what is asserted in the sentence, as evidence for the existence of God, only if they have already accepted a religious idea of God. It is only given such an assumption that the sentence 'there is a physical universe' functions as a reference to something which can be characterized as evidence for God's existence. I have difficulty in seeing how someone who does not already believe in God, could even be in a position to entertain the thought that the existence of the physical universe constitutes evidence of God's existence.

My fifth objection concerns how the reference to what is observable is to be understood. We recall that Swinburne in arguing that theism is more probable than naturalism, refers to a fundamental natural orderliness which cannot be explained scientifically:

> [A]lthough a scientific explanation can be provided of why the more specific powers and liabilities of bodies hold (e.g. why an electron exerts just the attractive force which it does) in terms of more general powers and liabilities possessed by all bodies (put in Hempelian terms – why a particular natural law holds in terms of more general

natural laws), science cannot explain why all bodies do possess the same very general powers and liabilities. It is with this fact that scientific explanation stops. So either the orderliness of nature is where all explanation stops, or we must postulate an agent of great power and knowledge who brings about through his continuous action that bodies have the same very general powers and liabilities (that the most general laws operate) and, once again, the simplest such agent to postulate is one of infinite power, knowledge, and freedom i.e. God (Swinburne 1979, 140f.).

Let me repeat the phrase 'science cannot explain why all bodies do possess the same very general powers and liabilities', i.e. why the most fundamental natural laws function as they in fact do. When Swinburne argues that theism is more probable than naturalism, it is mostly about a comparison between theistic and naturalistic explanation. In this respect, there is thus no problem in science lacking the capacity to clarify the circumstance mentioned. There is no problem if one accepts the earlier mentioned distinction between scientific 'why' questions which according to some, are really 'how' questions, and metaphysical 'why' questions.

Swinburne thus tries to answer the metaphysical 'why' question but he does it as if it were a factual question. I do not mean that we can rule out that the answers to metaphysical 'why' questions might be statements of fact in other contexts. It follows from my critique of metaphysical and semantic realism that as far as the actual answering of metaphysical 'why' questions is concerned, it is not an issue of statements about matters of fact.

For reasons which I shall presently give, I want to assign metaphysical questions to the existential questions about the meaning of life which as I shall show in the next section, consist of two types of meaning, namely phenomenological existential meaning and theoretical meaning. I do not, therefore, exclude the possibility that for certain people only statements about matters of fact can in practice have an existential function. What I mean, is that the sentences of metaphysics irrespective of whether they function in other contexts as statements about matters of fact or not, fulfil then an existential function when as answers to existential 'why' questions, they are experienced as existentially adequate. For this purpose, metaphysical sentences can take the form of statements about matters of fact, but they do not need to do so, nor need they be understood in this way. My reason for placing the metaphysical 'why' questions in the sphere of the existential, is because the metaphysical 'why' questions are intended to give meaning to life. Metaphysics is involved in giving meaning to how we are to understand our lives in a reality which we are part of and to which we consciously relate and interact with. Metaphysics is certainly not necessary in order to obtain an answer which can be experienced as an adequate answer to existential 'why' questions as far as meaning is concerned, but when metaphysics is involved, it plays its role precisely in relation to the existential 'why' questions about the meaning of life and existence.

This aspect leads me to my sixth objection which, to a certain extent, recalls the third objection. When Swinburne asserts that everything which occurs in nature does so in accordance with fundamental natural laws, this is not a statement of fact, but a conceptual remark about how we speak about processes and events in nature. It is not a question of observation, and can, therefore, not form a basis for arguing for the superiority of theistic explanation in regard to the question of why the most fundamental natural laws function as they do. Neither can it constitute evidence for the probability of God's existence. Since the probability of God's existence requires the superiority of the theistic explanation in the respect mentioned, the foundation for Swinburne's probability argument for the existence of God collapses. Let me show what consequences the above objections have for talk about God.

2 The character of religious utterances

A common reaction is that religious utterances are either meaningful in which case they are statements, or meaningless and not worth having, if they are not statements. I shall show that this is not the only basis for classification. In order to show this, I shall introduce two distinctions which I claim, provide a better basis for classification in the sense that the latter allows us to develop the desirable external or 'outside' perspective in relation to religions and their secular counterparts which I argued for in Part I. At the same time, it draws attention to the function which both religious and non-religious views of life play in people's lives.

The first distinction is as follows: it is something to assert i.e. to maintain in the form of a statement, that God has such and such characteristics, and then to show with the help of conceptual analysis and logical deduction what consequences follow from the statements about God's properties. One of the classic discussions in this respect is the so-called theodicy problem i.e. how far are God's infinite love and omnipotence reconcilable with the existence of evil and suffering in the world. It is on the other hand quite a different matter when e.g. it seems natural to speak about God, to reflect about what can be reasonably be said, must be said, and may not be said about God in order for the idea of God to remain existentially adequate. The following example illustrates this second aspect.

Many children in a part of northern Tanzania become ill and die. The youngest child in a missionary family also becomes ill but the parents succeed in flying it to a university hospital in Sweden and the child is saved.

They are about to translate their experiences, their happiness and gratitude to God into statements that God is love. But they refrain from doing so because the parents of the children left behind in Tanzania, had begun to wonder why God in this case did not allow them to share in his love, but gave it only to the white family. This does not prevent the missionary family or the other families from turning to God in their different existential situations and with the help of differing existentially adequate ideas. It is not even ruled out the both groups speak of God as love. This is then however not a conceptual analysis which determines the meaning of the concept of God. What can be reasonably said, must be said and may not be said about God in order for the idea of God to be existentially adequate, is supported instead by the existential insights into what it means to be a human being.

The second distinction is between the hypothetical character of pronouncements about God, on the one hand, when they are characterized as statements and the tentativeness with which at least some believers speak out, on the other. Someone who like Swinburne holds that pronouncements about God are factual statements, and moreover like him strive to demonstrate the probability that God exists or that the resurrection has taken place, treat pronouncements about God as in principle of the same hypothetical character which characterizes any factual statement whatsoever. I have already given my philosophical reasons why I do not consider religious sentences as factual statements on the same logical level as factual statements in science and tested experience. I shall not therefore repeat them here but content myself with reminding the reader that the assumption about God and God's properties is not in a position to generate testable hypotheses.

Instead I wish to advocate a kind of tentativeness or caution which is linked to a view of life's function in providing existentially adequate expressions for what it means to be a human being. This function is such that the aspect of experienced existential adequacy cannot be ignored, as far as pronouncements about God and other religious pronouncements are concerned. Since it is a question of an experience of existential adequacy, it is certainly a personal dimension. Given that we are the biological and social beings that we in fact are, the personal dimension does not imply solipsism. Since the existential experience of what it implies to be a human being i.e. to live with life's inevitabilities despite a difference in expression is an experience which we human beings share, and expressions can be critically compared and judged. The question of the experience of existential adequacy is in large measure a question of the meaning of life which implies that pronouncements about God have their function in relation to the question of life's meaning. Let me briefly mention some important as-

pects of the question of the meaning of life in relation to the material definition of truth according to which 'true' means to be in agreement with reality as conceptualized by us and which offers resistance in our existential
experiences of what it means to be a human being i.e. to live with life's
inevitabilities. I shall return to this question of different material definitions of truth.

The meaning of life

Let me apply a distinction between phenomenological and theoretical
meaning which is very fruitful for my purposes and which is due to Martin
Holmberg. In the case of phenomenological meaning, the focus is on "the
impact of life, the (positive) feeling that living my life gives me." Here it
is a question of what can be experienced, being in some sense a justification of my life. In the case of theoretical meaning, the focus is instead on
the fact "that life in some way communicates something to us, that there is
something to understand about life" (Holmberg 1994, 30). Here it is a
matter of what is understandable explaining my life. According to Holmberg, it is not simply a question of the role which meaning plays in a human being's life, as phenomenological or theoretical meaning. There is
also a temporal aspect with respect to the past, the future and the present.
Meaning with respect to the past is

> what we are trying to establish when we are treating the past as a kind of jigsaw puz-
> zle, and we are trying to put the pieces together in a satisfying way, to a coherent
> whole that makes sense. Asking about past-time meaning, thus, primarily means ask-
> ing about meaning in the theoretical sense, which has to do with the intelligibility of
> life (Holmberg 1994, 37).

Theoretical meaning is involved not only in the case of the past but also in
the case of the future. Here it is a question of

> the kind of meaning we are asking for when projecting ourselves forwards in time,
> when we are trying to find direction. Is there any telos for my activities that will grant
> meaningfulness to my life (Holmberg 1994, 37)?

Then we have meaning with respect to the present. In this particular case it
is by contrast a question of phenomenological meaning. The issue of
meaning with respect to the present arises most often through an experience of meaningless,

> when nothing seems to matter, when there doesn't seem to be any point in doing
> anything rather than the other. ... Life is here not about the past and it is not about the
> future. It is a question about a quality of life that is presently missing. ... As what is
> felt as lacking is a certain experience or feeling, here we clearly have a focus on
> meaning in the phenomenological sense (Holmberg 1994, 37).

Holmberg points out that theoretical meaning in one sense can be seen as a necessary precondition for phenomenological meaning (Holmberg 1994, 31). I prefer to understand it in the following way: If it is not to be simply a question of feelings of pleasure or discomfort, but is to be identified by the person having the experience and his or her surroundings as a feeling of meaningfulness or meaninglessness, preconditions for conceptualization are needed. These are to be found in what is grasped as theoretical meaning. In another sense, phenomenological meaning can be seen as a necessary precondition for theoretical meaning (Holmberg 1994, 31). This is to be found in the circumstance

> that both past time meaning and future meaning are in a way secondary to present meaning. When there is present meaning (when present meaning is present) neither past-time meaning nor future meaning become problematic in the way they do when there is no present meaning (when present meaning is absent). We ask about the meaning of past events because we are *now* frustrated, grieving, discontented etc., and we ask about future meaning thinking that there must be some project or other that will render life meaningful *now*, that will provide present meaning (Holmberg 1994, 38).

This doublesideness as regards meaning in relation to the experiencing subject, implies among other things that the question of meaning i.e. the question of the meaning of life, cannot be treated as a question of knowledge and truth in the sense of a correspondence with natural or supernatural facts which has happened in many traditional treatments in the philosophy of religion which are based on metaphysical realism. As I have shown, we cannot work with the same concept of meaning in all contexts and above all not with a concept of meaning which presupposes semantic realism's general application of the principle of bivalence. As a result, my criticism of religious metaphysical realism is strengthened. It is more reasonable to work with different concepts of meaning and thereby with different material definitions of truth.

Given that the question of existential adequacy is a part of the question of the meaning of life, I would like to introduce the distinction between knowledge and insight. As far as I can see, it is by means of the expressions of religion and views of life, that we are able to impart insights about what it means to be a human being i.e. to live with life's inevitabilities. In this respect, religious pronouncements are cognitive. They are cognitive, not because they are empirically testable, but because they constitute expressions for our experience of life's inevitabilities. In order to strengthen my argument for the importance of this distinction, I want to clarify my approach to realism (namely internal or pragmatic realism) by developing its pragmatic dimension. With the help of this position, I can then explain how even insights into what it is to be a human being, can be critically examined. It does not suffice merely to have some sort of diffuse intuitive ideas about it. The ideas must also be able to be formulated, communicated and criticized. Some people hold that these conceptualizations should be interpreted as knowledge and truth claims which should then be critically examined like any other similar claims. I shall oppose this view by showing that the question of the critical examination of insights into what it is to be a human being, are related to a material definition of truth quite different from that which arises in connection with claims to knowledge, that is expressed in testable hypotheses and that refers to the observable. The formal minimal definition, on the other hand, is common to them all. However, let me first of all say a bit more about what I mean by internal realism's pragmatic dimension.

3 Pragmatic realism

My aim in this book, as I have said before, is to make use of our inescapable, realistic intuitions which serve as different initial assumptions. We have a body which continually bumps into other bodies. Reality offers resistance in the sense that we cannot carry out any action whatsoever. However it also offers resistance in another way. Existentially our realistic intuitions are concerned with experiences of joy, love, happiness, suffering, guilt and death. They are tangible realities in our lives which we cannot ignore because they are involved in determining how we act and live. In the majority of cases, we are able to go pretty far on the basis of our realist intuitions and the experiences which are based upon them. For this reason, I would also like to take account of the fact that we normally have at our disposal practical intuitions, and therefore formulate them in such a way that (1) we certainly do not advocate the kind of realism which is afflicted with all the difficulties which are inherent in metaphysical realism and (2) we avoid throwing the baby out with the bath water by rejecting every form of realism. For this reason and with reference once again to Putnam's philosophical approach, I shall develop a form of pragmatic (or internal) realism and show what consequences it has for our attitudes to the phenomenon of religion.

I am obviously aware that our way of philosophizing both influences our view of religion and the practice of religion, including the practical rejection of religion, even although philosophical reflection is quite distinct, for example, from theological thinking. In philosophical reflection, the influence is a resulting effect, whereas in theological reflection, the effect is itself part of the goal of the reflection. If for philosophical reasons, one chooses a form of metaphysical realism, it tends to strengthen attachment to certain types of religious approach and strengthen opposition to others. This is true also when one chooses pragmatic realism. As I have already made clear, in the present work, I have chosen a philosophical and not a religious or theological starting point. For reasons which are explained above all in Part II, and which I shall return to in this part, I have also chosen pragmatic realism rather than metaphysical realism as my starting point. I do not therefore propose to discuss the connection between religion and philosophy seen from a religious angle. If the choice of religious approach is what is of primary interest, one approach to religion will tend to go better with e.g. metaphysical realism while another approach fits in better with pragmatic realism. Investigating philosophical questions from a theological or religious standpoint is certainly an important task, but it is no longer pursued with a philosophical purpose in mind. For this reason, even in the case of religion, it is not a relevant counterargument against developing a philosophically pragmatic (that is to say, internal) perspective, to assert that it is inconsistent with the traditional religious view of religion's essence or with religious self-awareness. Note that this does not necessarily rule out that the believer recognizes the practical consequences which the philosophical critique has for religious practice and the teaching which rests on it. Recognition of one's religious life in religious practice thus does not necessarily coincide with an established religious view about religion's essence and the associated official religious self-image. Such a view, in turn, rests upon particular philosophical presuppositions.

To dismiss a philosophical perspective, which in relation to religion is an view from the outside, is tantamount to denying that it is legitimate to have a philosophical purpose. There are religious fundamentalists who will go so far. Philosophy is considered certainly as something important, but philosophical investigation is subservient to religious or theological ends. Given that religions have not always been a positive thing for human beings, I hold that a philosophical critique of religion deserves a hearing. There are naturally different ideas about how one should go about it. In the present work, I argue for a view and critique of religion which is based on pragmatic (or internal) realism. As far as the internal aspect is concerned, I would underline that by internal realism I do not mean something that is the polar opposite of some kind of external realism. The aim is hopefully to put forward a philosophically defensible form of realism i.e. a philosophically defensible view of the conceptualization of our realist intuitions irrespective of the type of truth claims involved, whether religious or not.

Realism's pragmatic or internal aspect

Regarding the character of internal realism, Olof Franck in one of his works succeeds rather well in formulating the central issue. His formula-

tion is certainly based above all on how the internalist looks upon reference, but it succeeds nonetheless in showing clearly how the pragmatic (or
internal) realist differs from what I have called the metaphysical realist. It
is characteristic for internal realists not to onesidedly emphasize either the
referring subject or the supposedly existing referent.

> There is no doubt that the referring subject plays an important role in the referential
> process, but this takes place in combination with the reality of which it forms a part.
> Human beings do more than *discover* supposed objective relations between language
> and reality, but they also do less than *construct* such relations. What they do is to *es-*
> *tablish* them, by connecting on the one hand with their language and on the other with
> the reality as they experience it. It is human beings who, historically, have used lan-
> guage to formulate their relation to stones, horses and fields, but this naturally does
> not mean that some such relation cannot exist at all. It is certainly not necessary and
> eternal, but it is not because of that completely incidental. History links us to reality
> and all its objects; we learn to use the language we have inherited to refer and thus to
> express an ontological linkage to what we are talking and communicating about. Our
> linguistic means of expression are obviously not unchangeable but the linguistic con-
> texts in which we operate and with which we are linked, provide a framework for how
> we can and ought to describe and explain what we experience in ontological and
> epistemological terms (Franck 2002, 22).

It is a question of thinking in terms of both-and. Both the subject's conceptualizing activity and the fact that reality offers resistance, has to be
noted. For this reason, metaphysical realism seems pointless in its one-
sided emphasis on a reality which is independent of us and which is initially intrinsically unconceptualized.

The issue is not that metaphysical realism cannot be implemented in
practice because we never come into contact with reality in itself. If we
consider the failure of metaphysical realism to lie in its inability to pin
down reality, we are nonetheless still chained to a controversial metaphysical realist view. It is characteristic of such a view that in the use of
words such as 'representation' and 'correspondence', on the one hand, we
certainly follow the grammar for the everyday concepts of representation
and correspondence. On the other hand, we empty these concepts of their
content inasmuch as they are deprived of their original delimited area of
use.

Recalling the later Wittgenstein's talk of different kinds of philosophical pictures, I would like to emphasize that not every such picture is to be
condemned, just because it is a philosophical picture. When it comes to
discussions about metaphysical realism in general and more particularly
about metaphysical realism in the religious domain, we ought to distinguish between two kinds of realist philosophical pictures: (1) the first picture of realism is that which is implicitly arises from our various sorts of
interaction with the world in which we live and to which we consciously
need to relate. This picture for practical reasons must be respected. It

would in fact be utterly stupid not to respect it. (2) The second picture of realism is, on the other hand, an abstraction which has arisen because words such as 'representation' and 'correspondence' have been lifted out of the original context in which they are used and elevated to the status of critical norms against which the original applications have to be tested. This picture risks leading to a completely unproductive philosophical exercise. From our human perspective, there is in practice an indissoluble relationship between language and reality. This also applies to a distinction such as that between the linguistic and non-linguistic, or between the real and the unreal. In my view, metaphysical realism fails to observe that this is the case, or if it does accept the distinctions, deals with them in a problematic way. Thus it is certainly the case that perception, as a mental act, is not something linguistic and that we can perceive something indefinite simply as some thing without there being anything linguistic being involved in the picture. If, however, we perceive something as something definite, either directly or after some reflection, then language in terms of given concepts is involved in the picture, both as regards such fundamental concepts like substance, time, space, person and identity which are a prerequisite for any kind of conceptualization, as well as more specific concepts which are involved in various specific conceptualizations. Metaphysical realism constructs an ontology around our connection with language by looking upon language as representing, or corresponding to reality as such. However metaphysical anti-realism is no solution either. As I have demonstrated earlier, metaphysical anti-realism constructs instead an ontology around our connection with language, by giving up the distinction between linguistic and non-linguistic.

In spite of my criticism of anti-realism, I concur in the view that for human beings language and reality are, in a definite sense, dependent on one another; more correctly, we must link them to each other in order to be able to relate ourselves to reality. Even when we distinguish between linguistic and non-linguistic and between real and unreal, we do so with the help of language. When we speak of experience and knowledge, we cannot, therefore, speak about unstructured matter on the one hand and linguistic interpretation on the other. Does not such a view entail that truth is relativized?

A supposed relativization of truth

This would naturally be the case if truth were defined in epistemic terms. In the scientific context, it would mean that truth was defined, for example, as evidence, confirmation or verification while in the context of views of life, it would mean that truth was defined, for example, as experienced meaning. The relativistic consequences of such a definitional strategy are obvious. A definition of truth in epistemic terms would not only allow us to hold two statements contradicting one another but where there is equal evidence for both, as true. In the actual case, such a definition would in fact force us to maintain that both statements, given that there is equal evidence for both, are true. Once we have accepted that truth is to be defined in epistemic terms, and it turns out that it is possible to adduce admittedly distinct but nonetheless equally cogent evidence for two statements which contradict one another, we have no choice other than to accept the truth of both mutually contradictory statements. The consequences are disastrous. A contradiction considered as a compound statement has the truth value 'false' and since an implication of the form p implies q is always true when p is false, irrespective of the truth value assigned to q, it is possible to derive any statement whatsoever (including a false one) from a contradiction. In this case, it is no longer meaningful to work with the distinction between truth and falsity, which in turn implies that a necessary part of the basis upon which our consciously chosen standpoint rests, is destroyed.

It is, therefore, inappropriate to define truth in epistemic terms. For this reason, it is equally important to distinguish between meaning and truth. When we wish to know what the truth of something consists in, the question is related to the respective context in which it is raised. This involves clarifying the conceptual presuppositions for the respective context and includes, in certain cases, also references to methods and procedures which allow us to decide that something which is asserted to be the case, really is the case. The sense in which something which is asserted to be the case, really is the case, is not, however, caused by these methods and procedures. The following example explains what is meant.

In order to decide if there is a chair in the next room, we need to know what a chair is. Let us imagine a tribe whose members never sit but either stand or lie down when they are not in motion. They neither possess the concept of chair, nor any idea of chairs, and cannot have it either because they live in such a way that the concept of chair has no function. Such people cannot participate in answering the question whether there is a table in the next room since they lack the conceptual prerequisites for the context of meaning in question. Whether there is a chair in the next room, is not caused, however, by the conceptual presuppositions for being able to answer the question. Whether there is a chair in the next room or not, depends on whether it is there or not. In order to answer this particular question, we, however, need the relevant necessary conceptual presuppositions.

The metaphysical realist is careful not to define truth in epistemic terms and to distinguish sharply between meaning and truth. Despite this, the arguments of the metaphysical realist remain erroneous which Phillips among other points out:

> Realism tries to say something important but confuses it. What it wishes to say is that whether something is the case is independent of what we say or think. Notice that this is a thesis about *truth*, and it wishes to emphasise an important point, namely that we cannot make truth-claims at will. For example, I *cannot* say there is a chair in the next room, yet having nothing to do with the familiar ways in which we would check this fact. What do I mean when I say I *cannot* say ... I mean that if I said 'There is a chair in the next room', while ignoring the familiar ways of checking. *I would not be making an assertion at all. I would not be saying anything.* But what these procedures lay down *is the sense, not the truth* of the proposition 'There is a chair in the next room.' The procedures do not make the proposition 'There is a chair in the next room' true. What *that* depends on is there being a chair in the next room (Phillips 1993, 197).

I agree about emphasizing the importance of the distinction between meaning and truth so that we do not define truth, for example, in terms of meaning. As far as the definition of meaning is concerned, I would like to go one important step further, and distinguish between a formal aspect and a contentual, material aspect. The formal aspect means that a statement is true if and only if what it asserts is the case. This minimal Aristotelian definition is so minimal that it has not been taken for a definition but instead is looked upon as a formal requirement which every proposal laying claim to be a definition of truth, must satisfy. If we regard the function of the minimal Aristotelian definition of truth in this way, then the idea of different, contentual, material determinations or definitions of truth is not ruled out. Taking account of the different functions which sciences and views of life have in our life, I propose to use this possibility and to reckon on two different material definitions of truth, a material definition of truth which applies to the sciences and another material definition of truth which applies to views of life and thus also to religion.

Put simply, the task and function of the sciences is to provide us with knowledge about the nature of reality in order that we can deal with the empirical resistance which reality, so to speak, offers us. The task and function of views of life – both religions and their secular counterparts – is, once again to put it simply, to provide us with insights about what it means to be a human being i.e. to live with life's inevitabilities such as suffering, guilt, death, happiness, joy and love. Such insights can, however, only be conveyed and handed on if our views of life provide conceptualizations which we regard as adequate expressions for what it means to be a human being.

The religious metaphysical realist will naturally object immediately that my perspective gives no room for the transcendental as the central component of religion. I would remind the reader that my pragmatic realist approach is in relation to religion a view from the outside which assigns statements about the transcendental to the religious domain. The philosophical perspective we adopt naturally has consequences for how we concretely understand and employ statements about the transcendental. Arguments for, or against, the reasonableness of a philosophical perspective, however, ought to be philosophical rather than religious. Otherwise, it is impossible in a democratic and respectful way to react to the growing pluralism regarding views of life which was mentioned in the Introduction. Philosophers can no more enter into religious discussions about God and *qua* philosophers make judgements about the religious value of ideas about God, than they can enter into scientific discussions about scientific theories about black holes and judge the empirical adequacy of such theories. On the other hand, philosophers can devote themselves to an analysis of philosophical presuppositions and critically scrutinize claims which are made on the basis of these presuppositions in scientific or religious discussions with regard to views of reality.

Given the internal pragmatic realism which I advocate, we have the following consequence: if we leave aside formal sciences such as mathematics and logic, 'to be true' means, in the context of the sciences and the tested experiences of ordinary life, 'to be in agreement with reality as it is conceptualized by us and which offers resistance in our observational experiences'. We have to know what there is and the nature of the causal connections which exist, in order not merely to live but to be able to live a fulfilling life.

Nevertheless as human beings, we are not robots, but are continually confronted with choices which are conditioned by the fact that we are a part of the reality which we must interact with and relate to. We do not always know what the consequences will be of our actions, but we are, nonetheless, responsible for how we deal with the consequences. It does not suffice merely to have knowledge about the nature of reality. We also need something which appears meaningful and valuable to us so that we can have a compass to show us how our knowledge is to be applied. It is here that we find the function and task of views of life. What is meaningful and valuable, must be something that involves us personally: otherwise, it is not meaningful and valuable. I shall return to the necessity of this subjective aspect. In the case of views of life, 'to be true', therefore, means 'to be in agreement with reality as conceptualized by us and which offers us resistance in our existential experiences'. When this is applied to the religious domain, this definition means that statements about a personal God are true if and only if they are in agreement with the reality as conceptualized by religious people and which offers them resistance in their existential experiences. At the end of this section, I shall return to the question of the adequacy and truth of statements about God.

Thus even if we reckon with the possibility of different material or contentual definitions of truth, the distinction between definitions of truth and criteria for truth is still valid. Just like the minimal formal Aristotelian definition of truth, the two material definitions of truth which have been put forward, say nothing about which statements in their respective domains are true. In order to accomplish that, we require criteria. These, however, vary according to the domain of application. With respect to the question of knowledge, the criteria are freedom from contradiction and agreement with reality as conceptualized by us and as we encounter it in our observational experiences. With respect to the question of what it means to be a human being, the criteria are instead coherence and agreement with reality as conceptualized by us and as we encounter it in our existential experiences.

In the application of the respective set of criteria, it is important to note that there is an asymmetry between necessary and sufficient conditions. If in the one case, a statement contains a contradiction, or if it does not agree with reality as conceptualized by us as we encounter in our observational experiences or if, in the second case it is incoherent or fails to agree with reality as conceptualized by us as we encounter it in our existential experiences, then we do not treat it as true. In this respect, the criteria for truth are necessary conditions for truth. Every time the necessary conditions are not satisfied, this is sufficient to declare that the statement in question is false. On the other hand, the converse, namely that a sentence is true whenever both conditions are satisfied, does not hold. From the fact that both conditions are fulfilled, it does not follow that the statement is thereby proved to be true. We can still be mistaken. But for practical reasons, it would be imprudent in such a situation not to accept the statement as true. In this way, there is a connection between the two concepts of truth and rationality. The application of the truth criteria have primarily a critical and eliminative function, not a confirmatory one. By applying the criteria for truth, we can decide which statements are false and can be ignored. This concludes what I have to say about the internal aspect of the pragmatic (or internal) realism which I argue for and about the consequences for the religious domain which follow from it.

I shall now pass to examining the pragmatic aspect of pragmatic (or internal) realism and its consequences for the religious domain. This transition is entirely in keeping with how Putnam looks upon the relationship between internal realism and pragmatic realism:

> The key to working out the program of preserving commonsense realism while avoiding the absurdities and antinomies of metaphysical realism in all its familiar varieties ... is something I have called *internal realism* (I should have called it pragmatic realism!) Internal realism is, at bottom, just the insistence that realism is *not* incompatible with conceptual relativity (Putnam 1987, 17).

Let me distinguish between two types of pragmatism, namely (1) a pragmatism in which we find an analogy to a definition of truth in epistemic terms and (2) a pragmatism which is more akin to an attitude. Exactly as before, I would like to investigate, also in this case, the risk for the relativization of truth.

Different kinds of relativism

As far as the first kind of pragmatism is concerned, truth is defined partly as experienced meaning, partly as a successful solution of a problem. If truth is defined as experienced meaning, then on account of the meaning experience's subjective character, there would be as many truths as there are individuals with their individual experiences of meaning. The opposite to 'truth' would then be 'that which has not been experienced by me as meaningful' and there would no longer be any place for the distinction between 'that something is found to be true' and 'that something is true'. Even the definition of truth as the successful solution of a problem leads to similar relativistic difficulties. A problem is always a problem in a particular place, at a particular time, and for particular people i.e. in a particular context of meaning. Let us suppose that in a particular context of meaning, we treat the solution of a problem as a successful solution. However, this solution simultaneously entails consequences for another context of meaning which are such that, in this context, it is rejected as unacceptable. By defining truth as the successful solution of a problem, in such a circumstance, we would have no intersubjective criteria which would allow us to communicate between the two contexts of meaning. In order to survive and also to live a fulfilling life, we need among other things to know the nature of reality. It, therefore, does not suffice to have experienced something as meaningful, or to have access to a solution of a problem which our own group considers successful.

Truth is thus neither an experience of meaning, nor a successful solution of a problem. Nevertheless, it would be imprudent to ignore both what experience has taught us are successful solutions to problems, and what we in fact experience as meaningful when we try to discover partly what we mean by truth and partly what is true. From this perspective, pragmatism is more an expression of an attitude and one which is characteristic of internal realism. I shall give an account of how Putnam makes use of Wittgenstein's critique of relativism to show how an internal realist can still distinguish between 'that something is found to be true' and 'something is true'.

The form of relativism which, according to Putnam, Wittgenstein attacks, is usually called 'methodological solipsism'. A methodological solipsist is, according to Putnam, a non-realist and verificationist who certainly has accepted that truth ought to be understood as being in one way or another related to some form of rational acceptability, but who, nevertheless, still maintains that all justification ultimately takes place in experiences which all of us have our own private knowledge of. Thus I have *my* knowledge of which of *my* experiences would verify that snow is white and someone else has *his* or *her* knowledge of which of *his* or *her* experiences would verify that snow is white. In this way, the statement that snow is white has a different meaning for each person with *his* or *her* individual knowledge of which of *his* or *her* experiences verify the statement (Putnam 1981, 121f.).

Putnam judges the way in which Wittgenstein criticizes solipsism methodologically as an excellent objection to relativism in general.

> The argument is that the relativist cannot, in the end, make any sense of the distinction between *being right* and *thinking he is right*; and that means that there is, in the end, no difference between *asserting* or *thinking*, on the one hand, and *making noises* (or *producing mental images*) on the other. But this means that (on this conception) I am not a *thinker* at all but a *mere* animal. To hold such a view is to commit a sort of mental suicide (Putnam 1981, 122).

Putnam supplements Wittgenstein's argument by asking how the relativist might possibly attempt to maintain the distinction between really being right and believing that one is right.

> The relativist might borrow the idea that truth is an *idealization* of rational acceptability. He might hold that X is true-for-me if 'X is justified-for-me' would be true provided I observed carefully enough, or whatever. But subjunctive conditionals of the form 'If I *were* to ..., then I would think such-and-such', are, like all statements, interpreted differently by different philosophers (Putnam 1981, 122).

The problem is the following. If the relativist means that the conditional sentences about what would be the case, if this and this were the case, are themselves true in an absolute sense independently of how we would justify them, then the relativist is being inconsistent since he or she in that case reckons with at least one set of absolute truths. If on the other hand, the relativist is consistent, and asserts that even the conditional sentences about what would be the case if this and this were the case, are not absolute either, it becomes difficult for such a person to argue for why we should choose the relativistic view. The solution to this dilemma for Putnam is to be an internal realist.

> A non-realist or 'internal' realist regards conditional statements as statements which we understand (like all other statements) in large part by grasping their *justification* conditions. This does not mean that the 'internal' realist abandons the distinction between truth and justification but that truth (*idealized* justification) is something we grasp as we grasp any other concept, via a (largely implicit) understanding of the factors that make it rationally acceptable to say that something is true (Putnam 1981, 122f.).

In one respect, this is also a form of relativism in the sense that questions of truth are reduced to questions about what makes it rationally acceptable for us to say that something is true. It would be unwise to reject this form of relativism because of pragmatic reasons i.e. because it would be unwise to ignore how we humans, as the beings we are, learn how to use the factors which make it rationally acceptable for us to say that something is true. I shall presently return to this pragmatic aspect.

In the interests of clarity, I would like to emphasize that the view of truth which Putnam presents, is not a definition of truth. For Putnam, 'internal realism' is the name of

> a picture of what truth comes to, rather than what most philosophers would call a "theory of the nature of truth" (by which philosophers today understand a reduction of the notion of truth to concepts which do not presuppose it (Putnam 1994b, 242).

Admittedly Putnam no longer this picture view in all of its details. For example, he no longer speaks about ideal epistemic conditions in connection with idealized justification since the phrase 'idealized justification' has been misunderstood. It has for example been misconstrued as though it were an actually existing state which we were headed for, but have not yet reached. This would be close to a metaphysical realist view which Putnam after all was arguing against. On the other hand, he still accepts the picture's intention, namely

> to connect the notion of truth to the way in which words are *used* (including the speech act of assertion) and to the notions of rational acceptability and of sufficiently good epistemic conditions, and I still believe that our understanding of the notion of truth is intricately interwoven with our understanding of those notions (Putnam 1994b, 242).

Truth and rationality are thus closely related to one another, and cannot be understood independently of one another. Nevertheless there is an important conceptual difference between them. The arguments for truth and the arguments that it is rational to hold something to be true, are not always identical. They are identical only when we are dealing with effectively decidable statements. As an example of such a statement, I earlier cited the example 'My desk ways 20 kg'. This is a statement, the meaning of which consists in its truth conditions. Furthermore, it is in a substantial sense either factually true or factually false since, in this particular case we know exactly what the truth conditions are and the means of deciding whether these truth conditions are satisfied or not. It is just this relation to our knowledge that puts us in a position to assert in this case that the reasons that it is rational to hold this statement to be true, are identical with the reasons for the truth of the statement. When it is a matter of other types of statement e.g. the statement 'It will rain next week', any direct reference to the truth conditions for the statement are ruled out. They are not yet present. In the case of this kind of statement, we require references to our experience of the fruitfulness of certain methods and procedures in deciding which statements can rationally be held to be true. Rationality is about what it is reasonable for particular people in a particular situation to hold to be true and to act accordingly. This definition of rationality should be seen in relation to the pragmatic aspect's allowance for the fact that we are the biological and social beings that we in fact are.

Rationality

As far as this determination of rationality is concerned, it is important to distinguish between two kinds of rationality. Given a particular goal or purpose, the question of rationality amounts to determining the best means of attaining this goal or purpose. Here we can speak of a goal-directed rationality. However, we all know that not every purpose is reasonable, and that there are different views about what purposes ought to be achieved. In order to discuss these views, and, above all, to be able to decide which goal or purpose it is sensible for us to attain, we require values as pointers or as a compass. Otherwise, we do know how we are going to be able to use our knowledge about the nature of reality and its causal connections. In this case it is not a question of *goal-directed* rationality but of a form of rationality which we can call *goal-selective* rationality.

According to my earlier proposal for a division of labour between science and views of life, it is not the task and function of the sciences to supply us with values which operate as pointers in the application of knowledge. This job is the task and function of our views of life inasmuch as they supply us with adequate expressions for what it means to be a human being i.e. to live with life's inevitabilities. Clearly the knowledge which the sciences deal with, is relevant for which expressions can be experienced as adequate in expressing what it means to be a human being. For example, a metaphysic which continues to incorporate the antiquated thinking of the natural sciences from periods in the past in the picture, presented by its view of life, of the place of human beings in the universe, would not seem to be as adequate an expression of what it means to be a human being, as a metaphysic which draws upon the present state of research. Note, however, that it is not the linkage to the sciences which determines the rationality of the aims and values which a view of life expresses. The sciences themselves cannot, by virtue of their status *qua* sciences, create values so that they function as a compass for determining the end which our knowledge of the nature of reality and its causal connections should serve.

Here I would support Georg Henrik von Wright's view of the relationship between religion and science. He admittedly speaks only about reli-

gion and not more generally about views of life as I do, but the point that
he makes can be generalized without any difficulty to views of life in general, including both religions and their secular counterparts. von Wright
does not deny that the development of science has had an enormous influence both for the values which have had the greatest impact and for the
aims which we have considered rational to achieve. Nevertheless it is not
the sciences themselves *qua* sciences, which create values. As von Wright
points out:

> Science is not a source of value. This is one of the differences between religion and
> science. But in addition, though science itself is value-neutral, its effects are not al-
> ways so. The new type of rationality which in the seventeenth century thrust to the
> fore in science, proceeded in the course of the ensuing century, to put its mark on
> ways of thinking in general, not least when it came to questions concerning social or-
> ganization and forms of government. The "rationalization" of social functions which
> was then initiated, has, despite repeated "romantic" counter-attacks, advanced victo-
> riously to our present age. It has been powerfully assisted by the rapid development of
> science-based industry. Social life bears increasingly the imprint of socio-technologi-
> cal thinking. It is entirely natural that, in a society where scientific-technological ra-
> tionality has attained an overshadowing importance, other forms of rationality and
> spiritual life have been devalued and have lost their vitality or have begun to crumble
> (von Wright 1986, 63f.).

The dominance of technological rationality does not rule out the possibility
that new values can be created and new sources of value suddenly flower
within a culture. This is possible, but what happens afterwards remains un-
predictable, nor can it be steered by scientific means. In Part V, I shall return to the question of how values arise. It occurs when we human beings
create and maintain them with the help of the conceptualizations which are
composed of the ideas, narratives and images associated with our views of
life. Here I want instead to pause to consider the difference and connection
between goal-directed and goal-selective rationality.

Goal-directed rationality may be criticized both from within the given
goal-means perspective and from an external perspective. Internal criticism
arises if the means proposed to attain a certain goal, or to realize a certain
purpose, in comparison with other means, are shown to less appropriate,
cheap, reliable etc. than it was first believed. The point to be noted is that
the goal itself is not questioned. Such external questions can arise when the
attainment of a certain goal or purpose fails to agree with our idea of a fulfilling life. A concrete example of this from Swedish working life is the
increasing effectivization of methods of production and the organization of
work in order to reduce costs and raise productivity. From a statistical
point of view, and despite the human wastage in terms of the number of
people who are burned out or find themselves thrown out of work, this is
still an efficient and rational method of creating economic welfare for at

least an important section of the population. The question, however, which an increasing number of people ask, is why the value of economic welfare should have priority over the value of human well-being.

It is not only goal-directed rationality which can be criticized in two ways. The same is true of goal-selective rationality. We can ask, for example, if the determination of a particular value is adequate, or we can ask if knowledge of particular causal connections between purpose and means does not have the effect of making certain values appear less realistic. Thus we know, for example, that a life in poverty caused by oppression, the abuse of power and the unjust distribution of even the most elementary necessities of life, render it virtually impossible for such values as love and consideration to have a place in the scheme of things. It is unreasonable in such situations to appeal to these values before we have first removed the obstacles to them.

Another connection between goal-directed and goal-selective rationality is the following. I would like to recall the role which the solution of a problem and the experience of meaning plays in pragmatism considered as a way of relating and responding to things. As has been remarked, even if truth can neither be defined in terms of the experience of meaning or in terms of the successful solution of a problem, it would be unreasonable to ignore what experience has taught us, are successful solutions of problems and from what we in fact experience as meaningful. The connection between goal-directed rationality and goal-selective rationality is to be found in the fact that problems cannot be viewed only from a theoretical perspective: we have to take account of experience as well. From a theoretical standpoint, there is a problem whenever there is a tension or a incompatibility between two poles or to put it another way, when something simply does not fit. This need not, however, mean that what does not fit, is actually a problem for someone. This occurs first when someone views it, or experiences it as a problem: in other words, when there is a experiential aspect to the matter. A problem as a phenomenon first exists when someone or other in fact experiences a tension or incompatibility between two poles as a problem. If something is not experienced as a problem, we would hardly think even of trying to solve it. Without accepted values which show that it is urgent, interesting or quite simply exciting to solve the problem, a solution would probably never emerge.

The reason why things are thus, I believe, has to do with the following circumstance. Here, some of my philosophical, anthropological presuppositions come into play. In comparison with other organisms, we human beings have a minimum of instinctive and reflexive reactions which are insufficient to solve the problems which confront us in life. These basic reactions must be complemented by what in the case of human beings, are

conscious reflections and rational decisions without which it would be impossible to act or solve the problems which have arisen. These conscious
reflections are many-layered. First come those reflections which lead to
knowledge about the nature of empirical reality. Secondly, there are the
reflections which lead us to supply ourselves with values as pointers for
how we should use this knowledge. Thirdly, there has to be, as Charles
Taylor formulates it,

> a close connection between understanding the order of things and being in attunement
> with it. We do not understand the order of things without understanding our place in
> it, because we are part of this order. And we cannot understand the order and our
> place in it without loving it, without seeing its goodness, which is what I want to call
> being in attunement with it (Taylor 1985b, 142).

Our reflections need in other words to contain epistemic, normative, and
experiential aspects. I shall return to the connection between these kinds of
reflections when I deal afresh with the realist aspect of my pragmatic (or
internal) realism. Before that, I need to go back and consider the objection
to pragmatism and pragmatic realism, which holds that a pragmatic approach to truth would necessarily imply a relativized definition of truth.

A normative view of truth

I have earlier presented my arguments against metaphysical realism by re-
vealing the problems inherent in one of their most important assumptions,
namely that of an intrinsically unconceptualized reality which is independent of us and to which our views of reality, if they are true, correspond. I
have also shown that metaphysical anti-realism provides no escape from
the difficulties, since it basically shares the aforementioned assumption of
metaphysical realism, to the extent that one accepts the critical idea of a
division between reality in itself and our views of it and then strikes out
the first part of this division. The mode of approach can vary. One way is
straightforwardly to deny the existence of such a reality. The problem is
simply that the possibility of denying something's existence presupposes
that we can form some idea of what we are denying, so that we can specify
exactly what it is that we are denying. Both the metaphysical realist and
the metaphysical anti-realist speak about an intrinsically unconceptualized
reality which is independent of us. The former asserts its existence while
the latter denies it. Both thereby presuppose that conceptually they have
access to something intrinsically unconceptualized and independent of us
which in the one case is said to exist and in the other case is said not to
exist. There is an inconsistency here which becomes a problem shared by
both the metaphysical realist and the metaphysical anti-realist.

Another sense in which the anti-realists reject the idea of an intrinsically
unconceptualized reality which is independent of us, is that they draw at-

tention to the realist's inability to specify a relationship of correspondence between true views about reality on the one hand, and how reality is on the other, and thus they hold that it impossible to speak about objective truth in any sense whatsoever. Because of their rejection of objectivity, the anti-realists run the earlier noted risk that the difference between that something has been found as to be true and that something is true is abandoned. If the criteria for truth are merely contextually given, we are unable then to criticize externally truth claims which are put forward in another context of meaning where other criteria apply. This means that we are taken aback when we are confronted with a situation in which the truth claims which apply in one context collide with the criteria which apply in another context. For example, it is asserted in certain social, cultural or ideological groups that children and women are better off if men admonish them, using physical punishment to back up their advice whereas people in other social, cultural or ideological groups believe quite the opposite, namely that children and women, and indeed anyone at all, are damaged by being oppressed and abused. If we accept anti-realism, in a situation like the one just described, we no longer have any criteria to decide which of the competing, contradictory truth claims is justified. In the final analysis, this means that in our practical intercourse with the world which we are part of and require to relate to, we are no longer able to maintain the logical distinction between true and false. Thereby we would have lost one of the necessary preconditions for rational decision making.

If we, therefore, wish to avoid landing in such a situation which would be disastrous for human life, does this not mean that the emphasis on precisely the pragmatic (or internal) character of the realism which I have proposed, should be relinquished? I shall show that this does not follow for the following reasons. The first stage consists in criticizing the relativistic view that truth ought to be defined in epistemic, pragmatic or other contextual terms. By focussing especially on a specific normative aspect, I shall then in stage two show that this does not imply the view of metaphysical realism, that truth consists in the agreement between statements and an unconceptualized factual state of affairs. I shall take as my starting point the following example which is due to Alvin Goldman.

A man is tried in court, accused of having committed a serious offence. The majority of witnesses identify the accused as the guilty party and the accused lacks an alibi. Although the accused is innocent, he cannot prove his innocence. Moreover, the person who has actually committed the crime has died, so that the accused given the circumstances has no way of defending himself. If we now define truth as legal proof or as evidence, in the case concerned it entails that the accused cannot be other than guilty. In actual fact, however, the accused has not committed the offence. According to Goldman, we should therefore adopt a view of truth according to which

> the only correct sense of 'true' makes truth independent of how well it can be defended. Its defensibility is a separate matter, which may depend on a variety of extraneous circumstances. Any innocent person accused of a crime surely wants the real truth to emerge; and the real truth is all that is normally meant by 'true' (Goldman 1986, 18).

Even the pragmatic (or internal) realist wishes to retain this view but holds that this does not imply the thesis of metaphysical realism, namely that truth consists in an agreement between statements or words on the one hand, and an unconceptualized factual state of affairs on the other hand. It is possible to present normative arguments for the crucial distinction between truth and justification and between truth and rationality. A good example of this way of arguing is expressed in a reflection of Murat Baç which was occasioned by Goldman's example of the condemned man who is innocent. Baç points out

> that there would most likely be certain practical differences between a community the members of which are convinced that there is no sense of truth other than what is agreed by them at any given time and another community whose members tend to believe that propositional truth is something independent of their best evidence: the former would sentence Goldman's really innocent man to death whereas the latter would, I suppose, be very hesitant about it. My point is that recognition of such a truth independent of our epistemic means might have a valuable meta-epistemic and normative function or use in our actions despite the fact that at a basic epistemic level it admittedly has no use (Baç 1999, 215).

As far as I can see, we need the normative view of truth as something independent of our epistemic capacities, as a warning designed to deter the making of arbitrary decisions and as an exhortation to be cautious in making categorical judgements of various kinds. This view of truth also allows us to relate different contexts of meaning to each other and to compare them critically. Thus in certain contexts, methods and procedures have been developed which are superior to those which are offered in other contexts. I shall presently give an example of what I mean. I would like merely to say that when I speak of 'superior' here, I mean 'more reliable' in the sense that we know in our practical intercourse with the world, by relating ourselves to a critical meta-level, how to apply in practice the logical distinction between true and false. Pragmatic (or internal) realism is characterized by our acceptance of both (1) the meta-epistemic view of truth that truth is independent of our epistemic capacities and (2) the insight that this view is not a criterion for deciding concretely which claims to knowledge are justified.

Let me illustrate the importance of accepting this normative view of truth and its function in our search for truth, by citing the example of the conflict between two contexts of meaning where in one of them, illness is explained in medical terms, whereas in the other it is explained in terms of the influence which evil spirits can have on human beings. Some believers are convinced that we must seek the causes of certain illnesses in the influence which evil spirits exert upon us. The sick can, therefore, be cured only if the evil spirits or the devil are driven out. Exactly as in the case of medical textbooks, there are also instructions for exorcists, and examples of successful exorcism are handed down from one generation of adepts to the next. Common to both contexts of meaning and explanation, is the fact that the work is carried out by means of contextually established methods. In this respect, there is no difference between the domains.

In another respect, however, there is a crucial difference. The exorcist's theories do not allow that in the critical division between better and worse explanations, one can even go so far as giving up, in certain cases, the theoretical assumptions for the hitherto established explanations. Such a critical attitude to one's own activity can, however, be found, at least in principle, in the field of medicine. I do not assert that doctors are always right, or that they always know which diagnosis to make, or which course of treatment should be adopted. Given the discussions which are continually being conducted, not only about confirmed but also about refuted hypotheses, they are much better placed to distinguish critically between better and worse explanations, and thereby to evolve a reasonable practical application of the logical distinction between true and false. Even if, for institutional reasons, it very often can take a long time for a change to take place, it is true, nevertheless, that in the medical context one is ready to abandon theories, when it is no longer possible to generate testable hypotheses with their help. In my opinion, there is no similar readiness to act in this way in the case of exorcism. Views about the underlying, divine and thereby genuine reality steers what is said about observable reality. The aim is not, as in medical contexts, to be able, with the help of theories, to generate testable hypotheses which will allow us to say what is true about what is observed. Rather the reasoning runs in the opposite direction: we take the observable as evidence for our views about the non-observable.

This kind of critical comparison between two explanatory contexts presupposes that (1) on the one hand we advocate the view of truth as being independent of our epistemic capacities in order to avoid defining truth in epistemic, pragmatic or other contextual terms which as I have shown, would have disastrous relativistic consequences, while (2) on the other hand we do not present this view of truth in the spirit of metaphysical realism with the claim that there is a relation of correspondence between an intrinsically unconceptualized reality and our explanations of it. If we see things in this way – and I hold that my critique of metaphysical realism and my arguments for pragmatic (or internal) realism has demonstrated that it is reasonable to look on things in this way – then what speaks in favour of the medical explanatory context is that it can accommodate testable hypotheses and claims to knowledge which are open to critical discussion, so that even the underlying theoretical assumptions are not ultimately immune from revision. The fact that in practice it is impossible to question everything simultaneously, is something quite different and cannot reasonably be taken as an excuse for the vacuous objection that the medical context also rests upon assumptions. It is not a matter of assumptions versus no assumptions at all, but rather deals with the assumptions which are the most reasonable for us to accept, given that we are the beings that we are.

In spite of my critique of metaphysical realism, I in no way mean that all conceptualizations would be equally good. Let me discuss two respects in which all conceptualizations are not equally good. The first concerns knowledge claims and the second deals with values as conceptualizations of a fulfilling life. With respect to the former, not all claims to knowledge are justified and some conceptualizations should not be characterized as knowledge claims at all, since we cannot adduce any evidence that is observable by human beings, which would speak for or against the supposed claim to knowledge.

However, we require suitable conceptualizations also in another respect. In order to survive and be able to live a good life, it is crucially important that we seek correct explanations of causal relations and take pains over true descriptions of fact. It is certainly necessary but not sufficient that in our practical intercourse with reality, we know how we ought to use our knowledge of its empirical dimensions. Note that the word 'know' and related words can be used in different ways. To have knowledge about e.g. causal relations i.e. to know in this sense, naturally places limits on what we can do, but nevertheless our actual choice of action does not follow from the nature of the causal relation. In order to know how in our practical intercourse with reality we can use our knowledge *inter alia* of causal relations, another form of knowledge is required. This is knowledge about how we, in relation to the values which we seek to realize by reference to what we consider a fulfilling life, decide what it is worth having knowledge about, and what it is worth applying it to. Since reality is always a reality which is comprehended and conceptualized by us, it is pointless to speak about an intrinsically unconceptualized reality which unambiguously decides which explanation and description is the only correct explanation and description. Given we are the beings that we are, we require, in addition to knowledge about empirical reality which is conceptualized by us, also ideas about values as conceptualizations of a fulfilling life. This is a precondition for our being able to know how we should apply our knowledge about empirical reality as conceptualized by us, to the complex reality which we live in, are part of, and need to relate to. Even here, a critical examination of which preconditions in this respect are better than others, is required. I have now reached the point where I can clarify my view of religion.

4 The function of religion

My critique of metaphysical realism and my arguments for a pragmatic (or internal) realism form the preconditions for my proposal for a division of labour between science and views of life. The idea behind this proposal forms a central part of my view of religion. My aim is not to defend an essentialist definition of religion whether of a religious or philosophical kind, but to create a philosophical model which allows us to reflect on the human phenomenon of religion. A defining feature of this model is that it does not presuppose metaphysical realist statements about an intrinsically unconceptualized transcendental reality. This model, however, simultaneously also rejects an anti-realist reductionism according to which religion is nothing more than e.g. an expression for distorted social conditions (Marx) or for neurotic desires (Freud). Instead I look upon religion as a human phenomenon which contains ideas about God, or something divine, or something transcendent.

I would like to set forth here a philosophical perspective which, in relation to religion, views things from the outside, and argue that belief in God does not need to be considered as supplying us with truths about matters of fact in order for it to be meaningful in people's lives. In a pluralistic society, such a perspective is also important in order to be able to examine critically the phenomenon constituted by religions. We know that not all types of religion ensure a fulfilling life. Like all human phenomena, religion cannot only be used; it can also be misused. The view of religion which I wish to propose, should be seen against this background. The fact that such a view may clash with the self-image of religions i.e. the way in which they perceive and understand themselves, is not, I hold, a reason against proposing an external perspective. The truth claims which are made on the basis of the various self-images are not always compatible with one another. There are numerous examples to show how such incompatibilities are not simply superficial conflicts but have led to disastrous consequences for people's lives. The conflict between Roman Catholics and Protestants in Northern Ireland is one example; the conflict between Moslems and Hindus in Kashmir is another.

As I have said, I would like to see the following division of labour be-tween science and views of life: the task of the sciences is to provide us with knowledge about the empirical reality which is conceptualized by us and which offers resistance in our observational experiences. In other words, it gives us knowledge about a reality of which we physically are a part and which at the same time we must relate to and interact with. By contrast, we obtain in views of life a conceptualization of the reality which offers resistance in our existential experiences of what it means to be a human being. This conceptualization also contains ideas about a fulfilling life, which functions as a compass when we come to apply our knowledge to causal relations for example. If the views of life are religious, they con-tain in addition to ideas about a fulfilling life, ideas about God or some-thing transcendental.

The question has been raised whether this view of religion, namely as a view of life, which provides us with ideas about a fulfilling life, is not nevertheless a form of reductionism. Is it not the case that religion in the way I see it and reflect upon it, is reduced simply to be a matter of values? I believe that this objection depends on a confusion, namely that which arises from mixing up a statement about content with a statement about identity of meaning i.e. synonymy. I shall illustrate what I mean with the help of William Frankena's criticism of G.E. Moore's so-called naturalistic fallacy. Even if this fallacy is exclusively discussed within ethics, Frankena's observation is of more general importance. I shall begin by briefly summarizing Moore's standpoint, then present Frankenas's criti-cism and finally making use of this criticism, I shall show that my view of religion is not reductionist.

I am naturally aware that, according to the metaphysical realist, my philosophical view of religion cannot be other than reductionist. However, the metaphysical realist on the basis of a philosophical position which I have shown to be highly problematic, does not determine what is meant by reductionist. The metaphysical realist, for example, has recourse to a non-epistemic use of the concept of fact, which in my discussion of the concept of statement, I have already criticized. For this reason, what I mean by non-reductionist must be seen in relation to my critique of both metaphysi-cal and semantic realism and to the pragmatic (or internal) realism which I advocate.

The naturalistic fallacy

The naturalistic fallacy is said to occur whenever it is claimed that the fun-damental normative property 'good' can be defined in terms of something else, in particular in terms of natural properties.

It may be true that all things which are good are *also* something else, just as it is true that all things which are yellow produce a certain kind of vibration in the light. And it is a fact, that Ethics aims at discovering what are those properties belonging to all things which are good. But far too many philosophers have thought that when they named those other properties they were actually defining good; that these properties, in fact, were simply not 'other', but absolutely and entirely the same with goodness. This view I propose to call 'the naturalistic fallacy' ... (Moore 1903, 10).

Moore holds that if someone mistakes one natural object for another by defining the one object in terms of the other, then there is no reason to speak of a naturalistic fallacy. On the other hand, there is every reason in the world to speak of a naturalistic fallacy when the same person confuses good which is not a natural object with something which is (Moore 1903, 13). According to Moore it is really a very simple fallacy.

When we say that an orange is yellow, we do not think our statement binds us to hold that 'orange' means nothing else than 'yellow', or that nothing can be yellow but an orange. Supposing the orange is also sweet! Does that bind us to say that 'sweet' is exactly the same as 'yellow'. That 'sweet' must be defined as yellow? And supposing it to be recognised that 'yellow' just means 'yellow' and nothing else whatever, does that make it any more difficult to hold that oranges are yellow? Most certainly it does not: on the contrary, it would be absolutely meaningless to say that oranges were yellow, unless yellow did in the end mean just 'yellow' and nothing else whatever – unless it was absolutely indefinable. We should not get any very clear notion about things, which are yellow – we should not get very far with our science, if we were bound to hold that everything which was yellow, *meant* exactly the same things as yellow. We should find we had to hold that an orange was exactly the same thing as a stool, a piece of paper, a lemon, anything you like. We could prove any number of absurdities; but should we be nearer to the truth? Why, then, should it be any different with 'good'? Why, if good is good and indefinable, should I be held to deny that pleasure is good? Is there any difficulty in holding both to be true at once? On the contrary, there is no meaning in saying that pleasure is good, unless good is different from pleasure (Moore 1903, 14).

Moore distinguishes between three classes of question in ethics. They are admittedly related to one another, but, nevertheless, they should not be confused. The first class contains only one question,

the question What is the nature of that peculiar predicate, the relation of which to other things constitutes the object of all other ethical investigations? Or in other word, What is *meant* by good (Moore 1903, 37)?

The two other classes of question concern the relation which the predicate 'good' has to matters and things. We can ask: what things, adhere to the predicate 'good', and in this case to what extent? What things are good in themselves? Or we can ask: What means are there at our disposal to make what exists in the world, as good as possible? What are the causal relations between what is intrinsically good in itself and other things?

It is however the first question, namely what is meant by 'good' which interests Moore the most. It is for this reason that he devotes special attention to a critical analysis of particular ethical theories, namely those which in their answer to the question of what is intrinsically good,

> all hold that there is only *one* kind of fact, of which the existence has any value at all. But they also possess another characteristic, which is my reason for grouping them together and treating them first: namely that the main reason why the single kind of fact they name has been held to define the sole good, is that it has been held to define what is meant by 'good' itself. In other words they are all theories of the end or ideal, the adoption of which has been chiefly caused by the commission of what I have called the naturalistic fallacy: they all confuse the first and second of the three possible questions which Ethics can ask, It is, indeed, this fact which explains their contention that only a singe kind of thing is good. That a thing should be good, it has been thought, *means* that it possesses this single property: and hence (it is thought) only what possesses this property is good. The inference seems very natural; and yet what is meant by it is self-contradictory. For those who make it fail to perceive that their conclusion 'what possesses this property is good' is a significant proposition: that it does not mean either 'what possesses this property, possesses this property' or 'the word "good" denotes that a thing possesses this property.' And yet, if it does *not* mean one or other of these two things, the inference contradicts its own premise (Moore 1903, 37f.).

Moore's criticism of the naturalistic fallacy has often been understood to mean that one derives an 'ought' from an 'is' and thus is a question of confusing 'is' and 'ought'. Frankena shows that Moore's criticism that there is a confusion is certainly correct, but that the type of confusion involved is different from the confusion over 'ought' and 'is'. Let me first of all summarize Moore's standpoint.

The point of Moore's thesis that the predicate 'good' is not analysable, is that it is not empirically analysable either. It is precisely the attempt to define value properties in empirical terms which Moore labels the naturalistic fallacy. According to him, in such an attempt to define the predicate 'good', two worlds are confused which should be kept apart, namely the natural world of things and the non-natural world of values. Moore shows that empirical definitions of the predicate 'good' are inadequate by pointing among things, to the following example: when someone says 'What we all desire, is something good', he is not then uttering the mere triviality 'What we all desire is something that we all desire'. This example shows that 'good' does not mean the same as 'what we all desire'. As a support for his ontological thesis which asserts that the property good is not identical to an empirical complex such as what-we-all-desire, Moore makes the observation that the linguistic expressions 'good' and 'what we all desire' have different meanings (Newen and von Savigny 1996, 110). This is where Frankena comes in.

Frankena shows that the naturalistic fallacy does not consist in the confusion of 'is' and 'ought'. Instead it is a question of confusing a contentual
statement in a particular language with a statement about synonymy in expressions in this language. If we must speak of a fallacy, then it is a question of "the process of confusing or identifying two properties, of defining
one property by another, or of substituting one property for another"
(Frankena 1939, 471). When this happens and the property 'good' is defi-
nitionally replaced by another property, it is not always certain that those
who are accused of committing the naturalistic fallacy, are indeed guilty of
that.

> [T]he only fallacy which they commit – the real naturalistic or definist fallacy – is the
> failure to descry the qualities and relations which are central to morality. But this is
> neither a logical fallacy nor a logical confusion. It is not even, properly speaking, an
> error. It is rather a kind of blindness, analogous to colour blindness. Even this moral
> blindness can be ascribed to the definists [or naturalists] only if they are correct in
> their claim to have no awareness of any unique ethical characteristics and if the intu-
> itionists are correct in affirming the existence of such characteristics ... (Frankena
> 1939, 475).

A person who confuses the moral judgement 'What we all desire, is good'
where the reasonableness or unreasonableness of the judgement is a matter
for argument, with the statement about synonymy that 'good' means the
same as 'what we all desire', commits the same mistake as anyone who
confuses the statement 'Bachelors are glad young men' which has content,
and where the truth of falsity of the statement is a matter of argument, and
the statement about synonymy that 'bachelor' is synonymous with 'glad
young man' (Newen and Savigny 1996, 110).

Charles Taylor is another philosopher who, from a somewhat different
viewpoint, looks at the supposed confusion between 'is' and 'ought' in the
case of the so-called naturalistic fallacy. He too points out that something
has been missed in the criticism of this fallacy. Whereas Frankena shows
that contentual statements and statements about synonymy should be distinguished, Taylor agrees certainly that they have a different logical character, but wants to show that there is still an important connection with regard to the meaning of the value predicate. According to Taylor, those who
in their critique of the naturalistic fallacy, have wished to isolate the
meaning of the predicate 'good' from all descriptive aspects, have too onesidedly focussed on the absence of logical relations between descriptive
and value predicates. The fact that we cannot find synonymy between descriptive predicates and value predicates, or that we cannot exhibit valid
deductions from 'is' to 'ought' statements, says nothing according to Taylor about the connections which can, nevertheless, exist between one concept and other concepts. He agrees that

the 'descriptive' meaning: 'good' does not *mean* 'conducive to the fulfilment of human wants, needs or purposes'; but its use is unintelligible outside of any relationship
to wants, needs and purposes ... For if we abstract from this relation, then we cannot
tell whether a man is using 'good' to make a judgement or simply express some feeling; and it is an essential part of the meaning of the term that such a distinction can be
made. The 'descriptive' aspects of 'good's' meaning can rather be shown in this way:
'good' is used in evaluating, commending, persuading, and so on by a race of beings
who are such that through their needs, desires, and so on, they are not indifferent to
the various outcomes of the world-process. A race of inactive, godless angels, as
really disinterested spectators, would have no use for it, could not make use of it ... It
is because 'good' has this use, and can only have meaning because there is this role to
fill in human life, that it becomes unintelligible when abstracted from this role. Because its having a use arises from the fact that we are not indifferent, its use cannot be
understood where we cannot see what there is to be not-indifferent about ... (Taylor
1985b, 88).

It is exactly this linkage to the kind of being we are, and to what, given
this perspective, is not a matter of indifference to us, which deserves to
have a central place also in our philosophical reflections about the phenomenon of religion.

A supposed reductionist view of religion

I would like to return to the question of whether my conception of religion
as a view of life, which can provide us with a conceptualization of reality
which offers resistance in our existential experiences of what it means to
be a human being i.e. a conceptualization which includes ideas about a fulfilling life, is a form of reductionism? Does my view of religion imply that
it is reduced to merely dealing with our conceptualized values, and because
of this, does it become a mere idea about a fulfilling life? In the light of
my account of the naturalistic fallacy, i.e. what it implies and what it does
not imply, I would assert that anyone who accuses me of reductionism, is
confusing my contentual demand that views of life should deal with values
and therefore have something to say about the question of a good life, with
the statement that 'religion' is synonymous with 'the provider of a good
life' or 'the creator and maintainer of values', a statement about synonymy
which I do not make. The supposition that religion as a view of life ought
to deal with what it means to be a human being i.e. to live with life's inevitabilities, in no way entails a reductionist, essentialist view of religion
to the effect that religion is no more than *X*, whatever that *X* might be. I
would represent a reductionist view of religion if I had held that 'religion'
means nothing but 'the provider of a good life' or the 'the creator and
maintainer of values' With reference to Taylor, the only thing I would assert, is that religion which undeniably deals with values, would be "unintelligible outside of any relationship to wants, needs and purposes", i.e.

outside of any relationship to what it means to be a human being and to live with life's inevitabilities.

Because I have constructed a philosophical perspective which in relation to religion is an external one, I neither say that religion is something more than this nor that it is only this. On the basis of the pragmatic (or internal) realism which I advocate, it lies outside the framework of philosophy to assert anything about what more religion could be. From this perspective, it is therefore pointless, for example, to speak about supernatural factual states as if they were on the same logical plane as common empirical factual states. For the metaphysical realist, this is naturally equivalent to denying supernatural factual states. From the standpoint of my pragmatic (or internal) realism, on the other hand, it is equivalent to showing why it is problematic to speak of supernatural factual states as if they were on the same logical plane as common empirical factual states, and why it is thus more reasonable not to speak about supernatural factual states at all. As we have noted, this does not exclude the possibility of speaking about God. Thus the concept of God, from the standpoint of pragmatic (or internal) realism, can be spoken about as a limit concept. What it is possible to do concretely and what should be done with the concept of God, however, does not belong to the domain of religion. On the other hand, a linkage to the issue of what it means to live with life's inevitabilities and to the question of a fulfilling life is necessary to allow a critical attitude also towards the human phenomenon constituted by religions and their secular counterparts.

My proposal for a division of labour between science and views of life should be seen in the light of this perspective. This linkage to us, as the beings we are, distinguishes my view from certain kindred coherentist views such as Dirk-Martin Grube's coherentist holism Grube 1998, 173–209). We seek both a way to escape the Scylla of foundationalism i.e. the demand that there is an ultimate non-deducible but identifiable foundation and yet at the same time avoiding the Charybdis of relativism. Here, however, our ways part company. Grube wishes to give holistic systems, in both scientific and religious contexts, as a whole, essentially the same realist basis where the coherentist aspect plays an important role. Nonetheless, coherentist criteria are not sufficient but must be supplemented with pragmatic criteria:

> The kind of legitimization which is involved in the case of pragmatic confirmation, is a legitimization *en bloc*. It is a question of whether a belief system taken as a whole has managed to capture something of reality and not whether a particular claim within the system represents reality or not (Grube 1998, 194).

The question is what these pragmatic criteria consist of. Given that Grube does not include a linkage to human beings, as the beings we are, it is the coherentist aspect which supplies the realist basis. For my own part, I have difficulty in seeing how the coherentist aspect can provide the realist basis if we do not have a metaphysical realism at bottom with the epistemic addition that coherence in a scientific or religious system guarantees that the system in question is a correct representation of reality. But then we land back once more with my criticism of metaphysical realism and the attempt to decouple the epistemic aspect from our communicational, conceptual and epistemic limitations.

When Grube compares scientific systems with religious systems, he argues from a deficiency which is inherent in scientific systems in order to cite this deficiency as a support for the religious systems' realist basis. He lets his comparison *inter alia* revolve round the demand for predictability in the context of natural science and points out:

> Also the criteria themselves do not constitute realist claims but when taken together with parts of our other knowledge they become so ... Even in the case of the statements of natural science, criteria such as the ability to predict do not in themselves indicate realism so that as far as this point is concerned, there is no basic difference when compared to systems of religious belief. In this case, there are no grounds for treating the latter as deficient with respect to making realist claims (Grube 1998, 208f.).

The question is however, what positive conclusions one is justified in drawing on the basis of this negative circumstance. In order to be able to discuss this question at all, I hold that a expressly stated relationship to us as the beings we are, must be established, while at the same time consistently maintaining that reality for us is always a reality conceptualized and understood by us, and that we cannot say anything about the nature of reality which is beyond our conceptualizations. This does not mean that I introduce the idea of a reality in itself. It means only that reality for us human beings is a conceptualized reality.

Since we are the beings that we are, with both observational and existential experiences, talk about conceptualized reality, bearing in mind my idea of a division of labour between science and views of life in our life, means, as has been said, the following: the task of science is to supply us with knowledge about the empirical reality conceptualized by us, of which we are part and which we simultaneously must consciously relate to and interact with. The task of views of life, by contrast, is to supply us with insights about what it means to be a human being. These insights also contain ideas of a fulfilling life which acts as a compass in applying our knowledge to empirical reality. It can be established that science and theories do actually function in this way. This naturally does not prevent the occurrence of other functions. This takes place when scientific results are used for ideological ends e.g. in scientific socialism or in scientism. It also occurs when for religious reasons one uses political means to remove the evolutionary assumptions underlying scientific research, on the grounds that some scientists do not support the theory of evolution on scientific grounds. Hopefully my view of science and views of life will assist in exposing such improprieties.

5 Two material definitions of truth

My proposed division of labour between the sciences and theories of life implies that there are two different material definitions of truth which are used when one speaks of truth in these two domains. The formal Aristotelian, definition of truth that a statement is true if and only if it is as it is asserted to be, is on the other hand, common to both. When it is a matter of knowledge, 'to be true' means, according to the material definition 'to be in agreement with reality as it is conceptualized by us and offering resistance in our observational experiences.' I am obviously aware that the image that reality offers resistance, is just an image. It is not a question of some philosophical thesis. The image expresses an experience which we all share. We see a wall and know that we cannot simply go through it. In order for us to avoid making a mistake, the relevant criteria to decide which statements are true and which are false, are freedom from contradiction and agreement between, on the one hand, statements about expected observations based on particular hypotheses, and on the other hand, statements about observations which have been actually made.

With regard to the question what it means to be a human being i.e. to live with life's inevitabilities, 'to be true', as we have noted, in another material definition, means 'to be in agreement with the reality as conceptualized by us and which offers resistance in our existential experiences of what it is to be a human being i.e. to live with life's inevitabilities.' As I shall show in Part V, moral experiences form part of existential experiences. The latter are something that we all share. We know what we are speaking about, when we speak of love, joy happiness, suffering, guilt and death. In order to be able to deal with them as the inevitable realities which they are in our lives, and to find existentially adequate expressions for them so that we can live a good life, the relevant criteria in order to decide which statements are true and which statements are false, are coherence and adequacy. The first criterion is more objective in the sense that it is a question of discovering how far the expressions and narratives of views of life fit together and display coherence. The second criterion is more subjective in the sense that the question of adequacy is ultimately a matter of experiencing expressions and narratives as being adequate.

I would point out that this is a matter of an interaction between, on the one hand, views of life providing us with expressions for what it means to be a human being i.e. to live with life's inevitabilities, and on the other hand, human beings who, when they no longer experience existing expressions as existentially adequate, create new ones. It is important to take note of this interaction when we want to draw up criteria for critically discussing different views of life.

Criteria for a rationally acceptable view of life

In the light of my idea for a division of labour between science and views of life, I would like to propose the following necessary criteria for a rationally acceptable view of life, bearing in mind the function of views of life. To avoid possible misunderstandings, I shall begin by saying what the question is not about. The proposal for criteria for a rationally acceptable view of life is not about what could be compared with a choice between having a view of life and not having it. A view of life, in some form or other, would seem to be an integral part of human life We need to accept values as pointers or as a compass in order to apply our knowledge to reality. We conceptualize these values and we can do it because existing views of life, when they function, supply us with adequate expressions for what it means to be a human being i.e. to live with life's inevitabilities. The discussion about criteria for a rationally acceptable view of life deals instead with how we can relate both to other people's views of life and to our own. For the sake of clarity, I should point out that the way of relating is always the individual's way of relating.

I would like to propose the following criteria as necessary for the rational acceptability of an individual's view of life:
(1) The view of life provides us with images, ideas and narratives about life's inevitabilities in which we recognize ourselves and the conditions of our life.
(2) The view of life provides us with images, ideas and narratives about life, as it could be, when it is at its best.
(3) With the help of the images, ideas and narratives of the view of life, we can experience the tension between how life could be when it is at its best, and how life, with all its inevitabilities, actually is.
(4) With the help of the images, ideas and narratives of the view of life, we can on the basis of this tension, develop a feeling for good and evil, right and wrong.
Criteria (1)–(4) refers to the function which existing views of life play in people's lives and to the circumstance that we are always, so to speak, born within a view of life. The criteria which follow, on the other hand, focus on what we can do more actively with the help of our views of life.

(5) With the help of the images, ideas and narratives of the view of life, we can conceptualize the feeling mentioned in (4) above and thus create, that is to say, constitute the values.

(6) With the help of this conceptualizing feeling and of the values that are constituted by its means, we can critically review not only how we apply our knowledge but also how we form our views of life in terms of social paradigms and institutions.

This last point is included because the convictions which we human beings experience as being important, for one reason or another, have a tendency to take on an institutional form in order that they can be maintained and communicated further. The critical review mentioned in (6) forms the practical point of contact between philosophy and views of life, in the sense that the critical review can lead to a modification of the existing conceptualizations associated with a view of life, or new conceptualizations, and as a result, even to new views of life. This work of modification and creation is, in such a case, an effect of philosophical reflection although it itself lies outside the framework of philosophy.

There is a problem with these criteria which requires a special addendum. The criteria which have been put forward could be considered to be satisfied even by someone who oppresses or marginalizes others. When such a thing happens, it results obviously in a life which is far from fulfilling for those who are oppressed and marginalized. How can we deal with this, especially since the person who oppresses and marginalizes and does so quite consciously, can seldom be convinced by argument? I would point out that a consequence of the pragmatic (or internal) realism which I have developed is that no values can be defended on the basis of metaphysical realism. This means that no-one's personal claim to a good life can have some sort of metaphysical priority. This naturally does not convince the person who oppresses and marginalizes others and does so quite consciously, but it gives the rest of us the resolution to continue along the path of argument, questioning the various kinds of absolute claim, and developing reasonable alternatives.

It is in this respect that my idea for a division of labour between science and theories of life which is based on my critique of metaphysical realism in general and metaphysical realism in the sphere of religion in particular, rules out metaphysical realism for theories of life. This does not mean that every form of realism is ruled out. In addressing the question of the realism of views of life, I need to remind the reader of two different material definitions of truth which were mentioned earlier. If 'to be true' means 'to be in agreement with reality as conceptualized by us and as offering resistance in our observational experiences' then realism is related to experience in the sense of observational experience. If 'to be true' means 'to be

in agreement with reality as conceptualized by us and as offering resistance in our existential experiences' then realism is related to experience in
the sense of existential experience of what it means to be a human being
i.e. to live with life's inevitabilities. Note that in human life there is a
practical connection between these two notions of conceptualized reality
since the first is part of the second and observational experiences form part
of the existential ones. This, however, does not remove the distinction
between these two kinds of experience and their function in our lives.

A characteristic feature of the pragmatic (or internal) realism which I
have presented, is that reality is always reality as it is comprehended and
conceptualized by us. In this reality, we encounter not only problems
which can be solved by being made to disappear, but also problems which
will always exist because we are the beings that we are. In other words,
they are problems which are solved by learning how to live with them in
the right manner. Seen in this light, the realism of views of life consists in
their capacity to furnish us with expressions which we can experience as
adequately expressing life's inevitabilities. In doing this, views of life provide us simultaneously with real life alternatives. As long as we human
beings are the beings we are, there will never exist a life completely devoid of violence and oppression. From this perspective, views of life are
Utopias. Nevertheless, for many human beings, it can even make a physical difference in the practical conditions of their lives, if there are people
who fight for peace, who are committed to loving their neighbour as themselves, or who strive according to their capacity to add to the good things
of this world – be it materially, culturally or otherwise – and to share that
goodness according to need.

Talking about God

What then are we to make of talking about God? I have now come to the
point where I can indicate how the question of God's existence is to be
treated from the standpoint of the pragmatic (or internal) realism which I
have sketched. Bear in mind that this perspective is, relative to religion, an
external one: it is therefore not a question of speaking about God in terms
of a particular religion.

The question of God's existence is to be viewed according to the pragmatic (or internal) realism which I have advocated, not in relation to theories, hypotheses and observations, but in relation to views of life, life
situations and existential experiences of what it means to be a human being
i.e. to live with life's inevitabilities. If an expression associated with a
view of life is seen to be an adequate expression of what it means to be a
human being, then this means subjectively that the expression is experienced as adequate by someone. Such an experience of adequacy does not

exist unless the expressions, images, ideas and narratives of the view of life are linked to one another in a coherent way. That, however, is not all.

As I have said before, it is a question of interaction. In order to experience the expressions, images, ideas and narratives of a view of life as existentially adequate, we must be able to recognize ourselves and the conditions of our life in them. A prerequisite for this is that we can conceive our lives as narratives with a past, a present and a possible future, narratives which express the meaning of life in our own life. In order to recognize our life's narratives in the expressions of views of life, we require that the expressions of these views of life are themselves narratives or parts of narratives. What in Christianity is called God, for example, is a figure in narratives where people recognize themselves and the conditions of their lives in such a way that they also relate to God as God is represented in the narratives. Narratives of religious and other views of life are not testable claims to knowledge. However, it does not follow from this that they are merely arbitrary expressions of diffuse feelings. They are cognitive in the sense that they communicate insights into what it means to be a human being. These insights emerge because we recognize ourselves and the conditions of our lives in these narratives simultaneously as we relate to the figures portrayed in them. In this respect, the narratives of religious and other views of life bear upon the lives we live.

Limit experiences play a crucial role in this. When we want to say something about the limitations which we encounter in our lives e.g. with regard to death, but also with regard to love, which sooner or later is put to the test, we do so *inter alia* in the form of beliefs. Although these beliefs are presented as truth claims, it is not a matter of testable claims to knowledge. Let me illustrate by giving an example of what I mean. We are familiar with the difference between actions which have been motivated by love and those which have quite other origins. We know what unreciprocated love is and sometimes we are uncertain and cannot decided what is what. Then we begin to wonder about what love really is. We do it with the help of novels, dramas, films etc. In connection with this, the idea of a pure or perfect love crops up, an idea which is not a testable claim to knowledge. We have come to the end of the road or to a limit where the idea of pure or perfect love is an expression of this limit. For believers, it is natural when there is talk of pure or perfect love, to speak of God. To say that God is pure love or perfect love is not an assertion about facts and therefore it is not a testable knowledge claim. It is a belief i.e. a supposition which believers can defend by showing the coherence of their own views of life composed of expressions, images, ideas and narratives and explaining how the latter relate to those things experienced as life's inevitabilities.

In passing, it is here that I would like to see a place for certain so-called dogmatic reflections about what on the basis of a religious conceptualization of limit experiences could be said about God, must be said about God and may not be said about God.

Such an internal way of treating things entails the following consequences for a metaphysical realist theology. With respect to God, metaphysical realism means *inter alia* that God's existence or non-existence is asserted to be a fact, and it is independent not only of whether we have knowledge about it, but also of whether we can have any knowledge of it at all. On the basis of my previous criticism of metaphysical realism and of the view that there are religious statements, I do not consider it meaningful to use assertions about God as factual statements. Assertions about God are not testable knowledge claims: thus the question of God's existence cannot be seen in relation to theories, hypotheses and observational experience.

On the other hand, the question of God's existence can be seen in relation to our own view of life and to the existential experiences of what it means to be a human being, which are associated with this view of life. The question of God's existence is thus partly a question about the coherence of the given religious view of life, and partly about whether the expressions associated with the view of life are adequate for expressing life's inevitabilities. The believer can do nothing other than take it for granted that God exists. This does not eliminate doubt, which in a religious context is something quite different from doubt about whether a knowledge claim is justified. The atheist can do nothing else than take it for granted that God does not exist which does not rule out the atheist wavering and showing an understanding for religious belief in God.

According to my way of seeing things, the difference between atheists and believers has, therefore, primarily to do with the following. The atheist denies the coherence of religious views of life and their capacity to help us in coming to terms with life's inevitabilities and living adequately. By contrast, believers maintain that their religious views of life are coherent and provide adequate expressions for what it means to be a human being. For the believer and correspondingly for the atheist, it is psychologically and even logically impossible to deny that which constitutes their own view of life. To presuppose or reject as the case may be, that which constitutes a view of life, is from this perspective not the same as denying or asserting the existence of these presuppositions as if we were dealing with some kind of object. Despite the fact that we cannot psychologically or logically deny that which constitutes our own view of life, it is nevertheless possible to criticize views of life, so to speak, from the outside. We all know cases where atheists have become believers and believers have given up their faith. This occurs when the expressions, images, ideas and narratives of our own view of life are no longer experienced as being adequate i.e. when we no longer recognize ourselves and the conditions of our lives in them. This is not simply a matter of individual psychology. It has also to do with the kind of biological and social beings we are, as well as with the resistance from reality as conceptualized by us which offers resistance also in our existential experiences.

The point of this line of argument is that belief in God does not need to be meaningless simply because we do not speak of God as something which exists independently of every conceptual framework, a view of God's existence which even a person such as Runzo whom we mentioned earlier – a philosopher of religion much influenced by Kant's philosophy and strongly critical of metaphysical reasoning – can free himself from. Given that we are the beings that we are, we need to take note of the fact that we do not live merely as biological beings but also that our existence takes place within a particular *life-world* (*Lebenswelt*). In this concept which we have taken from phenomenological philosophy, we gather to-gether everything to do with traditions, language, habits, and culture which is available to us human beings in our lives and which we use without al-ways thinking about it. Belief in God is in certain life-worlds quite simply a natural reaction. As we recall from Putnam's internal realism, the thesis of a reality which is independent of every conceptual framework is not necessary in order to retain the idea of objectivity. Depending on the con-ceptual framework, what is said within the conceptual framework in ques-tion, is objectively true or objectively false as the case may be. I shall now investigate the conclusions which we can reasonably derive from this and those which we cannot.

The adequacy of conceptions of God

I shall begin with a short account of Rudolf Carnap's idea about the differ-ence between internal and external existence questions (Carnap 1950), an idea which, in my view, contains a point which is relevant to my own pur-pose, and which further strengthens my critique of metaphysical realism. For Carnap, philosophical problems about existence are about the concep-tual frameworks which should be used for everyday life, mathematics, fa-bles, religious language, quantum physics etc. It is not a question of whether the entities which are defined in, or are constituted by, a given conceptual framework, so to speak, *really* exist. The choice of conceptual framework is determined by its relevance in relation to the activities which are considered necessary or desirable for the task in hand whether it is, for example, survival or the attainment of the good life or quite simply the solution of problems which give us pleasure to solve. After a particular conceptual framework has been chosen, substantial internal questions can then be asked: for example, are there prime numbers between 10 and 20?

Carnap thus does not reckon on some metaphysical concept of existence, relative to which all kinds of alleged entities should be judged. Instead we assume certain entities when they are part of a theoretical framework which best explains our experience. I shall in due course widen this perspective to embrace different kinds of experience, both observational and existential.

Metaphysical realists usually emphasize that the question of God's existence has nothing to do with conceptual frameworks. In contrast to the non-metaphysical view of ontological commitment, according to which there is no metaphysical concept of existence to which alleged entities could be related, metaphysical realism holds with respect to the issue of ontological commitment, that there is a general metaphysical concept of existence to which the existence of alleged entities e.g. that of trees, black holes and God, can be related. In using the phrase 'metaphysical concept of existence' I want to emphasize what is important for the metaphysical realist, namely that no human influence occurs. Existence is something that is independent of how we formulate it and even independent of whether there is anyone there who would be able to formulate it.

Let me point out some of the shortcomings of this point of view with the help of a thought experiment which Putnam asks his readers to perform:

> If you have a world in which there are two black 'atoms' and one red one, you can either say that there are three objects (the atoms), or that there are seven objects (the atoms and the various aggregates of two or more atoms). How many objects are there 'really' in such a world? I suggest that *either way of describing it is equally 'true'*. The idea that 'object' has some sense which is independent of how we are counting objects and what we are counting as an 'object' in a given situation is an illusion. I do not mean by this that there 'really' are 'aggregates' and there really are atoms and there really are sets and there really are numbers, and so on, and it is just that *sometimes* 'object' does not refer to 'all objects'. I mean that the metaphysical notion of 'all objects' has no sense (Putnam 1992, 120).

Putnam's example demonstrates two things. First of all, it shows that on the basis of one sort of logic there are three objects, while according to another sort of logic there are seven. Secondly, it shows that one sort of logic need not be inferior to the other, so that it is possible to have more than one true description of reality. Once a particular conceptual framework has begun to be applied, what is said within this framework is objectively true or false. Inside one of the conceptual frameworks, there are objectively three objects and anyone holding that there are seven, is saying something that is objectively false. If on the other hand, we apply the other conceptual framework, then it is objectively true that there are seven objects, and anyone holding that there are only three, is saying something that is objectively false.

From the above we might get the impression that the choice of conceptual framework is arbitrary so that we can theoretically choose any conceptual framework whatsoever, according to taste, and then assert that what we assert is objectively true or false. However matters are not quite so simple. Let me illustrate this by referring to my view about how science and views of life are related in different ways to human life, depending upon the different functions they have in our lives.

In the case of science, theories play a central role. Put very simply, I wish to treat a theory as a structured view about the possible nature of reality, which is always reality as it is conceptualized by us, and about how the various components of reality are related to one another. In the first stage, the theory is treated as something we have created or developed but where it is still unclear if there is anything substantial in the proposed theory. In the second stage, the theory is applied to a given area of investigation and hypotheses are generated about entities of various kinds. In the third stage, the hypotheses are tested to see if there is an agreement between the observations we expect on the basis of the hypotheses and the observations we in fact make. If there is such an agreement, a given hypothesis is at least not falsified, and in the best case may even be confirmed. Let us now suppose that because of new knowledge, a situation arises in which a particular theory can no longer be used to generate testable hypotheses. The theory is then no longer used to allow us to assert something about reality.

Not demanding correspondence between statements and an intrinsically unconceptualized reality, but instead demanding agreement between expected observations and statements about the observations which have in fact been made, is not the same as saying that there is no objectivity. How reality, so to speak, offers resistance in our observational experiences influences whether we can establish agreement. Through our experiences of resistance, reality determines what we can reasonably assert about it. This does not mean, however, that theories are true or false. To accept a theory is not the same as believing it is true. It is, as I have previously shown, a question of believing that it is empirically adequate i.e. that with respect to what can be observed, it is in a position to generate testable hypotheses and by means of them to assert what is true in the observable world (van Fraassen 1980, 18). In this way, there is a continuous interplay between observations, hypotheses, and theories, where the latter function as expressions for what reality might be like. The interplay takes place through our seeking to relate theories, via the testable hypotheses which they generate, to our concrete experiences of the empirical resistance which reality offers.

I shall argue analogously in the case of our views of life i.e. with respect, not to observational, but rather to the existential experiences which receive their conceptualizations in our various views of life. Given the differing functions which these two kinds of experience have in our lives, I shall not in the case of views of life speak about knowledge, but prefer instead a term such as 'insight'. I would recall that in contrast to the usual religious viewpoint, I want to assert that religions and indeed their secular counterparts as well, cannot provide us with knowledge in the usual sense of the word. In the case of the tested experiences of everyday life and above all of science, we have experimental procedures associated with observational evidence, which enable us to investigate critically whether our claims to knowledge are justified. In the case of the supposed claims to knowledge of religions and their secular counterparts, we lack such test procedures.

The following objection probably arises quite naturally. Even if I am working with two material definitions of truth, does truth not imply knowledge? And if I want to speak about truth, even with respect to religion, ought I not then reasonably to speak about knowledge also in religious contexts? In one particular sense, the objection is valid. But I would hold that I have essentially taken account of it in the following way. The point of retaining the formal minimal definition of truth and simultaneously introducing two material definitions was partly to take account of how, with respect to different dimensions of reality, we speak about truth, and partly to specify how taking account of the difference between observational and existential experience, we can critically investigate claims to knowledge, with respect to both science and views of life. It is certainly possible to speak about two material definitions of knowledge also and to distinguish between knowledge in the everyday and scientific sense on the one hand and religious knowledge on the other. I am not utterly opposed to speaking about different sorts of knowledge. However I am afraid that on the religious side one might, on the one hand, be tempted to take advantage of what we normally mean by knowledge because in practice it has shown itself to be rather reliable while on the other hand one is reluctant to submit religious knowledge claims to the kinds of test which such claims must undergo in ordinary life and science. In order to avoid confusions of this type, I prefer to speak about insight.

The fact that, according to my way of seeing things, we cannot speak about knowledge in the case of views of life, does not imply that they have nothing of importance to say about life e.g. about love, joy, happiness, suffering, guilt, and death. Let us suppose that we are reflecting about certain crises, for example when we leave youth behind us, and are forced to see our guilt and our limitations with respect to attaining fulfilling conditions of life, both for ourselves, for those who are closest to us and for others, or when we encounter death. In the first stage, our thoughts will reflect more general ideas about what it means to be a human being. These ideas also include other ideas about the tension between life as it could when it is at its best and how life actually is. In the second stage, the various ideas which have been suggested about what it means to be a human being are applied to the concrete situations of our life with all the suffering, sorrow, death, guilt, joy, love and happiness that they contain. All these are concrete realities in our lives although we cannot explain them, far less define them out of existence. Nevertheless we must find a way of expressing them, if we are to be able to live a fulfilling life. If we are able to recognize ourselves in these expressions, we experience them as existentially adequate.

Let us now suppose that on the basis of new experiences, we no longer experience the given expressions for suffering, sorrow, death, guilt, joy, love, and happiness as existentially adequate for expressing what it means to be a human being i.e. to live with life's inevitabilities. What then happens, is that these expressions, so to speak, fade away and vanish so that we need to create new expressions. This is analogous to what happens in the sciences when theories are no longer empirically adequate.

But is this not the same thing as depriving religious ideas of their truth content? It suffices for me to recall my earlier critique of metaphysical realism. The internal aspect of the pragmatic (or internal) realism which I have defended, applies to all our ideas. When applied to views of life, it implies that the ideas involved are no more about an intrinsically unconceptualized reality than are those of science. The difference between science and views of life, as has been said, has to do with the difference between observational and existential experiences. The former are conceptualized in tested experience and in the sciences, while the latter are conceptualized in our coming to terms with life's inevitabilities. From the internal perspective, the ideas of views of life about what it means to be a human being, are human products. Religious views of life are no exception to this. Existential experiences are no more a mere question of individual psychological perception than observational experiences are. They have also to do with the kind of biological and social being we humans are. In this respect, the ideas of views of life of what it means to be a human being, can also encounter resistance from life. It is therefore necessary to scrutinize them critically. Neither in the case of science nor in the case of views of life, is it a matter of definitively, once and for all, determining empirical or existential adequacy. Even in the latter case, it is more a question of continually adjusting our ideas about what it means to be a human being, through concretely experiencing the resistance which reality offers in a mixture of love, joy, happiness, suffering, guilt and death.

The crucial feature of the kind of pragmatic (or internal) realism which I have advocated, is that both our observational and existential ideas are ideas about the reality of which we are part, in which we live and with which we interact, and not about an intrinsically unconceptualized reality which lies beyond conceptual systems and practice. It is not a question of fiction *contra* reality, but of ideas which are exposed to continual testing in life. I have earlier argued, with reference to Putnam, that the question of the nature of reality can only be raised within a theory (Putnam 1981, 49), i.e. on the basis of a particular conceptual system. I would like to add that the question of the nature of reality in all the dimensions which it is capable of being experienced, can be meaningfully raised only within the framework of some kind of view of life which we always, in one way or another, have. These views of life can change, but we are never without views of life and their conceptualizations of our existential experiences. Earlier experiences, on the basis of which we develop theories and views of life, form the background for our conceptualizations of the resistance which reality offers. It is, however, always a question of a reality which we live in and are a part of. I do not deny that there is more than what we can conceptualize. I share also the realist's emphasis on the fact that it is not through our conceptualizations that we cause what is true. Nevertheless, it is always with the help of conceptualizations that we represent reality i.e. the conceptualizations which we, in relation to our observational and existential experiences, experience as adequate conceptualizations.

If the ideas associated with a conceptual framework are experienced as being existentially adequate with respect to what it means to be a human being, and if they also contain ideas of God, then, given the adequacy of the conceptual framework, it is logically and psychologically impossible to dispense with God. As the critique of metaphysical realism has shown, it is not meaningful, moreover, to demand that God really exists in some intrinsically unconceptualized reality, or indeed constitutes such a reality. It is not a question of arbitrariness since the choice of conceptual frame here is not unrestricted. We can relinquish a conceptual framework, both in the context of science and views of life, when it no longer provides, as the case may be, empirical or existential adequacy in relation to the problems which we confront in our lives. Objectivity remains possible, but it should be seen in relation to the continual adjustment of our ideas with respect to both our observational and existential experiences. From this perspective, there is no reason to demand of a belief in God that it must provide us with truths about facts for it to be meaningful in the lives of human beings. Seen from this perspective there is no need either to assert or deny the existence of such facts and obstinately to adhere to the idea that belief in God stands or falls depending on whether these facts exist or not.

It is obvious that this way of looking at things has consequences for the self-image of religions and their secular counterparts. However this is largely a matter for internal discussion within the view of life and falls outside the framework of this book. What, on the other hand, definitely does lie within its framework, is to substantiate the foregoing view that talk about observational and above all existential experiences is not simply a matter of individual psychology but is bound up with the fact that we are the beings that we are. In the last chapter of the book, I would like explore what this means philosophically. Whereas hitherto, I have primarily pointed out the problems and shortcomings of metaphysical realism in general and in the religious domain in particular, and have shown how certain problems which are inherent in metaphysical realism can be avoided if we accept a pragmatic (or internal) realism, in the remaining Part V of the book I would like to explain in more detail how on the basis of this type of realism, we can understand and critically investigate the phenomenon of religion without necessarily adopting a religious perspective or arguing religion out of existence in a reductionist way because it does not fulfil the requirements for a justified claim to knowledge.

Part V

Views of life and a fulfilling life

I shall begin the last part of the present work by reviewing the difference between a definition of views of life from the observer's viewpoint and from the viewpoint of the person acting. By acting, I mean our interaction with the reality which we, as the biological and social beings that we are, are a part of, live in, and consciously need to relate to, and interact with. I shall argue against the first perspective (i.e. the observer's standpoint) and in favour of the second (i.e. the actor's standpoint).

1 Perspectives on views of life

As an example of how views of life are interpreted in accordance with the first perspective i.e. from the observer's viewpoint, I would like cite the definitions which are due to Ingemar Hedenius and Anders Jeffner. Both definitions still largely determine Swedish discussions of views of life. What is at stake are the following normative questions: what can reasonably be subsumed under the concept of view of life, and how far are views of life, particularly religious ones, rational or non-rational?

According to an often quoted definition of Hedenius, a view of life consists of utterly general statements about life, about humankind and its history, and about the universe.

> To call a view, a view of life, I require that it contains a number of statements of belief of an utterly general kind about life and man or history or the universe, where such statements of belief may include, but not necessarily include, some assumption of a supernatural, holy and personal power ... If the view of life is not religious, then it must at least have some moral significance in the sense of being a background for convictions about what in the greatest generality is right and wrong (Hedenius 1951, 73).

Jeffner's equally often cited definition reads as follows:

> A view of life is the theoretical and normative assumptions which constitute, or have crucial importance for, a comprehensive picture of human beings and the world, and which forms a central value system, and expresses a fundamental attitude (Jeffner 1981, 13).

There are thus three components which form the kernel of views of life:

> First of all it is theories about human beings and the world – e.g. about the origin of the universe, about what distinguishes human beings from animals or about what happens at death. Secondly it is values and norms of a fundamental nature. The view of life specifies what is intrinsically good in life or the basic rules which we must follow if we want to live according to what is right. We call the component a central value system. ... The third component is somewhat more difficult to describe. When one studies different views of life, one sees that they often express a certain attitude to life – a way of experiencing the human situation in the world. There can be a fundamental note of hope or doubt embodied in the view, or a complex feeling which is difficult to label with a name. In future, we shall call this third component the fundamental attitude. Of course the three components cannot be isolated from one another. There are many links between them. In a view of life, theories about the world and human beings often have the function of motivating or supporting the central value system and the fundamental attitude (Jeffner 1981, 12).

The last sentence in the passage quoted shows that the theoretical assumptions when compared to the normative assumptions and the fundamental attitude, nevertheless, have a special role. For this reason, one can say that it is characteristic of the type of definition advanced by Hedenius and Jeffner that views of life are considered – entirely in the case of Hedenius and at least partly in the case of Jeffner – as kinds of theory which claim to be descriptions of reality. Such an emphasis has naturally repercussions for the type of religious critique or religious defence which is put forward. I shall not investigate any further Jeffner's approach to justifying religion, since his defence is constructed as an answer to the challenge presented by Hedenius' critique of religion. In his answer, Jeffner presupposes the same observer perspective adopted by Hedenius. For this reason, it will suffice for my purpose to concentrate on Hedenius' critique of religion.

Hedenius' critique of religion

Hedenius lays down that an investigation of the relationship between belief and knowledge is a task for the philosophy of religion, not for religion. The fact that belief is also associated with supernatural properties which can only be observed by the believer, is irrelevant in this context. When Hedenius philosophizes about the relationship between belief and knowledge, he does not make use of any sources of knowledge other than those which he customarily employs when he discusses philosophy (Hedenius 1983, 44). Apart from this basic starting point, Hedenius mentions three more specific presuppositions. The first is that religious belief, to a considerable extent, is composed of statements presumed to be true, but which cannot be verified scientifically (Hedenius 1983, 45). Hedenius labels the presupposition that religion is not simply a matter of piety, but is also a conviction that certain religious views and assumptions are true, "the psychology of religion postulate" (Hedenius 1983, 47). If belief were not similar to knowledge in this respect, in holding certain things to be true, according to Hedenius, it would be akin to a piece of music, and would no longer constitute a problem, as far as the relationship between belief and knowledge is concerned. There would no longer be any issue about truth.

Let me briefly interpolate a remark here, by saying that Hedenius is naturally correct if truth is materially defined in terms of agreement with how reality, as conceptualized by us, offers resistance in our observational experiences. His conclusion does not follow, however, if in the case of religion, we choose, as I have earlier explained, the material definition of truth in terms of agreement with how reality, conceptualized by us, offers resistance in our existential experiences. I shall return to this later on.

By allowing belief to be akin to knowledge, in the sense that belief is considered as a matter of holding certain things to be true, Hedenius means that the term "holding certain things to true" must be taken literally. In his opinion, a religious person means that God really is merciful, and that belief in Jesus will redeem us, just as non-believers hold that no religious belief can save us from death. For the religious believer, certain truths are "true in exactly the same sense that any other truths are concerning real states of affair" (Hedenius 1983, 48). So much for the psychology of religion postulate.

Hedenius' second postulate is the so-called language-theoretic one, namely "that the statements of religious language are communicable, so that their meaning can be understood even by people who do not accept them" (Hedenius 1983, 49). This does not rule out the possibility that the terms in religious statements can have a different meaning when they occur in non-religious language, or that religious speech is interpreted symbolically. The language-theoretic postulate's requirement entails neither more nor less than "that the dogmas which are conceivably symbolic must always be able to be translated into statements which are not symbolic, provided the translations are made sufficiently detailed and comprehensive" (Hedenius 1983, 52f.).

I shall shortly return to the implications of this requirement, but for the sake of completeness, I shall also mention the third postulate which Hedenius wishes to accept, namely the logical postulate. He considers that he does not require to say very much about it since in contrast to the other two postulates it merely states something self-evident, namely "that two truths cannot contradict one another" (Hedenius 1983, 56).

Let us go back to Hedenius' language-theoretic postulate, according to which symbolic statements must be translatable into statements which are not symbolic. Which statements then are not symbolic? They are those where "on the basis of purely logical and scientific reasons" (Hedenius 1983, 44) the views they involve, can be rejected or confirmed.

It would seem clear that Hedenius accepts a picture theory of language as an implicit foundation of his critique of religion. Language is considered as corresponding to, or representing reality. The ontological thesis which lies behind this view, is metaphysical realism which holds that there is a reality which is independent of our language, but which, nevertheless, in some way can be described and represented through our use of language. From this, it follows that everything that can be said about reality, can in principle be said in any language whatsoever. We have Hedenius' language-theoretic postulate which, as we have said, holds that "the dogmas which are conceivably symbolic must always be able to be translated into statements which are not symbolic, provided the translations are made sufficiently exhaustive" (Hedenius 1983, 53). Even although language variations occur because of slightly different ways of structuring reality, reality is, nonetheless, there to be discovered, in principle by anyone at all, since it is fundamentally the same for all.

The question of communicability rests in Hedenius – as I see it – upon the assumption that linguistic expressions refer to entities which exist, and upon the assumption that it is reason which, with the help of logic and science, allows us to discover what there is. I have earlier criticized this type of metaphysical realism which forms the basis of such a view. I have also shown that it is completely possible to maintain the logical distinction between language and reality, while at the same time holding that language plays a crucial role in understanding and conceptualizing reality and in constituting (that is to say, in determining) the difference between what is real and what is not. Language is not then seen as representational. As I have earlier shown, according to this alternative view of language, reference is linked to the constitution of reality. We do not cause reality, but given that we are the creatures we are, we constitute what is real with the help of the conceptualizations we develop. The question of communicability has to do with question of the function of the various conceptualizations in our different observational and existential experiences.

For this reason and in contrast to Hedenius, I do not wish to see views of life as a system of very general statements. More promising in my opinion is the alternative view, which looks upon the statements of views of life in relation to the question of the meaning of life, and upon a fulfilling life as an expression of what it means to be a human being i.e. to live with life's inevitabilities.

A fulfilling life

Just as I have distinguished between the observer and the actor/participant perspectives with respect to views of life, I would like to do the same with regard to the concept of a fulfilling life. Hereafter in my critique of meta-physical realism and in referring to internal, that is to say, pragmatic real-ism, I shall draw attention to normative aspects and how they are dealt with in the respective perspective which is adopted.

It is one thing from a metaphysical realist perspective to try and give a substantial definition of the good. How we relate to ourselves, to other people and to our surroundings in general, is subjected to examination on the basis of this idea and judged accordingly. It is, however, quite another thing to start from human beings' existential experience of a fulfilling life. In practice, both aspects can naturally interact. However, a difference arises if we emphasize the first aspect more than the second. Metaphysical realists see no problem in isolating the first aspect since they ascribe to values an existence which is independent of human beings, and about which human beings, via intuition, revelation or in some other way, can obtain knowledge. By contrast, pragmatic (or internal) realists look upon this approach as problematic, since they maintain that the question of what values there are, is a constitutive issue which depends *inter alia* on the fact that we are the human beings that we are.

Seen from this perspective, it is a matter of concretely and practically proceeding from those reasons and motives for our actions which we are able to share, so that eventually something emerges which we are prepared to accept as something morally good. From this perspective, the presuppo-sitions for a fulfilling life consists in a certain measure of happiness and well-being i.e. we view, at least seen subjectively, our lives as more or less satisfactory and we are not exposed to too much suffering. The precondi-tions to achieve this sort of balance between suffering and satisfactions, embrace the following:

(1) that we can view our own lives as meaningful i.e. as a coherent narra-tive,
(2) that in this narrative we can view ourselves as part of the world around us and of the universe at large, and
(3) that we see ourselves having a good relation to other beings, and here I mean not only human beings, but also animals.

It certainly lies outside the framework of the present work to examine questions relation to animal ethics. I should, nevertheless, like to indicate the importance of this aspect since it is the function of views of life to pro-vide us with adequate expressions for what it means to be a human being; and from the pragmatic perspective, human beings are to be seen not as isolated entities, but as beings who live in different kinds of relational networks which include both human beings and animals.

If we look upon the question of a fulfilling life in this way, there is no difference in principle between religious and non-religious views of life. In the case of religion, as Zackariasson points out,

> the goods of religion are linked to the way religious practices help people to reconstruct their views of life so that they are experienced to be more adequate responses to human life, with its potential and its limitations. They make possible equilibrium where more experiences are better integrated than before; consequently, they make possible a more significant life. ... [I]t means that religious practices enable certain people to integrate what they find significant into a conception of human flourishing. Their views of life are experienced as adequate in relation to the experiences of existential significance they make, as well as in relation to how we lead our lives. An important mark of adequacy is the absence of tension, or doubt. ... So a religious practice tells believers something important about human life, and without it, and without the communion and communication with God, life would in some respects be defective. It is this function of making our view of life into a response to life which is adequate, directing, and integrating that I take to make up the goods of religion. Religion offers resolution where a previously experienced tension is overcome (Zackariasson 2002, 143f.).

The remark that "[r]eligion offers resolution where a previously experienced tension is overcome", characterizes not only functioning religions but also functioning views of life in general. Irrespective of how in our views of life, we give expression to the various kinds of relational networks which we as human beings live in, the important point is the following. The function of views of life is not to provide us with knowledge claims which are tested to see if they agree with how reality, as conceptualized by us, offers resistance in our observational experiences. Instead, it is a matter of whether our understanding of reality agrees with how reality, as conceptualized by us, offers resistance in our existential experiences. Let me show the sense in which emotions play an important role in the matter of balance mentioned above.

2 The role of the emotions in our conception of reality

I shall begin with a terminological clarification. Where it does not cause a problem, I shall follow ordinary linguistic practice and employ the words 'feeling' and 'emotion' as synonyms. When I do make a distinction in the use of both words, it is to emphasize the presence of intentionality. When it is purely or at least primarily a matter of experiencing e.g. discomfort or well-being, I shall use the word 'feeling'. On the other, if, in my experience of well-being, I express, for example, joy, or in my experience of dis-

comfort, express, for example, anger, in other words joy and anger in relation to something or someone, I shall use the word 'emotion'.

When feelings are seen as non-intentional, then it is only a question of
agreeable or disagreeable impressions on the same level as hunger, thirst
and sexual drive. When feelings are perceived as emotions i.e. as intentional, it can occur on the basis of an evaluation or an evaluating attitude.
In Harvey Green's formulation, emotions are defined, or as I prefer to say,
constituted, when a desire and a belief are directed at the same object
(Green 1992, 97). He illustrates what he means with the help of the Stoic
idea of the four basic emotions of joy, sorrow, hope and fear. Thus we can
provide an analysis of these four emotions as follows (1) joy: a person A is
entirely convinced that a definite state of affairs p holds and A desires that
p (2) sorrow: A is entirely convinced that p and A desires not p (3) hope: A
believes to a certain degree (but is not entirely convinced) that p and desires p and finally (4) fear: A believes to a certain degree (but is not entirely convinced) that p and desires not p (Green 1992, 82).

With the help of examples of rage and fear, I would like to make a further distinction which is important, namely that between (1) emotions
where language plays a crucial role, both for the occurrence of the emotion
and the form it takes and (2) emotions where language is not necessary in
this respect. It is not the case that there is a radical difference between the
first group of emotions and the second. Depending on circumstances, it can
be a matter of (1) and/or (2). Thus rage as a phenomenon is not first possible after language has been developed. Even dogs that fight, can be in a
rage. On the other hand, the concept of rage and what it stands for in our
human forms of community, presupposes a language with the help of
which we can indicate that while rage is certainly something which involves primitive reactions, it is also something more than the kind of rage
which is exhibited by dogs in a fight.

Fear, too, is an emotion which can occur, so speak, without a language.
However, it is also as an emotion where language is important, for example, when it is necessary to learn what is dangerous and therefore to be
avoided. Although we can often learn without the help of language what is
dangerous, certain dangers are such that an encounter with them can, in the
worst scenario, lead to death. It is therefore better, for example, to listen to
experienced people's descriptions of different types of ice, paying heed to
their warnings. In this way, we learn to fear ice, before we venture out on
it when it may be too late. The descriptions and explanations offered by
these experienced people are a linguistic help in learning about what is to
be feared and avoided.

Language can also be significant in another respect when, for example,
it is a matter of taking control of one's fear when faced with the serious

consequences of an illness. The difference between these two examples is as follows. In the first case, the danger which thin ice constitutes, is independent of language and can cause fear without linguistic references. The descriptions and warnings about this danger do nothing to reduce the danger as such to our lives and the fear we have for ice. It is otherwise in the second case. The various descriptions and explanations of what causes our fear of the serious consequences of an illness, can lead to a change in the way the illness is experienced. Depending upon how we conceptually and existentially understand what it is that we fear, our fear itself can be changed: it may even disappear. In this case, emotions in a quite definite sense, are linguistically determined. They derive their implications from the fact that we are dealing with human self-understanding and thereby also with insights about what it means to be a human being i.e. to live with life's inevitabilities. When seen from this perspective, emotions possess cognitivity. What exactly does this cognitivity consist in?

The cognitive aspect of emotions

In very rough terms, cognitivity can be understood in two ways.
(1) We base the cognitive on the factual rather than the feeling aspect of emotions.
(2) We treat the cognitive as an integral part of emotions.
In support of the first view, it is customary to cite the fact that emotions can be influenced by factual reasons. A particular emotion can, for example, cease when I perceive that I am mistaken about its cause. I am first put out to discover that my typically kleptomaniac colleague has taken my fountain pen when he leaves my office. A chance exploration of my breast pocket, however, transforms this feeling into the painful recognition that the situation is not as I had believed.

Another perspective is to see the cognitivity of emotions as an integral part of the emotions themselves. I shall illustrate what I mean with the help of an example which is inspired by Martha C. Nussbaum's approach to the question (Nussbaum 1990). I shall not, however, begin immediately with this type of example. Instead I shall try to place her in relation to two differing points of view concerning moral judgements. A common view is that moral judgements, in contrast to factual statements, are evaluations. Another view is represented by R.M. Hare. He criticizes the first view by showing that it is not enough to say that moral judgements are evaluations. According to Hare, moral judgements are characterized instead by the property that they are binding. In relation to Hare's view, the position taken by Nussbaum with respect to the cognitivity of emotions can then be seen as an explanation of why it is not enough to follow in Hare's footsteps, in pointing out the logical connection between moral judgements and actions. Sometimes, a substantial explanation of why, in certain cases, there is no link between moral judgement and action, is needed. The following example which is inspired by Nussbaum's view of the cognitivity of emotions, may serve as an illustration.

Let us suppose that I, as a member of Swedish society, have publicly declared that racial discrimination is the worst thing I know. In so doing, I have made a normative statement i.e. a statement that is an evaluation. Let us now further suppose that on some occasion, I and others, are witnesses to how someone is persecuted and mocked because of their skin colour. In such a situation, I would be expected to show my abhorrence by intervening, provided that there is no danger to life, or that the person being persecuted would be worse off due to my intervention. As Hare points out, the character of moral judgements as evaluative is certainly correct, but to find out if the actual moral judgement really is a person's moral conviction, in other words that the person actually means what he or she say, the best way to study this is by examining the person's actions. By making a moral judgement like 'Racial discrimination is the worst thing I know', we commit ourselves to acting in a particular way in different situations. People whose actions are inconsistent with their moral judgements, thereby contradict themselves. Their actions show that they do not mean what they say (Hare 1952, 1).

Another explanation is that the people mean what they say, but they do not know what they are talking about, since they lack the capacity to recognize racism. This incapacity reveals itself in the fact that the person does not feel any abhorrence. A necessary prerequisite for intervening is thus lacking. Note that it is not a question of two separate steps, namely that we should first show our abhorrence, and then act. The point is that our abhorrence will be find expression in the action itself. If, subject to the stated proviso, namely that there is no risk to life or risk that the person being persecuted might end up worse off because of our intervention, we do not feel abhorrence and fail to show it by our intervention, our condemnation of racism is either not genuine, or else we are not in a position to identify the situation correctly. In order to identify the situation correctly as one involving racial discrimination, we require to have trained and developed our emotional capacity sufficiently to allow us to see that it is not a matter, for example, of justified self-defence on the part of the perpetrator, but of genuine racial discrimination. We need to have developed our emotional capacity, and this capacity must not be blocked, if certain descriptions of the situation rather than others, are to emerge, and certain actions, rather than others, are to seem natural. It is thus not the case that we first register facts and then, so to speak, emotionally colour them. In such situations, specific emotions are a prerequisite for a correct description of these situations. Let me explain in a little more detail what I mean.

Moral judgements as descriptions

With the help of unpublished material ('Emotion and Moral Judgment') which Linda Zagzebski has generously made available to me, I shall show how cognitive and affective aspects work together in our moral judgements. Her approach to this question provides me with a fruitful basis in trying to show in part how in certain circumstances emotions play a decisive role in our view of reality, and in part how emotions, in order to be conceptualized, presuppose views of life. I shall, therefore, give a fairly detailed account of Zagzebski's standpoint.

She holds that moral judgements are not simply an expression of feeling but have a motivational function. Moral judgements are also propositional in form i.e. they express a thought. When moral agents make moral judgements, they express them in the form of statements acknowledging the thought, or in other words the description, which the moral judgements contain.

The kind of moral judgements which Zagzebski has in mind, are not, for example, principles but judgements about something which the moral agent is confronted with, or is in some way related to. A characteristic of such moral judgements is that they contain what in certain discussions about the theory of values are called *thick* concepts. As examples of moral judgements containing thick concepts, Zagzebski cites the following: "She is pitiful"; "He is contemptible"; "That remark is rude"; and "That's a lie." What is typical of thick concepts which are expressed in words such as 'pitiful', 'contemptible', 'rude' and 'lie', is that they have a both cognitive and affective (or emotive) aspects which cannot be considered in isolation from one another.

As Zagzebski naturally is aware, there are theories of emotions according to which an emotion certainly has a cognitive and affective aspect while these aspects are not necessarily connected to each other. One of the reasons for looking upon these aspects as separate from one another, would seem to be that a cognitive state similar to that which occurs in emotions, can exist independently of an affective state. Conversely, an affective state similar to that which occurs in emotional judgements can exist independently of a cognitive state. The thesis on the division between the cognitive and affective aspects in emotions is usually linked to the view that the affective states are an answer to perceptual or other cognitive states, so that emotions first come into being when the world has been represented or described in a particular way. Zagzebski does not deny that certain emotional states are really nothing more than a response to some prior non-affective representation of reality. However it must be pointed out that all emotions are not simply such responses. In order to make the difference clear, Zagzebski compares the words 'nauseating' and rude.

The word 'nauseating' means descriptively simply 'that which causes a feeling of nausea'. Theoretically there is thus no limit to what can be nauseating. Whatever a particular person finds nauseating, is nauseating for that person. We can naturally doubt whether people understand the word when they apply it solely to things which other people do not find nauseating. The point, however, is this: the very fact that John Doe on some occasion calls something nauseating which other people do not consider nauseating, does not demonstrate that John Doe has failed to understand the meaning of the word, or is making a false statement. If something causes John Doe to experience a feeling of nausea or disgust, then it is nauseating to John Doe, irrespective of the describable properties the cause of his nausea may have.

In the case of the word 'rude', Zagzebski holds that things are quite different. The word 'rude' is associated with certain describable situations which typically give rise to people reacting with a feeling of being hurt, or of having their toes trampled on, or something similar. It would be a mistake – in other words we would not understand the meaning of the word 'rude' – if we were to hold that every conceivable situation could be rude. An older person, for example, might consider themselves wronged if a teenager did not surrender their seat in the crowded bus although in this particular case it is not a matter of a rude action since the teenager in question suffers from a circulatory illness. The grammatical distinction between 'nauseating' and 'rude' is that whereas we say that something is nauseating *to a particular person*, we do not use the italicized additional phrase, in speaking of something that is rude. The two words are thus associated in different ways both with the describable situations to which they are applicable and with the subjective states which these situations induce.

The word 'nauseating' is applied to everything which causes the subjective feeling of nausea or disgust. Theoretically there no limits to what can cause the feeling of nausea. If I call something nauseating, it therefore means that I do not draw attention to any descriptive quality other than the circumstance that I feel disgusted by something. This is not so in the case of the word 'rude'. Here too, in theory there are no limits to what can cause me to feel hurt, wronged or to feel that my toes have been trampled on. However not everything is rude, even if it perhaps happens to hurt me. Only things, actions or situations with particular describable properties besides the property of hurting me, are rude and in calling them rude we draw at least partially attention to these other properties.

Zagzebski reminds us that not every rude action need necessarily cause us to feel injured, wronged or that our toes have been trampled on. In this respect, the word 'rude' is similar to the word 'red'. A red object does not have to cause a sensation of red in order for us to be able to apply the word 'red' to it. At the same time, the very fact that beings with our emotional dispositions normally have a definite feeling of being hurt or wronged when they are confronted with rude behaviour, is a part of what the word 'rude' means. In the same way, the very fact that beings with out perceptual abilities normally have a sensation of red in the presence of red objects, is part of the meaning of the word 'red'.

This view has been criticized on the grounds that the affective aspect in not an integral part of what 'rude' means. Instead it is a question of a complex concept which links the possession of a certain descriptive property with something which causes a feeling of being hurt, wronged or having one's toes trampled upon. According to Zagzebski, this does not explain what is special with just this descriptive property compared to other properties which also cause one to feel hurt, even although it is not a question of a rude act or rude behaviour. If the relation between a given descriptive property and the feeling of being hurt is merely a causal relation, it is no different from the relation with other descriptive properties and the feeling of being hurt which these other properties cause. Nevertheless, there is a difference, and according to Zagzebski, it is the following. In the case of rudeness, the feeling of being hurt is not brought about by purely arbitrary features of the situation in question. Instead, it is a matter of feeling hurt because of certain features which are constituted in a such a particular way that they are the object of this particular feeling of being hurt.

Zagzebski uses the word 'construed' but bearing in mind Appelros' earlier discussed terminological proposal, I feel that the word 'constituted' provides a better formulation of Zagzebski's point. Furthermore, I would like to make an additional remark. The reason that this works in the way indicated, is that we have learned which actions and behaviour can properly be said to be rude, just as we have learned that feeling hurt on account of such actions is an adequate emotional reaction.

On account of its specific properties, rude action is the intentional object of the emotion of being hurt, being offended or feeling wronged. In comparison with such an emotion, the feeling of being nauseated has certainly an association with something which, in principle, can be anything at all, but not to some intentional object in the sense of a conceptually identifiable intentional object of just this feeling.

It is here that Zagzebski perceives how the concept which the word 'rude' expresses lies, so-to-speak, between purely descriptive concepts and concepts like those expressed by the word 'nauseating'. When I view something as rude, I feel injured because of the hurtful features of the situation which cannot fully be described independently of their property of being the intentional objects for the emotion of being hurt. Thus there is no purely descriptive property in the case of the object or situation that hurts, which accurately captures what exactly is hurtful. When we look upon something as rude, it is not a question of first identifying in it certain descriptive features and then looking upon them as having caused us to feel hurt and finally to see these two aspects together. Viewing something as rude, is quite simply to see that which is before us as the rude intentional object of the emotion of being hurt. The concept which the word 'rude' expresses, is one which joins together a descriptive and affective aspect in such a way that both aspects cannot be isolated from one another. For this reason, the concept which the word 'rude' expresses is an example of a thick concept.

When the descriptive and affective components in a thick concept are indissolubly linked with one another, it implies that there is an emotional state in which we look upon the intentional object of the emotion in a way which differs from the way in which we would have looked upon another intentional object, if we had not found ourselves in this emotional state. I shall presently address the issue of critically examining whether a thick concept is used correctly. An emotion is thus a complex state with both affective and cognitive aspects which are necessarily linked to one another. This is so, because according to Zagzebski, an emotion is a state of relating ourselves in a special way to something which is viewed as being rude, pitiful, contemptible etc. The intentional object of an emotion is that which is subsumed under a thick concept. When I feel offended, I view something as rude; when I feel pity, I find it pitiful; when I feel contempt, I view it as contemptible etc. Conversely the following is true. Whenever I view something as rude, I feel offended; when I find it pitiful, I feel pity; when I view it as contemptible, I feel contempt etc.

Because emotions combine the affective component with intentionality, they serve to motivate us. In contrast to non-intentional affective states such as certain impressions or feelings, there is in an emotional state something specific about the world around us, at which the emotion is directed and which leads us to react in just that way which is characteristic for the emotion in question. Thus if we are open to compassion, we see someone as pitiful and the feeling of pity motivates us to put a stop to the suffering towards which our pity is directed; if we are in love, we see the other person as the loved one and the feeling of love motivates us to treat them in a characteristically loving way; and we see someone as contemptible, if one finds oneself in a state of feeling contempt, and the feeling of contempt motivates us to express our contempt by showing our abhorrence.

Emotions can naturally be expressed in different ways. The way which Zagzebski discusses and which is interesting from my point of view, consists in using thick concepts i.e. the intentional object for the emotion is question is subsumed under the thick concept which is adequate for this purpose. This implies two things. Since my judgement expresses an emotion, it expresses a state which motivates me to act. Furthermore, since my judgement also maintains that some person, some object, or some matter of fact is subsumed under the thick concept, which is used for the intentional object of this emotion, its form is that of a statement. The statement is about the intentional object of the emotion. Furthermore when I, in my judgement, make the statement, I am in a cognitive state of conceiving the intentional object as being subsumed under the thick concept in question. If the intentional object is subsumed under the concept, the judgement is correct; if not, it is false. A judgement such as 'This is rude' can either be correct or false although it expresses emotions. What makes a judgement that certain behaviour is rude, correct, is that the behaviour *is* rude. Given that we know when I can rightly claim that behaviour is rude, behaviour is rude in principle for the same reasons that a piano stands in the corner, and that the sky is blue, namely that a piano does in fact stand in the corner and the sky is in fact blue.

Naturally an affective disposition is a prerequisite for being able to view behaviour as being rude. In a similar way, however, observational dispositions are necessary to be able to view the sky as blue. With the help of Zagzebski's arguments, I consider that I can maintain that there are moral states of affair. For reasons which I have presented earlier, I wish to preserve the expression matter of fact for empirical matters of fact. The formal minimal Aristotelian definition of truth applies to both. As regard the aspect which is covered by the material definition of truth, there is however the following difference. With respect to judgements about matters of fact, 'truth' means 'agreement with the reality as conceptualized by us, which offers resistance in our observational experience'. With respect to judgements about moral states of affair, i.e. with respect to moral judgements, the situation is as follows.

I have earlier shown how the conceptualization of values and the conceptualizations (linked to views of life) of existential experiences of what it means to be a human being i.e. to live with life's inevitabilities, are inter-related. Views of life help us to conceptualize the tension we experience between life as it could be at its very best and life as it actually is. In the process, we acquire a feeling for good and bad, right and wrong. Once more it is the ideas, images and narratives of views of life which, in giving meaning to life, conceptualize our feeling for good and bad, right and wrong. It is through this process that we determine or, as I prefer to say, constitute values. As regards expressions for existential experiences supplied by views of life, 'true' means 'agreement with reality as conceptualized by us, which offers resistance in our existential experiences.' Without such existential experiences, it would scarcely be possible for us to formulate our experiences of the tension between life, as it could be at its best, and life as it actually is. Without the experience of this tension, we would be unable to develop a feeling for good and evil, right and wrong, and to conceptualize values. In developing this feeling, we develop our emotional capacity and thus acquire emotional experiences. Since the emotional experiences of the intentional objects of the experiences are conceptualized in terms of thick concepts, we might say that moral judgements are 'true' in the sense of 'agreeing with reality as conceptualized by us in terms of thick concepts'. Thick concepts thus form an indispensable component in the conceptualization of existential experiences, and also form the essential link between observational experiences on the one hand, and existential experiences on the other.

Naturally there is a difference between affective or emotional capacities and observational capacities, just as there is a difference between developing a moral capacity for judgement on the basis of existential experiences about what it is to be a human being i.e. to live with life's inevitabilities, through the development of emotional capacities, and being able to makes statements about reality in a purely descriptive sense by having developed observational capacities. Nevertheless, both types of capacity are involved in determining our view of reality.

Drawing on the work of Michael DePaul, I would therefore like to present the idea of an analogy between observational and moral experience. Suppose we are breeding horses and we wish to note down all the differences in the appearance and behaviour of horses which we must know about. For this purpose, we must develop our observational capacity accordingly. Another example is the practical use of a microscope. The beginner learns what can be seen in a microscope, by first learning how to operate the microscope in order to acquire the observations. It is a matter of developing and extending our capacity for observational experience. The widening of observational experience does not consist in a quantitative addition in the sense that experience produces a belief which is then put on top of the pile of our previously accumulated observational beliefs. The widening of observational experience presupposes that the observational capacity has itself altered.

DePaul holds that something similar happens in the case of our capacity for moral experience. Here too, we are not given this capacity in some final form. In the same way that observations can function as a support for beliefs, only if we develop our capacity to observe, so too moral experiences offer support for moral judgements, only if we develop our capacity for moral experience. In particular the experiences which are represented in literature, theatre, film, music, art and – I would add – those conceptualized existential experiences of life's inevitabilities as they are conceptualized in the narratives associated with views of life, help us to change and develop our capacity for making moral judgements (DePaul 1993, 207).

I want to pause for a moment to consider how we are to understand the role of our existential experiences and the emotional capacity which is based on them, in the creation of values.

3 Emotions and the conceptualization of values

As a phenomenon, emotions are tied to individuals. Joy, sorrow, hope and fear are always the joy, sorrow, hope, and fear of a particular individual. In order to identify an individual's utterance as the utterance of a particular emotion, the emotions require to be conceptually identifiable and for this to be possible, they need in turn to be conceptualized. As far as emotions are concerned, where language plays a crucial role for both their occurrence and their expression, there is, moreover, an interaction between emotions as something conceptually identified and emotions as something experienced. It is here that we find the point of contact with the conceptualization of values.

Emotions are, in a twofold sense, part of a process of conceptualization. Emotions, in the sense of an emotional capacity, are a precondition for our being able to identify certain expressions as expressions for particular emotions. At this point, we may recollect the earlier example of racial discrimination, where we argued that the ability to correctly describe certain circumstances as an expression of race discrimination and not something else, was presupposed. Conversely, in order to have adequate emotions, it is presupposed that we have adequate conceptualizations at our disposal. The requisite conceptualization concerns naturally the possibility of being able in general to identify emotions, and to distinguish them from one other. The required conceptualization, however, is something quite different when it is a question of emotions which play a role for the so-called thick concepts. Here conceptualizations of values are also needed. Otherwise we would be unable to describe the circumstances as an expression of, racial discrimination, for example, and to react adequately with abhorrence.

The conceptualizations of values and the conceptualizations (associated with views of life) of existential experiences of what it means to be a human being, are linked in the following way. Thanks to the ideas, images and narratives associated with views of life, we have the conceptual preconditions to allow us to experience the tension between life as it could be, when it is at its best, and life as it actually is. In experiencing this tension, it is possible for us to develop a feeling for good and evil, right and wrong. The ideas, images and narratives associated with our view of life, then allow us to conceptualize this feeling and in this way to create values. Conversely, once we have accepted the values and can no longer experience the given expressions, associated with a view of life, as existentially adequate any longer, we can create new impressions and thereby alter a given view of life, or help to see to it that a new one emerges. It is thus a question of interplay.

In the relationship between the conceptualization of values and the conceptualization of existential experiences of what it means to be a human being, i.e. to live with life's inevitabilities, the concept of a good person plays an important role. This is so because our discussion about what our values mean in more concrete terms, also presupposes narratives about role models who, in some sense, exemplify how the values, created by us, can be lived.

The concept of a good person

An appropriate starting point for discussing this aspect of the foregoing process of conceptualization, is to be found in further unpublished material (on divine motivation theory) which Linda Zagzebski has generously made available to me. In this material, Zagzebski applies the theory about direct reference which has been developed by (among others) Hilary Putnam (Putnam 1975, 139–152) and Saul Kripke (Kripke 1980), to the expression 'good person'. For safety's sake, I would point out that Putnam and Kripke develop a theory of direct reference only with reference to natural kinds such as water and gold. To begin with, I shall briefly outline the main points in the theory and then show, with reference to Zagzebski, how this theory can be extended to apply also to good people.

What is characteristic of expressions for natural kinds is that they are defined by reference to some example of the natural kind which is to be defined. 'Water' is defined for example as 'that which has the same chemical structure as *that*' and 'gold' is defined as 'that which constitutes the same element as *that*'. In each case, the demonstrative pronoun 'that' denotes an entity which the person giving the definition, directly refers to e.g. by pointing to. This sort of definition presupposes a common basis of shared experience. Even in cases, where we are not acquainted with the nature of the entity to be defined, it is nonetheless still possible, with the help of the common basis, to construct a definition which is essentially related to the nature of the entity. The majority of us are not acquainted with the specific nature of gold, and for many centuries no-one knew this at all. This, however, did not prevent one from defining 'gold' in such a way that the expression's reference is still fixed even after gold's specific nature has been discovered. My use of the expression 'gold' refers thus to gold even although I do not know gold's specific nature. This is possible since with the help of shared experience, and via a chain of applications of conceptualizations with respect to gold, I can refer to gold and nothing else. For safety's sake, I would add that talk about e.g. gold's specific nature is not a description of an intrinsically unconceptualized reality. It is part of a particular conceptualization which accommodates a theory of metals with the help of which it has been possible to generate testable and confirmed hypotheses about what is called gold's specific nature.

The theory of direct reference can also explain how expressions for natural kinds can gradually change with respect both to the expression's connotation and denotation. Stereotypical beliefs about the referent play an important role in the use of expressions of natural kinds. These beliefs are suppositions about which entities in the world around us can be reckoned as instances of the natural kind in question. Changes in meaning can occur if new discoveries about the referent lead us to alter our stereotypes. Such changes can in turn cause us to choose other entities as referents for the expression of the natural kind in question.

Zagzebski sees an analogy between such expressions as 'gold' and 'water' on the one hand and expressions such as 'good person' on the other. Even if we are not in a position to give a god person's specific nature, we can nevertheless provide examples of good people. A good person is a person like *that*. Obviously different people and cultures associate different stereotypes with good persons. The occurrence of different stereotypes does not entail, however, that the *concept* of good person changes. The concept requires simply that the examples of good persons have certain similarities. The intended meaning of the expression 'good person' certainly changes with altered stereotypes, and it is further true that the intended meaning, as it is used in one culture, differs from that in another culture with different stereotypes. In contrast to the case of natural kinds like gold and water, this lack of agreement cannot be removed by discovering the nature of the referent on the basis of testable hypotheses. Nevertheless the possibility that we can agree about certain examples of good person is not ruled out. The explanation why we can identify paradigmatic good persons in other cultures, is because we are the beings we are, also with respect to life's inevitabilities. These inevitabilities are the common lot of human beings. The expressions for the existential experiences of life's inevitabilities may change, but the fact itself that we have indeed existential experiences of life's inevitabilities, constitutes a common basis of shared experience.

Narratives about good persons are needed in order to allow us to know what values mean concretely. But by referring values to existential experiences, are we not guilty of relativizing them and depriving them of their objectivity? This is undoubtedly the criticism which normative objectivists who also include values in their metaphysical realism, might make. I shall show that this need not be the case by briefly presenting my view of the ontological status of values.

The ontological status of values

According to the pragmatic (or internal) realist approach which I have adopted, values are a result of a process of conceptualization which begins with the circumstance that the reality we live in and form part of, also contains life's inevitabilities and expressions for them. Without established expressions, we would have to continually create new expressions in order consciously to be able to experience the tension between life as it could be, when it is at its best – or to formulate it slightly differently – how a fulfilling life could be for a good person and how it actually is, as a conceptually identifiable tension and not merely as some kind of discomfort. Without this conceptualized experience of tension, we would be unable to create concepts for emotions such as joy, sadness, hope and fear. Without such concepts, we would in turn also be unable to conceptualize what we comprehend as values. Seen from one perspective, values are therefore something which is created by human beings inasmuch as we develop and transform feelings into intentional emotions, critically discussing them with respect to ideas about a fulfilling life and citing examples of good people. From another perspective, we are always born into a particular society and culture with values which have been created by the experiences of earlier generations and which have been conceptualized in their views of life. In this sense, the existence of values antedates us.

This view of values together with my earlier pragmatic realist interpretation of knowledge have a quite specific consequence as far as the division between facts and values is concerned. Let me begin by presenting the usual way of understanding the logical distinction between fact and value. It refers, above all, to the difference between the criteria we apply in the case of factual statements and those we apply in the case of value judgements. Thus for example the empirical criteria which we refer to in testing the truth of factual statements are not, at least in the same way, applicable to value judgements.

But now there arises the much debated question about the ontological conclusion which follows from this logical distinction. In logical empiricism, represented e.g. by A.J. Ayer (Ayer 1936), outside of logic and mathematics only that which can be identified in what is empirically given, can possess objectivity. Whatever lies outside the empirically given, is therefore not objective. Since values are not numbered among empirical objects, they lie outside the domain of the empirically given. Values are therefore not objective; they are subjective. They are merely expressions of feeling.

If we argue in this way, there is, as I see it, a risk of confusing the logical and ontological sides of the matter. We cannot derive from the logical distinction between factual statements and value judgements the conclusion that values do not exist. I agree with the thesis of logical empiricism to the extent that values are really an expression of feelings. But we cannot then draw the further conclusion that values are nothing but an expression of feelings, in the sense that they cannot say something about the reality in which we live. As I have shown, feelings can do this, if we treat them as feelings which are conceptualized in intentional emotions.

In accordance with the theory of pragmatic (or internal) realism which I have developed, values do exist. This, however, in no sense gets rid of the logical distinction between fact and value. The distinction between fact and value is retained, but this does not entail that facts exist, but values do not. Earlier I have shown with the help of an example from the history of science what it means within a pragmatic (or internal) perspective to speak about the existence of facts. I shall briefly repeat the example in order to develop an analogous thought about what it means to speak about the existence of values. When the question was posed whether, in addition to the planets which were already known, there was a further planet, this was occasioned by changes in the then contemporary theories of the universe. This, however, does not mean that it was the sketch of a new theory which caused the existence of another planet. Nevertheless, there is a pragmatic (or internal) relationship between the theoretically conceived i.e. intentional planet and the actual constituted planet. Given its relevance for the observations which were expected on the basis of theory, the intentional planet is, so to speak, the logical presupposition for talk about the real planet. If the situation is such that theories have been developed which allow us to put forward testable and subsequently confirmed hypotheses, we have no alternative but to assert that there is a further planet. This is no proof of the planet's existence. However, given the prevailing theoretical and empirical circumstances, it would be unwise to deny the existence of another planet.

Factual states of affair considered as intentional objects with respect to our theories and observational experiences, are the logical presupposition for being able to talk about real factual states of affair. Analogously, we might say that values considered as intentional objects with respect to our existential experiences of what it means to be a human being, are the logical presupposition for being able to speak about values as real entities. In other words, the fact that we human beings are made in a certain way, implies that as human beings we have certain needs which have the effect of making us value what can satisfy them. Among other things, we value conceptual distinctions e.g. the concept of value which helps us to express and obtain what we seek to satisfy our needs.

Given the previously mentioned connection between the conceptualization of values and the conceptualization, associated with views of life, of existential experiences of what it means to be a human being i.e. to live with life's inevitabilities and given also that religious language offers certain people existentially adequate expressions, a similar type of argument can be put forward concerning God. For reasons which I explained at the end of Part IV, we can say that the intentional object God is the logical presupposition of God, constituted as real. I have shown that to insist, in addition, upon the metaphysical realist's requirement of, so to speak, real existence, is unsustainable.

I have also shown that sentences about God are not statements in the sense of testable knowledge claims. Instead they belong to the conceptualizations, associated with views of life, of the existential experiences of what it means to be a human being. Moreover, I have shown that these conceptualizations associated with views of life, do not lack cognitivity because of this. They concern the life which we live, being the biological and social beings we are. Conceptualizations of value and sentences about God are not equivalent. Given that God, as a limit concept, deals with the tension we experience between life when it is at its best and life as it actually is, it nevertheless forms part of the relationship between the conceptualizations of values and the conceptualizations of existential experiences, associated with views of life, and of what it means to be a human being. If we accept the pragmatic realism which I have argued for, it is certainly true that no more can be said about God's existence, but on the other hand we cannot say less in order to create presuppositions for a necessary – and in relation to religion – external, philosophical critique of religions and their secular counterparts.

After this digression, I want once again to focus on the issue of the conceptualization of values. Even if the logical distinction between factual statements and value judgements is maintained, there exists, nonetheless, a certain connection between the two. Values as conceptualized emotions are the precondition for correctly identifying and describing certain situations. I would remind the reader of the earlier example of racial discrimination. In order to describe the situation as one involving racial discrimination, it is necessary that we have developed our emotional capacity to the degree that we can deal correctly with a thick concept which finds expression, for example, in the word 'abhorrent' and which consists of both an affective i.e. emotive and a descriptive component. The development of emotional capacity is a prerequisite for giving certain descriptions of the situation and not others. For this, it is essential that values as the conceptualizations of the feeling of good and evil, right and wrong, are present. It is thus not the case that we first note certain facts and then, so to speak, colour them emotionally. Instead, the intentional object which we encounter, is described directly with the help of thick concepts which are expressed by such words as 'grim', 'abhorrent', 'admirable' etc. Because of the connection between the conceptualization of values and the conceptualization, associated with views of life, of the existential experiences of what it means to be a human being (i.e. to live with life's inevitabilities), I would also wish to include good and evil, right and wrong among the thick concepts.

As I have said, a thick concept is one which is not purely descriptive, but which contains also an affective aspect. We gain knowledge of thick concepts through affective states and continue to use them in cases where we find ourselves in an emotional state which is both cognitive and affective. In this sense, thick concepts remind us of the concepts of colour. A person who has never experienced the feeling which accompanies a particular thick concept, no more understands that concept than a person who has never had the sense impression of red, can understand the concept of 'red'.

The connection between facts and values does not only apply to situations which are described with the help of thick concepts. From a general point of view, both the acquisition and application of knowledge is associated with values and interests. If we had not created values, we would not know how to apply our knowledge. When then we are able to confirm, not only that certain knowledge claims can contribute better than others to solving our problems, but also the reasons why they do so, it is rational for us to act on the basis of these knowledge claims and not on the basis of anything else. It is thus a matter of training our capacity for knowledge. However, this is not sufficient. Unfortunately we do not always act on the basis of those knowledge claims which help more than others to solve our problems. The view of emotions and values which I have put forward here, naturally does not solve this problem, but it has the advantage of helping us to see the following, so that we do not need to land in the same situation. One of the reasons why we do not always act on the basis of the knowledge claims on which we rationally ought to act, can be namely that we have not trained the emotional capacity which is necessary to relate the knowledge claims to the circumstances, where correct identification and description require thick concepts. Because the view of emotions and values presented here helps us to see such connections, it can at least be the first step in the way to a fulfilling life for both ourselves and others.

It is characteristic of my view of values, that they are certainly, in one sense, an expression of feelings. Since it is a question of feelings which are conceptualized in intentional emotions, values cannot be eliminatively reduced to feelings. Thanks to the ideas, images and narratives in our views of life, we can experience a tension between how life could be when it is at its best and how it actually is. In this way, we can develop a feeling for good and evil, right and wrong. Once more thanks to the ideas, images and narratives in our views of life, we can preserve this feeling by conceptualizing it in values. The close linkage between values as the result of a conceptualization process, and our existential experiences of life's inevitabilities does not mean, however, that values can be eliminatively reduced to feelings. It is not feelings which function as our compass in the use we make of our knowledge, but rather values. However, they do so only if they personally involve us as something meaningful. Here once again, I widen the perspective by relating the values, seen in their context of views of life conceptualizations of the existential experiences of what it means to be a human being, to the question of the meaning of life.

To experience personal involvement

My way of taking a wider perspective is, like Mats Furberg, to fix upon an important point with regard to the question of the meaning of life, in order to determine more exactly the functions of views of life. "'To experience personal involvement' – to care about things, feel that they personally involve us – is not necessarily to have enthusiasm or passion" (Furberg 1975, 175). I shall distinguish personal involvement, from what, for want of a better word, I shall call commitment. When it is a case of commitment, we can argue for and against becoming involved in a particular political question, whether it is the education of children or the preservation of the local dance hall. When, on the other hand, something personally involves us, it means that something attracts us, or scares us off. Quite simply, we feel personally involved.

The situation that something positive or negative personally involves us, presupposes that we find ourselves in a particular situation. When people begin to speak of the meaninglessness of life, it depends in part on the fact that they no longer are related to something that attracts or scares us off i.e. we no longer feel personally involved. When we discuss the question of the meaning of life, it is sometimes the expression of a desire to know how experiences of life as something meaningless, can be avoided or overcome. An external precondition for not experiencing meaninglessness, is to be part of a context which provides one with ideas, images and narratives about what is valuable. An inner precondition for not experiencing meaninglessness, is that something involves us personally. For this, we require access to expressions which can be personally experienced as adequate for expressing what it means to be a human being, that is to say, to live with life's inevitabilities. There thus exists an indissoluble bond between (1) ideas, images and narratives about what it means to be a human being (2) an experience of meaning and (3) the issue of personal identity.

Let us recall the earlier two-way connection between emotions and description. My experience of a particular emotion in a particular situation, depends in part upon how I interpret the situation which in turn depends on the concepts and expressions at my disposal. Furthermore, the extent to which I view concepts and expressions as adequate, depends on the correlation between my own emotions and the emotions which, on the basis of human experiences of what it means to be a human being, have been conceptualized, in particular social and cultural circumstances, in values. In order to relate myself in practice to these values, I need to have access to the narratives of views of life, in which these values find expression and in which I can recognize myself and the conditions of my own life.

Here, it is opportune again to talk about so-called thick concepts. As we recall, these are concepts which are composed of descriptive and affective components, and which, moreover, incorporate both culturally conditioned and personal experiences. Because such concepts are linked to particular historical, social and cultural contexts, they are forever changing in response to the changes in the contexts and in our social roles and relations to each other. In this process, narratives, myths and so on, play a crucial part both in defending and criticizing the different views of reality which we encounter through our experiences of how reality, so to speak, offers resistance. The narratives direct our attention to various aspects of reality in which we live and are a part of. They do it by giving faces to people, who just like us, have to live with life's inevitabilities, but do so in circumstances with which we are not familiar. The narratives place us in a position to test in fantasy how it would be to live various types of life so that we become more fully conscious of the consequences which various attitudes to oneself and others can lead to. In this way, we learn to understand not only other people better, but also ourselves, and how we can live with life's inevitabilities, so that our life is fulfilling.

With regard to this function, there is a close connection between narrative, play and fantasy. These allow us to extricate ourselves from our situation and allow us, not only to live in another way but to live in an *alternative* way. By the latter is meant that we actively choose another orientation to our lives, despite the various constraints imposed on us, to a greater or less extent. Play, narrative and imagination allow us to see our own situation from a different angle, which means that we can develop the capacity to live on different levels, in different dimensions or whatever we wish to call it. A life with imagination in adult life is in part a successor to the child's play activity. A life with fantasy provides the required nourishment for our capacity to enlarge our life situation (Taylor 1985, 158). We need this enlargement in order to allow us to experience consciously the tension between life as it could be, when it is at its best, and life as it is as a matter of fact. In this way, values can be experienced as something precious.

Conclusion

Here I would like to refer to what I said earlier about the function of certain narratives as life narratives, and return both to the difference between observational and existential experience, and the distinction between empirical and existential adequacy. In doing this, I want to summarize how in this book, which has been written against the background of a growing multiplicity of views of life, I have achieved my dual purpose of showing that it is imprudent to dismiss religion categorically as something irrational or unreasonable and, at the same time, showing how religion can be seen as a human phenomenon which can be submitted to philosophical analysis and criticism.

As I have said, in order to experience my life as meaningful, it is necessary that I can see it in the form of a narrative with a past, a present and an opening leading to a future. The adequacy of the various view of life narratives is judged from the perspective of my own life, on the basis of whether I can recognize my own life's narrative among them. From the perspective of the views of life, their narratives provide a background in terms of which I can recognize my own as a narrative and – should the question of meaninglessness arise – as a meaningful one.

The crucial criterion in this context is adequacy, and more specifically, adequacy in relation to existential experience. I reiterate that this sort of experience must be not be conceptually confused with what I earlier called observational experience. Experience as observation means, very roughly speaking, what can be referred to our five senses. In particular, perception and observation play a crucial role for human beings. Although observations are theory-laden, we can nevertheless formulate a relation between the observations which we expect on the basis of given theories and the observations which we in fact make. This must not be confused with experience understood as existential experience. If nothing personally involves us, there is no reason for us to choose consciously either the one or the other course of action. For something to personally involve us, we are required to look upon something as valuable. We do this in relation to the image of human beings we have formed. If such a image is not merely to be borrowed from others, existential experiences of our own regarding what it means to be a human being i.e. to live with life's inevitabilities, are required.

Both observational and existential experiences have subjective and objective aspects. In the case of observational experience, the subjective aspect consists in the fact that an observation is always a particular individual's observation. This entails that we must always reckon on the possibility of error. Nonetheless, objectivity is not ruled out. Because we share certain concepts, we can critically compare observations. Inversely we can also critically investigate our concepts to see how the observations which are expected on the basis of our theories, are in agreement with the observations that in fact are made. If the concepts of our theories are no longer suitable for generating testable hypotheses, they and the associated theories are no longer worth having.

As far as existential experience is concerned, the subjective aspect arises because the experiences of love, joy, happiness, suffering, guilt and death are *my* experiences. This means that the experience itself cannot be shared. What on the other hand we can share, are the expressions for life's inevitabilities, so that we can understand what with the help of these expressions, we are speaking about. Even the expressions for life's inevitabilities can be discussed critically with respect to their adequacy.

What then does adequacy consist in? The answer naturally varies depending on whether we have in mind observational experience or existential experience. As far as I can see, with regard to observational experience, the following is true. Statements about observations and hypotheses about what is observable, are either true or false. One the other hand, the theories which allow scientists to generate testable hypotheses, are neither true nor false. However, as van Fraassen, among others, emphasizes, theories are nevertheless related to the nature of reality in the sense that when they are fruitful, they are empirically adequate i.e. help us to say something about what is observable (van Fraassen 1980, 12).

Analogously, I would like to define adequacy with respect to existential experience, in the following way. The expressions for the existential experience of what it implies to be a human being, are true or false, but not in the sense of agreement or non-agreement with reality as it is conceptualized by us and offers resistance in our observational experiences.' Instead, the expressions for the existential experience of what it implies to be a human being, are true or false, in the sense of 'agreement or non-agreement with reality as it is conceptualized by us and offers resistance in our existential experiences.' Views of life as some kind of system are neither true nor false, whether in the first sense since views of life cannot be transformed into testable knowledge claims, or in the second sense. On the other hand, they are existentially adequate or inadequate, depending on whether they supply expressions which agree with reality as it is conceptualized by us and offers resistance in our existential experiences. If religions wish to be able to play a role in human lives, their views, images and narratives need to be existentially adequate.

As I have demonstrated, a foundation based on the fact that we are the beings that we are, is not necessarily the same thing as a reductionism that seeks to remove religion altogether. Religions have a function in human life, and I have also shown how starting from my position of pragmatic (or internal) realism, we can talk philosophically about God's existence. But on the particular question of the nature of statements about God, this is a matter for human beings who look upon reality in a religious light. Moreover, I have shown the way in which religions can be investigated critically and thereby can be improved in regard to the role they play in the lives of human beings. My aim has been to make use of a critique of metaphysical realism and the development of a position of pragmatic realism, to produce conceptual tools for views of life which will allow us to say that it is imprudent to dismiss categorically religion as something irrational or unreasonable while simultaneously requiring that religion too should be seen as a human phenomenon and in that light be subjected to a philosophical analysis and critique without any restrictions imposed by essentially religious arguments.

Both points are important in order for us to take into consideration that religions by virtue of being views of life, have an important function in the lives of human beings. The job of these views of life is to supply us with existentially adequate expressions for what it means to live with life's inevitabilities such happiness, love, joy, suffering, guilt and death. In order to live a fulfilling life, we need conceptualizations about all such things. As is the case with everything human beings do, there can be fatal consequences, when we apply conceptualizations, including those relevant here, in the wrong way. It follows that the truth claims associated with views of life, including religious ones, must be submitted to critical examination. My contribution has been to create the theoretical presuppositions for this by developing in relation to the view of life in question, an external philosophical position which is important as a platform in a society which has become increasingly pluralistic. To this end, I have chosen a way of philosophizing about religion which consistently keeps to our human capacities with their possibilities and limitations, and refrains from asserting anything about that which lies outside our capacity to reasonably say something about.

Instead I have developed what one might characterize as a pragmatic realist philosophy of religion. This is more a way to reflect and cannot, therefore, be summarized in a list of definite theses. This was possible with metaphysical realism because in contrast to pragmatic (or internal) realism, it ascribes to philosophy the capacity to be able, first of all, to come with knowledge claims about what there is, namely a reality which in itself is unconceptualized; and secondly, to come with knowledge claims to determine in what sense the things that are, do exist, namely equipped with certain properties and standing in certain relations, in a manner which is completely independent of the way in which we human beings conceptualize it. I have argued that the only reasonable perspective which we human beings can reasonably construct, is a pragmatic one which takes into account that we are the beings that we are. This is the pragmatic aspect. The realist aspect consists in accepting that reality is always a reality which is understood and conceptualized by us human beings, where our understanding and conceptualizations are based on experiences of how reality offers resistance.

As regards our experiences, I have introduced the distinction between observational and existential experiences and have placed them in relation to the fact that the sciences on the one side, and religions and their secular counterparts on the other, have different functions in our lives. The tested experience of everyday life and the sciences provides us with empirically adequate theories which allow us to generate testable hypotheses, and in this way say something about what is observable. Views of life, including religions, furnish us with existentially adequate images, ideas and narratives which allow us to conceptualize values. In so doing, they say something about what it means to be a human being.

I have shown that this is not synonymous with reductionism with respect to religion. An important consequence of my critique of metaphysical realism and my proposal for a pragmatic (or internal) realism is expressed in the following distinction. It is one thing if we define religion in terms of human needs and human perspectives, which is something I myself do not do. It is quite another thing to discuss, as I have done, the concepts of objectivity and truth, even in the case of religion with its pronouncements about the divine and the transcendent, on the basis of the only perspective which we human beings have access to, namely the human perspective. This is not reductionism. It is to take religion seriously as the human phenomenon that it is for us human beings.

Bibliography

The bibliography only lists titles which are mentioned or referred to in the text. As a result, it does not aspire to provide a comprehensive guide to all that has been written on the questions in hand. It is purely a list of works which I cite or use for the purpose of my own arguments.

Agazzi, Evandro
- 2000: 'Observability and Referentiality', Evandro Agazzi and Massimo Pauri (eds.): *The Reality of the Unobservable. Observability, Unobservability and Their Impact on the Issue of Scientific Realism.* Dordrecht: Kluwer, 45–57.

Alston, William P.
- 1996: 'Speaking Literally of God', Michael Peterson, William Hasker, Bruce Reichenbach, and David Basinger (eds.): *Philosophy of Religion: Selected Readings.* Oxford: Oxford University Press, 365–386 (First published in Axel D. Steuer and James W. McClendon (eds.): *Is God GOD?* Abingdon Press, 1981.)
- 1996: *A Realist Conception of Truth.* Ithaca: Cornell University Press.

Appelros, Erica
- 2002: *God in the Act of Reference. Debating religious realism and non-realism.* Aldershot: Ashgate.

Ayer, Alfred
- 1936: *Language, Truth and Logic.* London: Victor Gollancz.

Baç, Murat
- 1999: Propositional knowledge and the enigma of realism', *Philosophia, Philosophical Quarterly of Israel* 27:199–223.

Blackburn, Simon
- 1993: *Essays in Quasi-Realism.* Oxford: University Press.

Brümmer, Vincent
- 1993: 'Wittgenstein and the Irrationality of Rational Theology', James M. Byrne (ed.): *The Christian Understanding of God Today.* Dublin: The Columba Press.

Butchvarov, Panayot
- 1995: 'metaphysical realism', Robert Audi (ed.): *The Cambridge Dictionary of Philosophy.* Cambridge: Cambridge University Press, 488–489.

Carnap, Rudolf
- 1950: 'Empiricism, Semantics and Ontology', *Revue Internationale de Philosophie* 4:20–40. (Reprinted in Rudolf Carnap, *Meaning and Necessity: A Study in Semantics and Modal Logic*, 2nd ed. Chicago: University of Chicago Press, 1956.)

Churchland, Paul M. and Clifford A. Hooker (eds.)
- 1985: *Images of Science: essays on realism and empiricism, with a reply from Bas C. van Fraassen.* Chicago: University of Chicago Press.

Clark, Peter and Bob Hale (eds.)
- 1994: *Reading Putnam.* Oxford: Blackwell.

Cohen, Robert S., Risto Hilpinen and Qui Renzong (eds.)
- 1996: *Realism and Anti-Realism in the Philosophy of Science*. Dordrecht: Kluwer.
Conant, James
- 1990: 'Introduction', Hilary Putnam: *Realism with a Human Face*. Cambridge, Massachusetts: Harvard University Press, xv–lxxiv.
Cupitt, Don
- 1991: *What is a Story?* London: SCM Press.
Dancy, Jonathan
- 1985: *An Introduction to Contemporary Epistemology*. Oxford: Blackwell.
DePaul, Michael
- 1993: *Balance and Refinement. Beyond Coherence Methods of Moral Inquiry*. London: Routledge.
Devitt, Michael
- 1991: 'Aberrations of the Realism Debate', *Philosophical Studies* 61:43–63.
Dummett, Michael
- 1978: *Truth and Other Enigmas*. London: Duckworth.
- 1991: *The Logical Basis of Metaphysics*. London: Duckworth.
- 1993: *The Seas of Language*. Oxford: Clarendon Press.
Elgin, Catherine Z.
- 1996: *Considered Judgment*. Princeton, New Jersey: Princeton University Press.
Ellis, Brian
- 1979: *Rational Belief Systems*. Oxford: Blackwell.
Eriksson, Stefan
- 1998: *Ett mönster i livets väv: Tro och religion i ljuset av Wittgensteins filosofi*. Nora: Bokförlaget Nya Doxa.
Farrell, Frank B.
- 1994: *Subjectivity, Realism and Postmodernism: the recovery of the world*. Cambridge: Cambridge University Press.
Fine, Arthur
- 1984: 'The Natural Ontological Attitude', Jarrett Leplin (ed.): *Scientific Realism*. Berkeley: University of California Press, 83–107.
Flew, Antony
- 1955: 'Theology and Falsification. The University Discussion A', Antony Flew and Alasdair MacIntyre (eds.): *New Essays in Philosophical Theology*. London: SCM Press.
Franck, Olof
- 1998: *Tro och transcendens i Ulf Ekmans och Kristina Wennergrens författarskap. Om teologisk realism och referentiell identifikationsteori i två samtida trosuppfattningar*. Studia philosophiae religionis 20. Stockholm: Almqvist & Wiksell International.
- 2002: *Förtryckets grundvalar. Norm och avvikelse i argument om homosexuellas, invandrares och kvinnors rättigheter*. Studia philosophiae religionis 22. Stockholm: Almqvist & Wiksell International.
Frankena, William
- 1939: 'The Naturalistic Fallacy', *Mind* 48:464–477.
Furberg, Mats
- 1975: *Allting en trasa? En bok om livets mening*. Lund: Bokförlaget Doxa.
Goldman, Alvin
- 1986: *Epistemology and Cognition*. Cambridge, Massachusetts: Harvard University Press.

Grace, George W.
- 1987: *The Linguistic Construction of Reality.* London: Routledge.
Green, O. Harvey
- 1992: *The Emotions: A Philosophical Theory.* Dordrecht: Kluwer.
Grube, Dirk-Martin
- 1998: *Unbegründbarkeit Gottes? Tillichs und Barths Erkenntnistheorien im Horizont der gegenwärtigen Philosophie.* Marburger Theologische Studien 51. Marburg: N.G. Elwert Verlag.
Hare, Richard Mervyn
- 1952: *The Language of Morals.* Oxford: Oxford University Press.
Hedenius, Ingemar
- 1951: *Att välja livsåskådning.* Stockholm: Bonniers.
- 1983: *Tro och vetande.* Stockholm: Askild & Kärnekull Förlag. (First published Stockholm: Bonniers 1949.)
Heimbeck, Reaburne S.
- 1969: *Theology and Meaning.* London: Allen and Unwin.
Henriksen, Jan-Olav
- 1999: *På grensen til Den Andre. Om teologi og postmodernitet.* Oslo: Ad Notam Gyldendal.
Herrmann, Eberhard
- 1995: *Scientific Theory and Religious Belief. An Essay on the Rationality of Views of Life.* Kampen: KokPharos.
Hick, John
- 1993: *God and the Universe of Faiths: Essays in the Philosophy of Religion.* Oxford: Oneworld Publications. (First published London: Macmillan 1973.)
- 1995: *A Christian Theology of Religions: The Rainbow of Faiths.* Louisville: Westminster John Knox Press.
Hilpinen, Risto
- 1996: 'On Some Formulations of Realism, or How Many Objects are there in the World?', Robert S. Cohen, Risto Hilpinen and Qui Renzong (eds.): *Realism and Anti-Realism in the Philosophy of Science.* Dordrecht: Kluwer, 1–10.
Holmberg, Martin
- 1994: *Narrative, Transcendence & Meaning. An essay on the question about the meaning of life.* Studia philosophiae religionis 16. Stockholm: Almqvist & Wiksell International.
Jeffner, Anders
- 1981: 'Att studera livsåskådningar', Carl-Reinhold Bråkenhielm, Carl-Henric Grenholm, Lennart Koskinen and Håkan Thorsén (eds.): *Aktuella livsåskådningar. Del 1. Existentialism, marxism.* Lund: Bokförlaget Doxa, 11–21.
Kirk, Robert
- 1999: *Relativism and Reality: A contemporary introduction.* London: Routledge.
Koistinen, Timo
- 2000: *Philosophy of Religion or Religious Philosophy? A Critical Study of Contemporary Anglo-American Approaches.* Helsinki: Luther-Agricola-Society.
Kripke, Saul
- 1980: *Naming and Necessity.* Cambridge, Massachusetts: Harvard University Press.
Leplin, Jarrett (ed.)
- 1984: *Scientific Realism.* Berkeley: University of California Press.

Mackie, John Leslie
- 1982: *The Miracle of Theism. Arguments For and Against the Existence of God.* Oxford: Clarendon Press.
Magnus, Bernd
- 1995: 'postmodern', Robert Audi (ed.): *The Cambridge Dictionary of Philosophy.* Cambridge: Cambridge University Press, 634–635.
McDermid, Douglas
- 1998: 'Pragmatism and Truth: The Comparison Objection to Correspondence', *Review of Metaphysics* 51:775–811.
McNaughton, David
- 1988: *Moral Vision: an introduction to ethics.* Oxford: Blackwell.
Mitchell, Basil
- 1973: *The Justification of Religious Belief.* London: Macmillan.
Moore, George Edward
- 1903: *Principia Ethica.* Cambridge: Cambridge University Press.
Mäki, Uskali
- 1996: 'Scientific Realism and Some Peculiarities of Economics', Robert S. Cohen, Risto Hilpinen and Qui Renzong (eds.): *Realism and Anti-Realism in the Philosophy of Science.* Dordrecht: Kluwer, 427–447.
Newen, Albert and Eike von Savigny
- 1996: *Analytische Philosophie. Eine Einführung.* München: Wilhelm Fink Verlag.
Nussbaum, Martha C.
- 1990: *Love's Knowledge. Essays on Philosophy and Literature.* New York: Oxford University Press.
Patterson, Sue
- 1999: *Realist Christian Theology in a Postmodern Age.* Cambridge: Cambridge University Press.
Peterson, Michael, William Hasker, Bruce Reichenbach and David Basinger
- 1991: *Reason and Religious Belief. An Introduction to the Philosophy of Religion.* Oxford: Oxford University Press.
Phillips, Dewi Zephaniah
- 1970: *Faith and Philosophical Enquiry.* London: Routledge & Kegan Paul.
- 1988: *Faith after Foundationalism.* London: Routledge.
- 1993: 'How Real Is Realism? A Response to Paul Badham', Runzo, Joseph (ed.): *Is God Real?* London: Macmillan, 193–198.
Putnam, Hilary
- 1975: *Mind, Language and Reality, Philosophical Papers. Volume 2.* Cambridge: Cambridge University Press.
- 1981: *Reason, Truth and History.* Cambridge: Cambridge University Press.
- 1983: *Realism and Reason. Philosophical Papers 3.* Cambridge: Cambridge University Press.
- 1987: *The Many Faces of Realism.* La Salle: Open Court.
- 1988: *Representation and Reality.* Cambridge, Massachusetts: MIT Press.
- 1990: *Realism with a Human Face.* Cambridge, Massachusetts: Harvard University Press.
- 1992: *Renewing Philosophy.* Cambridge, Massachusetts: Harvard University Press.
- 1994a: *Words and Life.* Cambridge, Massachusetts: Harvard University Press.
- 1994b: 'Comments and Replies', Peter Clark and Bob Hale (eds.): *Reading Putnam.* Oxford: Blackwell, 242–295.

- 1999: *The threefold cord mind, body, and world*. New York: Columbia University Press.

Runzo, Joseph
- 1993: 'Realism, Non-Realism, and Atheism: Why Believe in an Objectively Real God?', Joseph Runzo (ed.): *Is God Real?* London: Macmillan, 151–175.

Runzo, Joseph (ed.): *Is God Real?* London: Macmillan.

Scott, Michael and Andrew Moore
- 1997: 'Can Theological Realism Be Refuted?', *Religious Studies* 33:401–418.

Sellars, Wilfrid
- 1956: 'Empiricism and the Philosophy of Mind', Herbert Feigl and Michael Scriven (eds.): *Minnesota Studies in the Philosophy of Science, vol. 1*. Minneapolis: University of Minnesota Press, 253–329.

Stenlund, Sören
- 1987: 'Tankar om realism', Olof Franck, Eberhard Herrmann, Martin Holmberg, Björn Sahlin and Peder Thalén (eds.): *Mystik och verklighet. En festskrift till Hans Hof*. Delsbo: Bokförlaget Åsak, 142–166.

Stenmark, Mikael
- 2001: *Scientism. Science, ethics and religion*. Aldershot: Ashgate.

Stigen, Anfinn
- 1983: *Tekningens historie, Bd 1: Oldtiden, middelalderen, den nyere tid til 1600-tallet*. Oslo: Gyldendal Norsk Forlag.

Swinburne, Richard
- 1979: *The Existence of God*. Oxford: Clarendon Press.
- 1981: *Faith and Reason*. Oxford: Oxford University Press.
- 1993: *The Coherence of Theism*. Revised edition. Oxford: Clarendon Press. (First published 1977.)

Taylor, Charles
- 1985a: *Human Agency and Language. Philosophical Papers 1*. Cambridge: Cambridge University Press.
- 1985b: *Philosophy and the Human Sciences. Philosophical Papers 2*. Cambridge: Cambridge University Press.

Toulmin, Stephen, Richard Rieke and Allan Janik
- 1979: *An Introduction to Reasoning*. New York: Macmillan.

Trigg, Roger
- 1997: 'Theological realism and antirealism', Philip L. Quinn and Charles Taliaferro (eds.): *A Companion to Philosophy of Religion*. Oxford: Blackwell, 213–220.

van Fraassen, Bas C.
- 1980: *The Scientific Image*. Oxford: Clarendon Press.

Vardy, Peter
- 1990: *The Puzzle of God*. London: HarperCollins.

Wainwright, William J. (ed.)
- 1996: *God, Philosophy and Academic Culture. A Discussion between Scholars in the AAR and the APA*. Atlanta: Scholar Press.

Ward, Keith
- 1990: 'Truth and the Diversity of Religions', *Religious Studies* 26:1–18.

Wittgenstein, Ludwig
- 1953: *Philosophical Investigations*. Translated by G.E.M. Anscombe. Oxford: Blackwell.
- 1966: *Lectures and Conversations on Aesthetics, Psychology and Religious Belief*. Edited by Cyril Barrett. Oxford: Blackwell.

- 1989: *Werkausgabe Bd. 6: Bemerkungen über die Grundlagen der Mathematik.* Frankfurt am Main: Suhrkamp.
Wright, Crispin
- 1987: *Realism, Meaning and Truth.* Oxford: Blackwell.
- 1994: 'On Putnam's Proof that We Are Not Brains in a Vat', Peter Clark and Bob Hale (eds.): *Reading Putnam.* Oxford: Blackwell, 216–241.
Wright, Georg Henrik von
- 1986: *Vetenskapen och förnuftet. Ett försök till orientering.* Stockholm: Bonniers.
Zackariasson, Ulf
- 2002: *Forces by which We Live. Religion and Religious Experience from the Perspective of a Pragmatic Philosophical Anthropology.* Studia philosophiae religionis 21. Stockholm: Almqvist & Wiksell International.

Indices

Index of Names

Index of Subjects

Abstract

The book deals with what is one of the central issues in the philosophy of religion, namely the problem of realism: do we human beings have access to a reality in itself, assuming that such an idea makes sense at all, or only to reality as it is conceptualized by us? Both the approaches of metaphysical realism and postmodern relativism are rejected. Instead an alternative approach called pragmatic realism is presented and developed. It embodies two main lines of thought. First of all, it stresses that reality is always reality as conceptualized by us. But at the same time it does not rule out objectivity. In the case of a good life, that is to say a fulfilling life, a notion of objectivity is presented on the basis of certain reflections about how conceptualized reality can be said in certain respects to offer us resistance.

Religion in Philosophy and Theology

Editor
INGOLF U. DALFERTH (Zürich)
Advisory Board
HERMANN DEUSER (Frankfurt/M.) . JEAN-LUC MARION (Paris)
DEWI Z. PHILLIPS (Claremont) . ELEONORE STUMP (St. Louis)
HENT DE VRIES (Amsterdam)

For a complete catalogue please write to the publisher
Mohr Siebeck • P.O. Box 2030 • D-72010 Tübingen/Germany
Up-to-date information on the internet at www.mohr.de